NADIR SHAH

NADIR SHAH

SIR MORTIMER DURAND

GYAN

Published by

GYAN

Gyan Publishing House
5, Ansari Road
Daryaganj, New Delhi-110002
Phone: 011-47034999, 9811692060
E-mail: books@gyanbooks.com

Distribution Network
gyanbooks.com
India, USA, Canada, UK, Australia, France

ISBN : 978-81-212-9484-3 (PB)
First Published, 1908

2nd Impression 2023

Printed at: Gyan Press, Delhi.

NADIR SHAH
Author: SIR MORTIMER DURAND

NADIR SHAH

Swan Electric Engraving Co. Ltd

Nadir Shah

(From the picture at the India Office)

NADIR SHAH

BY

SIR MORTIMER DURAND

1908

INTRODUCTION

In the course of the eighteenth century, a Turkoman soldier of fortune, Nadir Kuli, better known to the world as Nadir Shah, raised Persia to the first place among Oriental powers; and notwithstanding the insane hatred which during the latter part of his life he showed towards his sensitive and quick-witted people, who had fought well for him, he is regarded by Persians of the present day as one of the greatest of their national heroes. This book is an attempt to make his character and times more familiar than they are to English readers.

After some doubt, I have written it in the form of a romance. I have done this partly with the hope of giving it more life and colour, partly because the existing accounts of Nadir Shah, whether Persian or European, are hardly the material from which exact history could now be written. Many controversies have arisen even about the career of Napoleon. Considering that Nadir Shah spent his life fighting in Asia, and died before Napoleon was born, it is natural that in his case the facts should sometimes have become hopelessly obscured. For example, the blinding of his favourite son, Reza Kuli Khan, is generally regarded as the turning-point of Nadir's career; but though all agree about this, I found it impossible when I was in Persia to make sure of the time and place at which the tragedy occurred, or of some other circumstances connected with it. Altogether, after endeavouring in vain to reconcile the evidence, written and oral, with regard to many incidents in the great conqueror's life, and to fill up gaps in the information, I have preferred to deal with the subject from a point of view other than that of the historian. By this I do not mean that I have written a story which I believe to be inconsistent with known facts. On the contrary, I have done my best throughout to treat known facts with proper respect. But the book does not pretend to be a history.

The stories of Nadir's dream, and of the Shirázi and Ferrash, were told to me, almost word for word as I have given them here, by one of the Shah's ministers, a typical Persian of the old school, easy-going and genial and witty, who to my great satisfaction used often to enliven our official interviews, and lead me away from awkward diplomatic points, by some excursion of the kind. He said the stories were told to him in his youth by a very old and very holy Mujtehid, who had heard them fifty or sixty years before from the Ferrash himself, who helped the lady to escape from the camp, with considerable plunder, on the night of Nadir's death, and afterwards married her and settled down as a country gentleman.

The descriptions of Persian scenes, and of Nadir

Shah's surroundings, have been drawn from notes taken down on the spot, or from accounts left by eye-witnesses. They are as accurate as I could make them.

H. M. D.

2nd August 1908.

CONTENTS

LIST OF ILLUSTRATIONS

CHAPTER I

In the King's pavilion, surrounded by the tents and camp-fires of a great army, three men were drinking together and talking over the scenes of a memorable day.

They lay on soft carpets, after the Persian manner, propped up by cushions, and all of them seemed thoroughly at their ease and free from constraint.

Nevertheless it was evident that one of the three was of superior rank. His carpet was spread upon a wooden platform or 'takht,' richly carved and inlaid, while the other two lay upon the ground to right and left of him. Except for some jewels in his turban, his dress was simple, but his eyes and manner were those of a man used to command. The strong, black-bearded face, tanned by exposure to sun and weather, and the tall, powerful frame, spoke of the camp rather than the Court. He was, in truth, the greatest soldier of his day, Nadir Kuli, the Turkoman robber-chief who had made himself Shah of Persia. He had freed his country from a foreign yoke, routing the Afghans and Turks in many battles, and forcing the Russians to give up the provinces they had seized. Now he was encamped on Indian soil, attacking the great empire of the Moghuls, whose army had been defeated by him a few days before.

His successes had not been due to courage alone.

An Englishman of that day wrote of him what might have been written of Napoleon. 'In the conduct of his wars he ever preferred stratagem to force. His marches were always amazingly rapid, and his progress so irregular and contrary to the ordinary rules of war, that he confounded his enemies.'

Yet Nadir looked what he was, a man good at close quarters. By his side, in place of a sceptre, lay the battle-axe he had carried through all his fields—a plain fighting weapon, which had taken the life of many enemies. It was always ready to his hand, and had won for him the name by which he had long been known—Topuz Khan—The Lord of the Axe.

The man to his right was very different in appearance. He had the dark eyes and thick black eyebrows of the Persian, and a face that must once have been handsome. But the regular features had lost their fineness, and the eyes, though still intelligent and bright with humour, were discoloured and sunk under heavy lids. His round thighs and shoulders gave evidence of sedentary work and want of exercise. This was Mirza Ali Akbar, the keeper of the records, whose duty it was to receive and lay before the Shah all petitions which might be submitted. Practically he had become the Shah's chief minister. He had shown himself a clever and useful servant, with a special talent for finding money to meet his master's perpetual needs, and he was besides an amusing companion, with a bottomless fund of laughter and anecdote.

The last of the three was little more than a boy. The down was still soft on his chin, and his frame was not yet filled out. But he gave promise of growing into a man of great size and power, and he had already shown himself a brave soldier. He was not a Persian, but an Afghan called Ahmed Khan, whom the Shah had taken prisoner in the storm of Kandahar, on his march to India, and had since kept 'at the royal stirrup.' He too was one day to be a famous conqueror.

No man worked harder than Nadir Shah. Like all really great men, he knew that the secret of abiding success is untiring industry. But in the evening, when he ended the long day's work which had begun at sunrise, he liked to retire to his tent with one or two of his people, and to forget for a few hours, over his food and his wine-cups, the labours and cares of his life. Then he unbent entirely, and became again, as he used to say, Nadir Kuli, not Nadir Shah, encouraging those about him to talk and laugh as if he were one of themselves.

At these informal supper-parties all mention of public business was forbidden.

The Shah and his companions had made a hearty meal, for Persians and Afghans alike have magnificent appetites. Pile after pile of rice and roast lamb, served in various forms, had been set before them, and partridges, and young chickens stewed in vine leaves, and grapes, and long white melons, the Shah's favourite fruit, brought for hundreds of miles by fast camels in the wake of the army. They had slaked their thirst with deep draughts of wine, the generous wine of Shiráz, which sparkled like molten gold in the golden goblets. And now they were lying back on their cushions at peace with the world. The Shah's servants had cleared away the dishes, and after pouring warm water over the hands of each, had left on the carpet a tray of sweets and a squat wood-stoppered flask of Shiráz, while they prepared the 'kalián' or water-pipe which follows a Persian dinner.

The Shah was the first to break a short silence.

'It is strange,' he said in his deep voice, 'that the Indians have not yet sent the slaves they were ordered to send. By the head of my father they will repent it if there is any trickery.'

It was a shameful tribute that he was awaiting; but like other eastern conquerors he exacted it from every beaten enemy. The Moghul Emperor had come to the Persian camp that day to sue for peace. He had returned after some hours of bitter humiliation, and as he left the Shah's pavilion, his officers had been reminded that they had orders to send at once fifty of the most beautiful maidens of India, and as many slave boys, for the Shah's approval. The Shah was expecting them now, and with some impatience. He had already in his camp hundreds of women of various nationalities, Persians and Georgians and others, whom he had distributed among his chiefs and soldiery. But the women of India, except a few peasants, he had not yet seen, and it was said that they were not without beauty.

Ali Akbar drained the goblet of Shiráz and put it down beside him. His cheeks were flushed and his eyes were bright. 'The Indians will not dare to disobey,' he said. 'Whose dogs are they that they should trifle with the orders of the King of Kings? But they have hardly had time as yet to collect the slaves and send them.'

Then he turned with a laugh to Ahmed Khan. 'What are the black women like? You should know, boy as you are, for Kandahar is near to Hindustan. Tell the King about them. Are they slender as the cypress, and are their eyes like the stars of night? They say you are a poet, and can make verses like Háfiz. Let us have a stanza or two. You have hardly drunk or spoken to-night. Speak now for the service of the King.'

Ahmed Khan coloured at the ring of contempt in the voice of the older man. 'I know nothing about the women of Hind,' he said, 'and it is not my custom to talk about women. I serve the King with deeds, not words.'

The Persian threw himself back on his cushions and burst into a peal of laughter. 'He does not talk about women. He serves the King by deeds, not words. Ai Afrîn! Afrîn! Bravo! Bravo! So young and yet so mighty,' and his fat sides heaved with his mirth.

Ahmed Khan answered hotly, 'There is nothing to laugh at. But a man who has drunk a camel load of Shiráz will laugh at anything.'

Ali Akbar only laughed the more. 'He sees nothing to laugh at. Oh the buffalo calf, the Afghan buffalo calf! When God had many asses, why did He make the Afghan?'

Nadir bent down and laid his hand on the boy's shoulder. There was laughter in his eyes too, and it had stung Ahmed Khan. But now he repressed himself. 'You have spoken the truth,' he said. 'You have done good service, young as you are. Ali Akbar meant no harm. It is his way. He would laugh at his grandfather's beard.'

As the Shah spoke there was a noise outside the pavilion—the tramp of horses, and the voices of men, and the shrill trumpeting of an elephant. Nadir sat up and listened. A servant came in, stepping softly in his woollen socks over the felts and carpets that covered the floor. He made a deep reverence before the Shah's seat, and stood with his eyes cast down. 'What is it?' Nadir said.

'I beg to represent for the service of the Shah that the Indians have sent a present, an elephant and some horses, and a hundred slaves.'

Nadir's eyes brightened. 'Ah,' he said. 'At last. Bring the slaves into the outer tents, and tell me when all is ready. I will come and see.'

When the man came back the Shah rose, and telling the others to follow him, he walked out of the tent where he had been sitting. First he went to see the animals, which were standing outside in the torch-light. There was a tall elephant with hanging 'jhûl' of cloth of gold, encrusted with precious stones, and a row of horses richly caparisoned. The elephant lifted its trunk and saluted at a signal from its driver. The Shah loved horses as much as women, but it was too dark to see them properly then. He would inspect them in the morning when there was light. 'Now show me the slaves,' he said, and a negro in attendance led the way to a long tent brightly lighted, and carpeted with soft felt. Ranged along both sides of it were fifty boys in clothing of embroidered muslin and brocade. The Shah walked down the tent looking to right and left, and ordered that the boys should attend his Durbar or Court next day. Then the negro led him to a second tent, where the Indian girls were assembled. In the middle of the tent, an embroidered slipper in his hand, stood a black eunuch who had come in charge of the girls, and had been marshalling them to receive the Shah.

As Nadir entered they all bent low with an Indian 'salaam.' There were many beautiful faces there, and many graceful forms, for Indian women yield to none in loveliness of face and figure. But as Nadir looked down the room, one of the girls especially struck his fancy, and walking to the middle of the line, where she was standing, he stopped before her. She was tall and slight, with black hair and dark eyes, but with a complexion as fair as that of many Europeans. A bright flush was in her cheeks, and she held herself erect, with a touch of defiance which singled her out from the rest.

'Who is this girl?' Nadir said to the eunuch in Persian.

'My Lord, a maiden of the Rajputs.'

The girl looked the Shah in the face. 'A Rajputni, but no maiden,' she said. 'I have been a wife.'

The eunuch stepped forward hastily, and raised his slipper as though he would have struck her across the mouth. The next instant he recoiled in alarm, for with a sudden movement the girl had drawn a dagger from the breast of her dress, and though she held it quietly across her, point downwards, there was no mistaking the warning in her eyes.

To right and left of the Shah were standing Ahmed Khan and Ali Akbar, whom in the licence of camp life he had taken with him. As the dagger flashed in the lamp-light, Ahmed Khan stepped quickly forward with uplifted hand, between the Shah and the fiery girl. Ali Akbar as quickly sprang backwards. 'God save us!' he exclaimed, in alarm.

Nadir looked over his shoulder and smiled contemptuously. Ali Akbar coloured. 'I am a man of the pen, not a man of the sword,' he said with an uneasy laugh.

Nadir turned from him in silence. He drew Ahmed Khan back into his place, and stood before the girl with a look in which there was something of admiration.

'Give me the knife,' he said sternly. The girl looked in his face, hesitated an instant, and obeyed. Nadir took the weapon from her and thrust it carelessly into the shawl he wore about his waist.

'Do you know,' he asked, 'what is the penalty for drawing steel in the King's presence?' The girl did not answer.

'It is death.'

She remained silent, but he saw the heaving of her heart under the tight bodice. He turned to the eunuch.

'Mannerless dog,' he said, 'you may thank God that you are the servant of the Emperor. But for that the rods should have broken every bone in your body.'

Then he passed slowly down the lines of startled women, and looked them over carelessly one by one. As he came back, past the point where the Rajputni was standing, his eyes fell on her again, and lingered a moment.

He returned to the tent where he had dined; but he seemed to be in no mood for further talk. He dismissed his companions with a curt word of farewell, and went into the Anderûn, or women's quarters.

CHAPTER II

When the King had entered the tent in which he usually slept, he took his seat on the takht prepared for him, leant back on his cushions, and remained for a few minutes in silent thought.

The remembrance of the scene he had just witnessed seemed to be pleasing to him, for a faint smile came into his face. He drew the dagger from his waistband and looked at it curiously. 'A woman's toy,' he said to himself, 'but she would have used it, and it was enough to frighten two men. Men! She is more of a man than either of them! How beautiful she looked!' He put the dagger down on the takht beside his axe, and paused a moment. Then he called for a servant. 'Send me the Agha Bashi.'

The Agha Bashi or chief eunuch came at once. He was a tall negro, with a sad but pleasant face. In all the great King's following there was perhaps no one whom he trusted so thoroughly, and with reason, for the man was worthy of trust. He had the fidelity of his race for those he loved, and he loved Nadir, who had rescued him from ill-treatment some years before and had given him service. A quick eye for character and a half-generous, half-calculating kindness to men who were in trouble had won Nadir many friends. He never did a wiser thing than when he promoted the grateful African to the charge of his Anderûn, a charge which meant close attachment to his person, and considerable power.

'You know what happened just now when I was looking at the Indian women.'

The negro bent his head. 'I know. I saw it all.'

'The girl is beautiful.'

'Beautiful as a Peri.'

'I want to see her alone.'

The negro looked troubled. 'Ba chashm—on my eyes be it, but——'

'Well, what is it? You think there is danger, that the Indians have sent her here to do me evil?' and Nadir laughed.

'She is only a weak girl, and the Shah is stronger than the hero Rustem, but . . . I trust no woman, least of all one of these Indians. She is not like other women.'

Nadir laughed again. 'A woman who can do what she did is more to be trusted than a lying Persian. Send her to me.'

The negro hesitated. Nadir laid his hand on the man's shoulder with a touch that was almost a caress.

'I know, I know,' he said, 'and you do well to be careful. But there is no danger. Send the girl here.'

The last words were quietly spoken, but they were a command. The Agha Bashi laid his hand on his heart and bent his head again. 'Whatever the Shah wills,' he answered, and passed out.

A few minutes went by, and then the hanging curtain at the doorway was held aside, and the Rajput girl stepped into the Shah's presence. The curtain dropped behind her. After a quick glance round the room her eyes fell, and she stood before him in silence. For some seconds he did not speak, but gazed at her steadily, and even in the dim lamp-light he could see that with all her proud carriage, her breast was heaving and her hands shook as she arranged a fold of her dress about her. He could see too that his first impression had not been false. Though very young, she was beautiful as few women are, and the delicate Indian dress displayed rather than hid the gracefulness of her slight but deep-bosomed figure. At last he spoke. 'Come nearer,' he said, 'and stand in front of me.' She walked forward and stopped again, within a few feet of him.

'Look up, girl, and answer my questions, and see that you speak the truth.'

She raised her eyes, and looked at him. His face did not seem unfriendly.

'You are frightened, girl. What is it?'

'I am not frightened, but, my Lord, you said that . . . that for what I had done the punishment was death.'

'Let your heart be at rest. I meant only to warn you. You are forgiven.'

She put her hand to her forehead. 'The King is great and merciful. What am I that I should trouble the King? God knows I meant no harm. But I will not be beaten by eunuchs.'

Nadir smiled and held out the dagger she had surrendered to him. 'Take it,' he said. 'Maybe you will want it again one day, but do not draw it too readily.'

She put it back in the breast of her dress.

'How is it that you speak Persian?'

'My Lord, I have lived at the Moghul Court. Every one there learns to speak Persian.'

'What is your name?'

'My Rajput name was Meera Bai, but I have been called by another name, Sitara.'

'That is easier, and it is a lucky name. Now answer

me. What made you speak as you did in the tent? Is it true?'

The blood came into her face.

'Yes, it is true.'

'But why did you say it? Did you not know that you were playing with your life?'

'Yes, I knew it; but what is life to me? And I did not think the King would kill me. I thought he would send me back and punish the Moghuls for deceiving him.'

'Why should I punish the Moghuls?'

'Why should you not?' she answered bitterly. 'Is it fitting to lay before the King of Kings the food half eaten by a dog?'

'You have no love for the Moghuls?'

'Does a woman love those who have slain her kindred and brought her to shame?'

'Then why did you wish to go back?'

'My Lord, I am a Hindu. I feared I should be given to one of the King's soldiers and taken away beyond the mountains, to the land of the man-sellers. I would die rather.'

Nadir thought of his Turkoman horse, with their flat Tartar faces and filthy sheepskins, a horror to the clean and delicately dressed Indians.

'My spearmen are rough folk,' he said. 'So the Indians fear them?'

'Yes, my Lord. Dreadful tales are told about them in the Moghul camp.'

'What do they say?'

'I hear people say that their horses are as large as elephants, and breathe fire as they come galloping into the fight; and that the riders have the heads of wild beasts, bears and tigers and lions.'

Nadir laughed aloud. 'Fools and cowards!' he said.

The girl's head went up. 'Without doubt there are cowards among them, but there are many brave men. Many are Rajputs.'

Nadir smiled. 'They could do nothing when they met my troops.'

'My Lord, they have no leaders. The Moghul lords know nothing of war, and many are faithless to their salt. What is the Emperor himself but a woman, and less than a woman?'

Nadir agreed in his heart, but he answered with pretended sternness: 'Girl, you are speaking of a King.' He always stood by his order.

'Forgive me, my Lord. But he has not seen war. If one like the Shah had led the Indians they would not have fled.'

She spoke in simple earnestness, and Nadir saw it. Her words pleased him more than the extravagant flatteries of the men about him.

'You do right to speak well of your people,' he said. 'But tell me your own story. What have the Moghuls done to you?'

Her face clouded over and her eyes grew hard.

'My Lord, I am nothing. What can I say that the King would care to hear?'

'But I wish to hear it. Tell me all from the beginning. There is nothing to fear.'

She paused a moment and collected herself.

'My Lord, I am a Rajputni of the tribe of the Rahtors. My father was a Thákur—a chieftain—and his name was well known in our country. He had held his fort and his lands against all men, and my brothers, too, were strong and brave.

'As our custom is, I was married when I was a child, but I remained in my father's house. Before they came to take me away to the place where I was to live . . . there had been foolish talk about me.'

'What did they say? That you were beautiful?'

She flushed hotly. 'These things are said without reason.'

Nadir smiled. 'They did not lie,' he said. 'Go on.'

'My Lord, it was the ruin of our house. For some time there had been a Moghul force not far off making war on another Thákur, who had raided across the Moghul border. He was at feud with us, and the Moghul leader had made friendship with my people, so that we feared nothing. One night some of his men had come to my father with a message, and had been received into our fort. We had a fort on a hill, and at the foot was a village of reed huts with a thorn fence round it. It was not a great fort, but it was strong for our country. It had often been besieged and never taken.

'Suddenly a little before dawn there was a noise of firing and shouting, and my people woke from their sleep to find that the gateway had been opened, and that the Moghuls were rushing up the stone slope into the fort, killing every one they could see. They had crept up in the darkness, and the gates had been opened by their men inside.'

Her voice faltered, but she controlled herself and went on quietly:

'We were not thinking of any treachery, and they were ten to one. My father and brothers fought, as our people have always fought, but what could they do? They had not even time to kill the women, and we found ourselves in the hands of the Moghuls. The huts below had been set on fire, and one or two jumped from the walls of the fort into the flames and became 'sati,' pure. The rest were taken, and I among them. My hands were bound with handkerchiefs, and I was tied upon a camel.'

'Faithless dogs! And then?'

'All that day and night and all the next day we marched fast, for the clansmen were said to be gathering to rescue us. On the second evening the Moghuls had reached safety in the great fort of Ajmir, and I was taken from the camel and put on a charpai—a string bed. Then an old woman came and told me all the evil had been done for my sake, that a young Moghul lord had heard of me and sent the troops to carry me off. She said he was young and handsome, and that he would take me into his zenána, and that it was a great honour for a Hindu girl.'

Her eyes flashed and her breath came fast. 'What did you say?' Nadir asked.

'My Lord, I thought of my father and my brothers. I said that I was a Rajputni and that no Moghul dog should touch me, and I know not what more.'

'You spoke well. And after that?'

'The woman laughed. She was an old woman with an evil face, and as she leant over me I saw my "putli," my image, in her eyes, head downward, and I knew she was a witch. Then I was frightened and begged her to help me; but she only laughed and said I was a fool, and left me alone.'

'And after that?'

'Afterwards he came and stood looking at me. He was not a warrior like my people, but soft and womanish like the Lords of the Court, and I hated him. He spoke to me, and I answered I know not what. I was mad with grief and anger.'

'You did well. And then?'

'Then he grew angry too, and said he would tame me, and at last he struck me on the mouth.' She clenched her hands.

'Cowardly hound! And then?'

'My Lord, I was bound and helpless. What could I do?'

She covered her face with her hands, and a sob broke from her.

Nadir sprang from his seat with an oath, and laid his hand on her shoulder. She shrank back and shook herself free. He stood gazing at her with rage in his eyes.

'By Allah! he shall die the death of a dog.'

She shook her head and controlled herself. 'He is dead.'

'Alhemdulillah! Praise be to God! Tell me the rest.'

'For some days more I remained in Ajmir, and then we marched away to the north. I wanted to kill myself, but I could not. They used to untie me to let me eat, and then they bound my hands again with twisted handkerchiefs. They said I should remain so until I grew quiet.

'One night when we were in camp, and had marched far from my country, the old witch came again and jeered at me, and I said I would resist no more if they would untie my hands. I was broken with grief, and I could not bear the pain any longer. I thought that if I could get free I should find some way of killing myself, and I promised.

'Then they unbound me, and I was married. A

Mulla, a priest, came and said some Mussulman spells, and made me repeat their cursed "kalima."'[1]

'Girl, you are blaspheming our holy faith.'

She looked up quickly, and saw a mocking light in Nadir's eyes.

'And then?'

'My Lord, in the evening he came to me. If he had said a kind word then, I might have given in, for I was worn and broken, but he laughed and made me hate him. Then I thought of my people again, and as he tried to take me I snatched at the dagger he was wearing in his waistcloth, and struck him—once and twice.'

'You killed him?'

She shuddered and was silent.

'Afrîn! And after that?'

'After that I do not remember very well what happened, but no one had heard, and in the darkness I got away from the tent and into the fields. I walked as far as I could, and in the morning there was no one in sight.

'That day I lay hidden in the long grass near some water I had found by chance, and while I was lying there some men came riding along a track which passed close by me. I watched them in fear lest they should be searching for me, but when they came near I saw that they were Marwári traders, from my own country, though not of my blood. They stopped and drank water, and I heard them speaking in our language. Then I showed myself and spoke to them.

'They were afraid at first to do anything, for they had heard all about me, but after some talk they

[1] The kalima is the Mahomedan confession of faith. 'There is no God but God, and Muhammad is the prophet of God.' The Persians add, 'And Ali is the friend of God.'

said they would help me. So they took me away with them, and after a long time we came to Delhi, where the Court was. One of the Emperor's wives was a Rahtor princess from my own country, and was held in high honour. She was kind to me, and gave me shelter and food. I have been with her ever since. No one molested me, for I was the Queen's servant, and besides they said I was mad.

'But I was a burden to her, and when the Emperor's people came to-day to make up the number of the slave girls, she could not protect me any longer, and they brought me here. What more can I say?'

Nadir gazed at her in silence. She did not meet his eyes, but stood erect again, with the same touch of defiance which had attracted him at first. He had seen many women, but never, he thought, one like her, beautiful beyond words, and brave and impetuous, a woman worthy of himself. A sudden wave of passion came over him, something more than passion, a sudden desire to make that hot heart his own.

With the quick instinct which rarely left him, he felt that if he could win her love, the love of a slave girl, whose person and life were at his mercy, he would win what he had never known yet. And all-powerful as he was, he stooped to sue for it.

The very fact that she was what she was appealed to his masterful nature. He had taken pleasure in showing all about him that they were nothing but what he made them; that the King's will was the one power to which they owed honour or disgrace. He would show it them again, men and women, and the Indian slave should at his word become a Queen before whom all should bow.

She did not yield at once. Although he laid aside his rank and power, and appealed to her as any man might have done, with passionate admiration and entreaty, she was startled and shrank from his eager eyes. But what woman in her place would have resisted long? She, the helpless girl whom he could have handed over as he pleased to death, or the depths of dishonour, found herself wooed by the greatest King and conqueror of the age; and as he stood before her, tall and straight and comely, with words of praise and tenderness on his lips, she would surely have been more or less than woman if her wounded heart had not gone out to him.

'Oh, my Lord,' she said at last, with a great wonder and the dawn of a great joy filling her eyes, 'Oh, my Lord, what am I that I should find favour in the sight of the King? But if it is so indeed, then from this day I shall have no thought but to give my life for the King's service.' And with a swift movement she knelt and laid her hands on his feet.

Nadir raised her. 'You shall not be a servant,' he said, 'but a Queen. You said your Rahtor princess was the honoured wife of the Emperor of Hind. You shall be the honoured wife of a greater than the Moghul, and he and his women shall be as dust under your feet.'

He put her aside suddenly and called for the Agha Bashi, to whom he gave an order.

The negro came back soon after with one of the priests or mullas whom Nadir kept in his camp.

When the brief informal ceremony was over, the mulla went out. Nadir laughed. 'Pidr Sukhteh!' he said, 'son of a burnt father! what foolishness it is. But for your sake it is better.'

The Agha Bashi returned bearing a golden casket, which he opened and held before the Shah. It was full of jewels which glittered in the lamp-light.

'Come and choose for yourself,' Nadir said. 'You must wear to-night the ornaments of a queen.'

She made a quick gesture of refusal.

'But you shall wear them,' he said, and one by one he forced them upon her; a 'sarpîch' of diamonds for her head, and a broad armlet of emeralds, and golden bangles encrusted with gems for her slender wrists, and ropes of pearls for her throat and bosom.

When he had adorned her as he pleased, he led her to the takht on which he had been seated, and made her take her seat beside him.

As, many hundreds of years before, Esther the Jewess found favour in the sight of the great King Ahasuerus, so the Rajput girl had won the heart of his mighty successor. And deep in her own heart, born of his strength and tenderness, had come into being a love that would never leave it while she lived.

CHAPTER III

The morning mist had cleared away from the plain in which the Persian host was encamped. There had been frost, but in the bright Indian sunshine the air was warm and pleasant. The sky was blue, without a cloud.

Nadir Shah was to hold that day a great 'Durbar' to celebrate his victory over the army of the Moghul. Sitara, concealed from all eyes, in the upper story of a building where the Agha Bashi had placed her, stood gazing through a screen of marble fretwork at the opening of the pageant. Nadir, as his custom was, had risen at dawn and had been at work for some hours despatching the business of the day. Now that the sun was well up, and that the assembly was ready to receive him, he came out from his tents, and mounted his horse to ride to the spot prepared.

His approach was heralded by a mighty shout from the thousands who had gathered on the open space in the middle of the camp, and Sitara, her heart beating fast with excitement, saw her royal lover appear. Before him came a hundred of his 'Chaûsh,' in brilliant uniforms of green and silver, who called out his titles and invoked blessings upon him. 'In the name of God —the great and merciful. Victory to the King of Kings!—Victory!—Victory!' Then, alone, no man within ten paces of him, and none but himself on horseback, Nadir rode slowly past between the lines of his troops.

Soldier as he was above all, he knew the effect of pomp and show upon the imagination of the East, and to-day nothing was wanting to make the ceremonial one of impressive splendour. He had laid aside the simple dress he usually wore, and was arrayed like Solomon in all his glory. On his head was a golden helmet, encrusted with pearls and gems in the shape of a crown. To the right side of it were fixed three black heron's feathers, the badge of Persian royalty, clasped together by a large diamond. A crimson mantle lined with fur fell from his shoulders. Under it he wore a coat of cloth of gold. In the Kashmir shawl which was wound about his waist glittered a jewelled dagger. His riding-boots of soft crimson leather rested in stirrups of beaten gold. His charger, a tall grey Turkoman, moved proudly under him, its arched neck adorned with a rich collar of gold and precious stones. The bridle and headpiece and breast-plate were also of gold, and studded with jewels. But in his right hand, as if to remind all about him that Nadir the King of Kings was still Nadir the soldier, he held in place of a sceptre the plain battle-axe which his people knew so well.

At the foot of his throne the King dismounted. It was raised several steps above the ground, and surmounted by a cupola of gold, borne on golden rods. On each side of it stood a golden lion. Behind it were two lofty flagstaffs, from which floated the royal standards of crimson and yellow silk, embroidered with the Persian device of the lion and sun.

As the King took his seat, there was a thunder of drums and a blare of trumpets, and the whole of the great assembly before him bent low in salutation. Nadir bowed his head slightly in acknowledgment, and gave the signal for all to be seated who had a claim to the honour.

Sitara watched him with pride and wonder in her eyes. He seemed so great and glorious, so far removed from her, that she found it hard to believe all was not 'maya,' a delusion. Could it be true that she, the slave girl of yesterday, was now the beloved of that mighty being—almost a god, as he seemed to her?

But as she gazed, the assembly sank into order and silence, and her eyes wandered in womanly curiosity over the splendid scene.

Close behind the Shah's throne stood the green-coated Chaûsh, and the royal bodyguard, tall men in white uniforms, with cuirasses of steel. These were armed, like himself, with battle-axes; but their weapons, unlike his own, were ornamented with gold and silver chasing. A golden axe was embossed on each man's breastplate.

To right and left of the Shah's throne were five hundred slave boys, among them the Indians sent to the Shah the night before. These were marked out from the rest by their delicate muslins and embroideries, not less than by their dark faces and slender figures. A thousand young men of gentle birth, drawn up in single rank, enclosed the space set apart for the 'Durbaris.' Each held in his hand a silver-topped lance, from which drooped a pennon of crimson silk, with silver fringe and tassels. A few paces to the rear of the line of pennons, on all four sides of the enclosure, stood the Guards, a body of picked soldiers six thousand strong. They were formed up in close order, four deep, two ranks facing outwards, two inwards. These troops were clothed in white uniforms and turbans, with breastplates of polished steel, and armed with sword and musket. The only points of colour about them were the crimson four-pointed caps, round the base of which the white turban was wound, and a badge in the waistband which served to distinguish the men of the several commands.

Nadir might well look with pride upon those grand soldiers, hardened by his iron discipline and by years of war. Not all the East in arms would have broken that square.

Within the enclosure facing the throne, the chief men of Nadir's Court sat in long lines upon the carpets which covered the ground. Behind them, hundreds more stood in even ranks, marshalled by the King's attendants. All kept their eyes cast down, and not a word was spoken.

Outside the square, the men of the Persian army and its innumerable camp-followers had gathered to see what they could of the great ceremonial. Gazing down through her marble screen, Sitara saw them in their thousands; the fierce warriors who had marched triumphant from the Caucasus to the Ganges, and filled all Asia with their renown. They were of many nations, Turkomans with flat Tartar faces and huge fur busbies; black-bearded stalwart Afghans, in loose white clothing or 'postîns' of sheepskin embroidered with yellow silk; Bakhtiari tribesmen from the mountains of Central Persia, smaller men with a different type of face, wearing round caps of white felt; Georgians from the Caucasus, white-skinned and handsome and reckless; wild Kurds from the Western border, who were said to worship the devil; Arabs from the plain watered by the Karûn; Persian 'Kizlbash,' or red heads, so called from their scarlet caps, with scissor-clipped beards and long drooping moustaches, whose name was often applied to the whole army. Among the soldiers were women, the light loves of the camp, cloaked like men, and hardly to be distinguished from them.

As Sitara's glance wandered over the motley crowd, she was struck by the hush that had fallen upon it. In the words of an eye-witness who was present at one of these gatherings: 'Dieu! quelle vigoureuse administration! Dans ce camp immense, plein d'une multitude mêlée, on eût dit un seul homme, retenant son haleine, tant il y avait de modestie et de crainte.'

Sitara's eyes went back to the master of them all, seated under his golden canopy. He waited a few moments, with a proud joy in the display of his power, and then his deep voice broke the stillness. She was too far away behind him to hear what he said, but the strong tones reached to the farthest limits of the assembly in front of him. He spoke slowly, with the dignity and natural eloquence which seem to be the birthright of the East. If his words were not free from oriental hyperbole, they were the better suited to his hearers. He began, as ever, by giving God the glory. It had pleased the Most High, he said, before whom all men were as the dust of the earth, to make the humblest of His creatures a conqueror and a king. Praise be to His name. And now it had pleased Him to vouchsafe to his servant another victory such as the world had never seen.

By the favour of God, the host of the idolaters had been scattered. The men of Hind had come up to battle with pride and boasting, till the plain was black with their elephants and horsemen, and now what were they? The soldiers of Islam had rushed upon them like lions, and their hearts had turned to water. Thousands had been hurled into hell, and those who had found safety in flight were cowering behind their entrenchments, not daring to face the royal troops in the open 'maidán.'

The Emperor of Hind had presented himself at the royal footstool, and had sued for mercy, and this slave of the Merciful, remembering that the sword and clemency are twins, had set his heart at rest.

The troops of Islam would now march on the capital, and if any of the black men ventured to raise again the standard of rebellion, they would be ground to powder.

Then Nadir announced that as a thank-offering for the victory, he had ordered a general distribution of rewards, in which all present would share. Their leaders would be honoured with 'khilats,' robes of honour and presents, according to the valour they had shown, and every soldier would receive a gratuity of three months' pay.

The Persians passed their hands over their beards, and a low murmur of applause made itself heard, but Nadir raised his hand to command silence. 'It is nothing,' he said. 'Remain faithful in the service of the King, and be assured that Nadir, the son of the Sword, will never forget the man who shows himself ready to throw away his life in the fight for the sake of Islam.' He paused, and then added with something of sternness in his tone, and something of mockery in his eyes: 'And you who are not men of the sword, you also be assured that faithful service will not be forgotten. You who are men of the pen, and you priests, let your service be done, and your prayers be offered, for the welfare of Islam. Be faithful and devoted, as these poor servants and priests of God, the men of the sword, have been faithful and devoted. Then it will be well with you. What more shall I say?'

For a moment there was silence, and then at a sign from him there was a roll of drums, with which mingled the shouts, no longer repressed, of the triumphant soldiery.

As the clamour died away, a score of richly clothed attendants advanced into the Durbar square, and passed down the lines, swinging before them jewelled censers from which rose clouds of perfumed incense. After them walked others bearing golden trays covered with sweetmeats, and golden vases from which they distributed atar of roses. The men who had not the privilege of a seat on the carpet, and had remained standing, were similarly honoured, but the censers and vases and trays used for them were of silver instead of gold.

While the distribution went on, Nadir sat motionless under his canopy, one hand resting upon the head of the golden lion at his side, one holding his battle-axe. When all was over, and the attendants had replaced their censers and vases on two golden tables in front of him, he rose slowly, stood for a moment drawn up to his full height, looking proudly down on the silent ranks before him, and then, with a gesture of farewell, descended the steps from under his canopy, and mounted his horse. As the Turkoman stepped forward, champing its golden bit, and arching its neck, the martial music broke out again, and once more the voices of the Chaûsh rose in a triumphant shout, 'Victory to the King of Kings!—Victory!—Victory!'

And the Indian girl, hidden behind her marble lattice, saw him as he passed look up towards her. He made no sign, but she knew that in all his glory he was thinking of her, and her face flushed with a passion of pride and joy.

THE MOGHUL EMPEROR MUHAMMAD SHAH

From Fraser's 'History of Nadir Shah,' 1742

CHAPTER IV

In the camp of the victorious Persians the day was one of triumph and rejoicing. In the camp of the Moghul Emperor it passed in very different fashion.

The evening before, as Nadir told his soldiery, the Moghul had presented himself at the footstool of his conqueror to sue for peace. He had suffered bitter humiliation. At the entrance to the Shah's camp, he had been forced to leave behind the scanty retinue he had brought with him, and to go on almost alone to Nadir's tent. There, it is true, he had been received with some show of the ceremony due to a king. Nadir Shah had come out as he alighted from his litter, had embraced him and bid him welcome, and had led him to a seat on the royal divan. But when the two monarchs were sitting side by side, and had made the customary inquiries after each other's health, Nadir had proceeded to inflict upon his beaten foe a merciless homily. He had reproached the Moghul with his weakness and indolence, his neglect of public affairs, his want of control and discipline over his officials and people, his rashness and incompetence in the field. 'You were so puffed up, with your own childish conceits and foolish resolutions, that you would not listen to the honourable overtures which I made, or consult your own interest, until at last by the assistance of the Creator of the World, and the strength of the arms of the victorious warriors, you have seen what has happened. Your army has been routed and scattered. And now you have cooped yourselves up in your entrenchments, with your elephants and your guns, not considering that if your enemy was stronger you could not remain in them without food or water, and if he were weaker it was unnecessary and disgraceful to let yourselves be besieged by him.'

Nevertheless, the conqueror went on, he would not make the Moghul pay the full penalty for his misdeeds. 'Hitherto your house has not injured the people of Persia. Therefore I shall not take the empire from you. But as your indolence and pride have obliged me to march so far and have put me to vast expense, and as my troops are fatigued and in want of necessaries, I must go on to Delhi. There I shall remain some days until my army is refreshed, and the tribute your ministers have promised has been paid to me. After that I shall leave you to look after your own affairs.'

To all this, and much more in the same strain, the fallen Emperor had been forced to listen. He had heard it in silence, his head bowed with shame. The descendant of a great line of warriors and kings, of Tamerlane and Humayun and Akbar, he had not dared, on the soil won by the swords of his forefathers, to say a word in answer to the contemptuous reproaches of the Turkoman soldier of fortune.

After he had been dismissed, the Moghul re-entered his litter and was borne away through the lines of the Persian army towards his own camp. Overwhelmed with misery and shame, he shrank back behind the embroidered curtains, hiding his face from the eyes of the rough soldiery of Irán, who had gathered here and there to gaze upon the show. Their bold, disdainful stare filled him with impotent rage, and though he understood little of their language, he writhed under the mocking laughter which broke out now and again at some witty gibe.

When he had passed the outer lines, and had been left to the escort of his own retinue, he pushed aside the curtains of his litter, and after a hasty glance round to see that he was safe, broke into a torrent of railing against the man who had humbled him. His shrill voice rose almost to a scream as he poured out his complaints and curses, now bemoaning with tearful self-pity the open disgrace to which he had been subjected; now angrily declaring that he was still a king, and that he would lead out his army himself to take a fearful revenge on the accursed barbarians. But his boasting imposed on none. The very tone of his voice, uncertain and querulous, betrayed his weakness; and the men about him, some of them traitors who had invited the enemy to India, paid little attention to his words. Looking from one to the other in piteous appeal, he could see that under the forms of respect they scarcely tried to conceal the disdain which filled them.

Their road lay across the plain where the battle had been, and as the litter was borne along at the slow pattering trot of the bearers, the wretched monarch saw around him horrible traces of the fight. Dead men lay on all sides, their bodies twisted into every sort of attitude, or swollen beyond recognition. They were all Indians, for the Persians had buried their own dead. The stench from the rotting corpses poisoned the air. Here and there a wounded man, still alive after days of thirst and torment under an Indian sun, moaned out a prayer for water, or a wounded horse stood with drooping head, patiently waiting for death. The Moghul, to do him justice, was not unkindly. He gave orders for the burial of the dead, and for help to be brought to the wounded. But his people took little heed of the order.

When the Emperor's litter arrived within the lines of his own entrenchments, he felt for the moment a little less miserable. The Indian army had lost heavily in the battle, and afterwards great numbers had deserted; but many thousands of brave fighting-men still remained, and the Moghul, encouraged by the sight of them, was almost tempted to try his fortune again.

In that frame of mind he entered his women's quarters, and called for his chief Queen. She had tried in vain to prevent his going as a suppliant to the Persian camp. Now she rejoiced at the change which seemed to have come over him.

'Ah, my Lord, she said, 'at last you speak like a king. You have been deceived by the traitors about you, but it is not too late. There are many still faithful to their salt, and you have lakhs of fighting-men, hundreds of thousands. Bring together those whom you can trust among your ministers, and tell them now that you have resolved to fight. You will see that they only want this to give them fresh heart. If you cannot attack the Persian dogs in their camp, you can send away your women and treasure, and fall back fighting. The Persians cannot follow you all over Hindustan. They are worn with their long marches, and they will grow weaker and weaker as they advance. Without your help they cannot find food, and their accursed troops will starve. Not one will recross the frontier.

Act now, to-night. Get your troops ready, and in the morning we will leave the entrenchments and march for Delhi. For God's sake do not delay.'

The Moghul seemed almost convinced, and she thought she had prevailed. He swore that he would fight, and vowed vengeance on the traitors who had beguiled him. But he could not make up his mind to act at once. He was faint for want of food, and he longed for the opium to which he had become a slave. It would be time enough in the morning, he said. He must have rest.

Then the Queen tried to spur his flagging spirit by reproaches and taunts. 'In the morning it will be too late. You will sleep till midday with your accursed wine and opium, and the Persians may attack at day-break. Then your face will be blackened indeed. Will you let your wives be carried off by Tartar dogs before your eyes?'

The Moghul only grew sullen. Come what might he would have his comforting poison, and secure an hour or two of peace and forgetfulness. 'I will hear no more,' he answered angrily. 'What does a woman know of State affairs? The Persian is nothing but a blood-drinking robber, and I have fooled him. He thinks I am going to make peace, and will do nothing yet. He is afraid to attack. Thousands of his men were killed in the fight, and he knows our entrench-ments are strong. Though he spoke great words, he was frightened. When he saw that I was angry he turned white with fear, and his heart became like water. I saw it. He was trembling. What is he? A dog and son of a dog.'

The Queen turned away with a gesture of disdain. She saw that for the moment she could do no more.

The ignoble craving was too strong to be resisted. The Moghul's heart was as soft as his effeminate limbs. Still she would not despair. He had shown some signs of spirit, and she hoped against hope that rest and sleep might bring him courage.

It was not to be. Wearied in mind and body the Moghul drank deep that night, and when the wine had done its work he turned to the treacherous drug which was sapping his life. Long after the sun was high he lay in his darkened room sleeping a torpid sleep. When he woke to consciousness, and the remembrance of the day before came back to his clouded brain, he turned on his cushions with a groan. At last he sat up and called to his people. His eyes were bloodshot, and his hands trembled as he held to his lips the cup of wine for which he had asked.

His servants brought him evil news. The Persian horsemen were riding far and wide on all sides of his camp. They had surprised and destroyed a detachment of Rajputs who were marching up to join his army, and a few wounded fugitives only had escaped to spread fear and confusion among the troops within the entrenchments. During the night, too, there had been many desertions, hundreds of men stealing away singly or in companies, under cover of the darkness. Grain had gone up to famine prices, even water was scarce, and the soldiers were murmuring.

The news was bad, and as the day wore on it was made worse by the Emperor's ministers. The peace party, traitors many of them, and mostly men of Persian or Tartar families, used his attendants to frighten him. Their natural love of exaggeration was stimulated by bribes, and as the Emperor was always ready, after the manner of the East, to listen to any one about him, the stories of the ministers had their full effect.

In truth, the state of things was bad enough. The whole army was disheartened by defeat, and by the feeling that they had no leader. There were many brave men among them, and the Rajput clansmen were ready as ever to follow their tribal chiefs to the death. But the chiefs were jealous of each other, and it needed a strong hand to weld together the clans into one fighting whole.

If the Emperor had taken command in person, and appealed to their loyalty, foreigner as he was in blood and creed, they would have responded to the call; but the Emperor was hiding his face in his women's quarters, and the nominal commander-in-chief was the arch-traitor who had planned the invasion.

Finally, the imagination of the Indian troops, always credulous and quick to exaggerate any tales of marvel or horror, had been appalled by the stories told round their camp-fires. To the comparatively civilised and polished Indians, Nadir Shah and his fierce soldiery seemed at best wild and savage. Now they were told, and half believed, that the Persian King was surrounded by supernatural beings, jins and demons with awful powers. Cowards who had fled from the field, or men in the pay of the traitors, described the Tartar spearmen as giants mounted on colossal horses, whose nostrils spouted fire. It was said that horseman and steed alike devoured the bodies of the slain, and that even elephants were killed like sheep by one thrust of the terrible lances. In vain some of the sturdy Jats and Rajputs scoffed at these tales. They sank deep into the hearts of the superstitious Indians. Throughout the doomed army of the Moghul there was idleness and disunion and doubt, and the shadow of a great fear.

And over against it stood the trained fighting-men of Nadir, diverse in nationality, like the Indians, but united by confidence in their great leader, hardened by years of warfare, and taught by an unbroken series of victories to believe themselves invincible.

It was at best a gloomy prospect that the Moghul had to face, and though the Persians made no attack in force, the day brought him little comfort. Stung by the reproaches of his Queen, and writhing under a sense of shame, he tried to find support for his flagging courage in the counsels of others. But he shrank from the one course which might have saved him. Instead of doing what she advised, taking command of the army in person, and announcing that he would fight to the end, he did the worst that could be done. He assembled his council and told them that he had three courses open to him. The first was to fight, the second to take poison and escape from the miseries of the world, the third to accept whatever terms Nadir Shah might impose. And though by fits he spoke boastfully enough, he let it be seen only too clearly that in his heart he inclined to the most shameful course of all. With such an example before them, his councillors did little to help him. One or two good soldiers spoke up and urged him to make a push for victory. Others remained silent or gave uncertain counsel. Others again magnified the dangers and difficulties, and showed that they regarded resistance as hopeless. The day passed away, and the Moghul remained undecided. His last chance had gone.

For two or three days longer the final decision was put off, but there could only be one ending to the long-drawn misery. The Queen still implored and upbraided by turns, and the wretched monarch still vapoured and vacillated; but day by day the state of the army grew worse, day by day the war party grew weaker and weaker, day by day the tone of the traitors became stronger and more confident. At last, mastered by the will of his conqueror, like a bird fascinated by a snake, Muhammad Shah stooped to the last depth of dishonour, and leaving his army, delivered himself up as a prisoner in Nadir's camp.

CHAPTER V

During the day of the Durbar, the Shah's Anderûn had learned with some curiosity, but no great surprise, that the Shah had taken to himself another consort.

The Indian girl had been installed by the Agha Bashi in a tent of her own, and two Persian women had been appointed to wait upon her. The scanty wardrobe with which she had come to the camp was supplemented by costly furs and robes suitable to her new dignity. Accustomed to the light and graceful dress of her own country, she thought them stiff and uncomfortable, but her women insisted upon teaching the poor barbarian how a Persian 'Khánum,' lady, should be clothed, and with a smile at their airs of superiority, she submitted. When she watched Nadir in his glory from behind her marble screen, she was attired as they thought fitting.

The Agha Bashi answered shortly enough all questions about her. But he made it clear that she was not to be molested, and the Anderûn decided to receive her with all outward respect. The Agha Bashi himself showed her nothing but kindness. He would have been good to her in any case for his master's sake, but he soon began to like her for her own. Though on the first night her impetuous action had startled him, he saw that she was different from the Shah's other women, and before a week was over her beauty and gentleness had fairly won his heart. Thenceforth the unsexed African was the most devoted of her friends.

To Sitara herself the week was a week of wonder and joy. In a few hours of that starlit Indian night, Nadir had made her his, body and soul, and the days that followed passed in a golden dream. They were lonely enough, for she hardly spoke to any one except her maids, but the loneliness troubled her little. The Agha Bashi came for a few moments now and then to see that all was well, and to give her such advice as she needed. He told her among other things that the Shah expected his ladies to do their marches on horseback, and one day he brought to the garden in which her tent was pitched, a trained Arab stallion equipped for the march. She had learned to sit a horse in her old Rajput home, and she mounted and rode the little Arab with an ease that delighted him.

'Afrîn! Khánum,' he said. 'Well done! You ride like one of the Shah's spearmen.'

Through the long afternoons she lay in her tent thinking of her kingly lover, or strolled about the walled garden, with its rows of plane-trees and rivulets of running water. Then the swift eastern darkness fell, and the noises of the camp gradually died away, and at last he came again, no longer in his splendour, but as she had first seen him, clothed in the plain white dress he usually wore.

At times, with his passionate bantering ways, masterful always but tender and caressing, he made her almost forget that he was anything but the strong-handed soldier who had stormed her heart. He was every inch a king, but he was more—he was every inch a man.

He would have none of her Persian robes. He liked to see her wearing the jewels with which he had adorned her, but the first time he saw her in her new attire, he stood looking at her with a frown. 'Never wear those things again,' he said. 'You are not a lying Persian. Alhemdulillah! Praise be to God! No Persian is to be trusted. See that you do not become like them.' She tossed the stiff garments aside with evident relief, and he soon forgot his displeasure.

In the intervals of his fiery passion he would lead her on to talk of her past life, of her own country and her Rajput clansmen, of the Delhi Court, and the men and women about the Moghul Emperor. He learned from her to look upon the discomfited Indians with kindliness. A country which bred such women must breed men too. Beaten as they were, he felt they were not to be despised. He used to laugh at her joy in the humiliation of the hated Moghuls, and loved to draw her on till her dark eyes flashed and the blood surged into her face at some tale of oppression or indignity to her people. In her impetuous womanly wrath she seemed to him more beautiful than ever.

For one short week the heaven of her happiness remained without a cloud, and then it was overcast. Nadir had begun to reflect. The first rush of his new passion was spent, and 'love's sad satiety' was upon him. He had been conscious throughout that the Indian girl had stirred him as no other had ever done; and the thought had begun to trouble him. Lover of women as he was, he had never allowed any woman to gain the least influence over his actions; and looking back upon the course of the last few days, it came home to him that he had perhaps let himself go too far. A chance word of praise from the Agha Bashi sent a flash of suspicion through his brain. 'The girl is well enough,' he said, 'but women are all alike. He is a fool who trusts any one of them.' And he determined to put a check upon himself.

So on the evening when the Moghul Emperor came as a prisoner to his camp, Sitara waited in vain for Nadir to raise the curtain of her tent, and at last she learned with a pang at her heart that he had gone to see another of his wives. Sooner or later the thing must have come to her. She was one of many, and could not hope to keep him to herself. Brought up in the traditions of the Mnse, she never thought of questioning his right to do as he pleased with his own. But human nature is the same all the world over. It was an Oriental who said 'Love is strong as death; jealousy is cruel as the grave.' And for Sitara that night the flames thereof were flames of fire.

Perhaps if she had known all she would have felt less miserable.

The woman to whose tent Nadir had gone was one for whom he had little love, well knowing her to be false and mischievous; but she was Ali Akbar's sister, and on that account it was well to humour her, for Ali Akbar was a useful servant. Moreover, she could be useful herself, for she had much information about all that was going on. Like many Persians she was intelligent and amusing. She could even read and write, an accomplishment very rare among eastern women. The time which Nadir passed with her was largely spent in talking over affairs, and this she resented, for though she cared nothing about him, it hurt her vanity. She would have liked his admiration to be warmer. But the Shirázi, as she was generally called, from her birthplace, was no longer in her first youth, and she had never been beautiful. She had the ruddy skin and dark eyes of the Persian, but her features were irregular, and the swarthy down upon her lip and chin was too strong to be becoming. Her thick eyebrows met in the middle. It was a clever, bad-tempered face, with some charm in it when she was laughing; but it was not a face to be trusted or loved.

The lady was childless too. She had prayed at many shrines, and more than once she had poured rose-water into the mouth of a dead dog on a Wednesday night, but even that had failed.

When Nadir's takht had been carried into the tent, and he had taken his seat upon it, she brought him a flask of Shiráz, and a white stoneware goblet.

She had at various times tried to secure his wavering affection by magical spells. Now, while he drank his first cup of wine, she closed her fingers one by one, each on a potent word, and when he was not looking opened them all together and fired a silent volley at him, her cunning eyes watching him closely to see whether the charm worked.

She then disposed herself upon the carpet by his side, and began to press and knead his muscular limbs in the manner of the East. Under the soothing influence of her lithe hands, Nadir settled down into comfortable rest, and she set to work to amuse him with the gossip, more or less indecent and malicious, but often witty enough, of which she was a mistress. Like most of his order he liked gossip, which he found useful as well as amusing. Soon he was laughing freely, and at times the deep base of his voice rose on the silence of the night far beyond the tent in which he lay. The night was one of triumph to the Shirázi.

She longed to get Nadir to speak of the Indian girl, but for a time she was afraid. At last, emboldened by his apparent good-humour and his careless caresses, which she hoped were the result of her new charm, she ventured to touch the subject.

'The camp is full of strange women now,' she said. 'The last batch of slave girls the Shah distributed to those on whom he conferred favours were Kafir girls of the Siah Pûsh—the Black Robes. Now that the camp is in Hindustan, the girls they are bringing are Siah Ru—black faces.'

Nadir did not answer. The woman stole a sidelong look at him, and quickly changed the subject. Nadir was a dangerous man to trifle with, and she saw she was going too far.

In fact, the main result of her attempt was the very reverse of what she imagined.

'Jealous,' he said to himself, 'jealous and spiteful as usual, like all the Persian women.' And his thoughts went back to the passionate, impetuous girl he had learned to love. 'Siah Ru!' he thought. 'She is beautiful as a dream. By Allah, you little Shaitán, you will repent the day if you try to do her evil.'

CHAPTER VI

HAVING satisfied his conscience by his visit to the Shirázi, Nadir let himself yield again to his inclinations, and during the few days that the camp remained stationary at Karnál, where he had halted after the fight, Sitara had no fresh cause for distress. Night after night he came to her tent, unannounced as his custom was, lifting the curtain at her doorway and walking in without a word.

One night early in March he came as usual. She had been waiting and hoping for his arrival, but he was late, and she had almost given him up. Her thoughts had gone back over the past week. As he entered she was lying on her cushions with her chin resting on her hands, and a far-away look in her eyes. His deep voice startled her from her dream.

'What, no "Khush Amadîd"—no welcome for me?' he said, and she sprang to her feet in confusion. But as she did so she saw that there was no displeasure in his face.

'Forgive me, my Lord,' she said, 'I did not hear.' She bent low before him and kissed the strong brown hand that was laid on her hair. He raised her with a smile. All the welcome a man could need was there in her eyes.

'You are forgetting me already,' he said. 'I have brought you something by way of remembrance,' and he held out to her an ancient seal which had been presented to him by a frontier chief. Simple as his dress usually was, he had a fondness for precious stones. He always wore one or two in his turban, and many were brought to him. The seal was beautifully carved from a single emerald, and represented a woman's figure which bore some resemblance to her.

'Take it,' he said. 'They tell me it belonged to Sikander Rûmi, Alexander the Great.'

She made a gesture of refusal. 'My Lord,' she said, 'you have given me too much already. I want nothing but your kindness.'

'It is my wish,' he answered. 'To-morrow we march for Delhi, and who knows what may happen? Inshallah, please God, you will never need it, but if at any time you want to come to me, send me the stone and you shall be received wherever I may be.'

She looked at him with a sudden fear. 'Am I not to go with the camp, my Lord?'

Nadir's eyes lit up with a smile.

'Let your heart be at rest. Where I go, you go, little one. But still take it—as a remembrance of Karnál.'

Sitara took the stone and pressed it to her forehead. 'I will never be without it—but Inshallah, I will never trouble my Lord with petitions.'

'That is settled then. Has the Agha Bashi taught you to sit a horse? In the camp women must be able to ride.'

'I can ride. The Agha Bashi says I am like one of your spearmen. A Rajput woman does not go in a litter like a Moghul lord.'

Nadir laughed. 'Always a hard word for the Moghuls. It is not well to despise your countrymen.'

'They are not my countrymen, my Lord. My people

hate them. They are Tartars and Persians. They have only been in India a little while.'

'Long enough to get soft. My men are Tartars and Persians too. But riding on the march is rough for a woman.'

He went on to speak of the country in front of them, and of the people who held it. He listened carefully as she described the route, explained where water and supplies were to be found, and told him many details which he wished to know.

'You speak like a Mîm Bashi, a Commander of a Thousand,' he said. 'I wish all my people had as much sense,' and late into the night he sat talking over the coming march, and the great city which was their goal.

Nevertheless he woke early as his custom was, soon after dawn, and left her. Hardly had he done so before the stir of preparation began. In the chilly morning light the attendants of the Anderûn, trained by years of campaigning, rapidly packed the mule trunks in which the baggage of the ladies was carried, and then the mules and ponies were as rapidly loaded up. The tents were left standing, as a 'Pîsh khaneh' or fore camp had gone on in advance.

The cold was still in the air as Sitara mounted her Arab for her first march with the camp, but the sun was bright, and she felt in all her young blood the joy of living. She rode astride, as did all the women, on a soft saddle of padded cloth, richly embroidered; and the little chestnut, whose coat shone with the metallic glint which one sees only in the East, tossed his head proudly in response to her light touch on the gold chain which formed his bridle. Horses in Persia are mostly grey, and according to a grotesque custom which still endures, the Shah's ladies in general rode greys with tails dyed crimson or orange. But the Agha Bashi had chosen the chestnut carefully for Sitara's comfort, and his long pasterns came down at each step, giving him the easy walk which makes such a difference on a march.

Nadir was a soldier who knew his business, and was not to be caught off his guard. In spite of the submission of the Moghul there was no sign of carelessness about the order of advance. His spearmen had for days been scouring the country in his front to a distance of sixty or eighty miles, and all seemed secure; but the main body was ready for anything that might happen.

The level plain, which stretched away in all directions as far as the eye could see, allowed the army to march on a broad front, and the whole of his great force was well closed up.

Twenty thousand of the best horsemen in the army covered its front, and immediately behind them rode Nadir himself at the head of his Guards, the 'Six Thousand,' who had been mounted for the march. In rear of the Shah, on the left of the great array, came the 'Kurk,' the Shah's women, escorted by armed eunuchs, and surrounded at a distance by several thousand musketeers, who cleared the way for them, killing or driving off any man found in their line of advance. To the right of the Kurk came the Moghul Emperor in his litter, with a few of his own people, in the centre of a great body of Kizlbash horse. On his right, again, were the principal Moghul chiefs and their retinues, disposed in separate parties some hundred yards apart. Between them rode Kizlbash horsemen, to prevent their joining and keep them on their proper course. In rear of the Kurk and the Indians came the main body of Nadir's troops, and then the artillery and baggage protected by a strong rear-guard. To right and left marched flanking parties of horse.

In spite of its great numbers, the Persian force, which was entirely mounted, advanced at a fair pace across the open plain; and Sitara, riding in the Kurk by the side of the Agha Bashi, enjoyed the life and grandeur of the scene. At first, as the Kurk crossed the battlefield of the week before, she was horrified by the things she saw about her, and she thought with a pang at her heart that among the troops of the Moghul were some of her own countrymen. At times, too, she came upon Indian villages which showed pitiable marks of the savage treatment dealt out by the Kizlbash horsemen who had cleared the front of the Kurk. But India was a continent, not a nation; and she had generations of fighting blood in her veins; and her pride in her soldier-king did much to soothe the feelings of indignation and sorrow with which these things oppressed her.

During the day's march, when the Kurk had remounted after the midday meal, a cloud of dust moving rapidly towards them from the front attracted her notice. As it approached there broke through it the glitter of lance points, and the Agha Bashi, who had pulled up his horse, with his hand over his eyes, called out, 'The Shah is coming, the Shah.' A moment later Nadir galloped up to the party of women. He was riding as usual a big Turkoman thoroughbred, over sixteen hands in height, which seemed to know it carried a king. Its long easy stride kept the small Arabs of the escort racing behind it. As Nadir reined it in, its nostrils flashed crimson in the sunlight, and a network of veins stood out upon the delicate skin. Nadir sat it with the ease of constant habit, his tall figure upright, his left hand hardly seeming to close on the chain bridle, and his right, which held his axe, resting loosely on his thigh. He carried no other weapon, and his dress was plain, worn for comfort on the march rather than show.

He seemed in the best of health and spirits. It was often noticed that when halting in a town or a fixed camp he was apt to become restless and impatient. His nomad blood was calling. Directly he was in the field again his restlessness vanished, and gave place to content. So it seemed now. The march had brought a bright colour to his face, and a happy smile to his eyes.

The Agha Bashi had dismounted and stood at his stirrup. Nadir rested his axe blade lightly on the negro's shoulder in his frank soldierly way, and spoke a few cheery words inquiring if all was well with the Kurk. The Agha Bashi laid his hand on his heart. 'By the Shah's favour. All is well.' Nadir turned to the Shirázi, who was well to the front, with her veil up, and a smile of welcome in her crafty eyes. 'Ah, Khánum,' he said with a laugh, 'I see you are none the worse for the ride. You are an old soldier, always ready, as hard as one of my Kizlbash.' The Shirázi flushed slightly. 'Those who follow the Shah's stirrup have need to be hard,' she said. 'There is little time for rest between the Shah's victories.'

Nadir's eyes wandered over the party to where Sitara was sitting on her horse, a few paces to the rear. He knew her in spite of her veil, and rode up to her. 'Tired, little one?' he said. 'No, my Lord.' She raised her veil. 'The horse is very easy, and now . . . I have seen you.'

Nadir smiled. 'Khudá Háfiz—God protect you—I will come to-night.'

He turned away quickly. 'Mount, Agha Bashi,' he said. 'We must push on. We have another league or two to ride. Khudá Háfiz,' and he touched the Turkoman behind the shoulder with the point of his stirrup, and was gone in a cloud of dust.

And the Shirázi cursed him under her breath. 'Sag zádeh,' she muttered. 'Dog-born and mannerless. May Shaitán take you and your black slave girl!'

CHAPTER VII

So the Persian army marched on for a week, until at last the domes and minárs of Delhi rose from the plain. The Shah's own camp was pitched at some distance from the city, among the trees and running water of a beautiful garden, and there on the night of their arrival Nadir came as usual to Sitara's tent.

He was in high spirits that night, for all had gone well on the line of march, and the great capital of the Moghuls, the goal of his ambition, lay defenceless before him.

Sitara received him with joy in her eyes and words of proud congratulation.

'My Lord must be content,' she said after Nadir had settled himself on his takht. 'He has conquered the whole world now.'

Nadir had begun to play, as he had a trick of doing, with a great blue sapphire he always carried about him.

'Not all the world yet,' he said with a smile, trying to balance the stone on the tip of his axe. 'The Lesghian robbers of the Caucasus have been giving trouble. They believe I cannot reach them in their mountains. And the Kings of Bokhara and Khiva are sending foolish answers to my messages, as the Moghul did. They think they are safe behind the Turkoman steppes. He has learnt that my arm is long, and by Allah they shall learn it too.'

'My Lord is thinking of fresh conquests already?'

'Why not? While any country remains to be conquered, what I have done is nothing.'

'My Lord, it is so much. What other King of Irán has been as great?'

'*Rást ast.* It is true. By the favour of God I have taught these Persian dogs what a King of Irán should be.'

'My Lord, forgive me if I am too bold. Why do you always speak with contempt of the Persians? Are they not the creatures of God, and your people?'

Nadir laughed. 'The creatures of God. Balé. Yes. God is great. It has pleased Him to fill the world with dogs and asses. What am I that I should say a word? But the Persians are not my people. I am a Turkoman.'

'But you are Shah of Irán, and there are many Kizlbash in the King's army. Why do you hate them?'

'Why should I not hate them?' A look of rage came into his eyes and his face flushed.

'Listen, and I will tell you. And once you have heard, never speak of it again.'

Nadir's face alarmed her. 'Tell me nothing,' she said hastily. 'I should not have spoken as I have. I want to hear nothing that it angers my Lord to remember.'

Nadir paused and began thinking back. The look of anger faded from his face. 'Listen, and I will tell you all from the beginning, as you told me.

'My father was a chief of the Afshar, and held the strong place at Kelát. When he died I was a child, and his brother, upon whose name be curses, seized the fort and took my place in the tribe. He betrayed me to the Turkomans of the steppes, the man-sellers, and for years I was a prisoner among the black tents in the desert. When I became a juwán, a young man, I escaped from the man-sellers and claimed the chiefship, which was my right, but he was faithless, and I was driven out from among my people.'

'Let my Lord forget those days. He has conquered the world now.'

'But I cannot forget. I was driven out with my brother Ibrahim, and being hungry we went to Meshed and took service with the Persian Governor. Soon I was given a troop of horse.'

'Were they Persians?'

'They were men from the north who spoke Turki, which is the language of men. We had many fights with the man-sellers, who used to make raids into Persian territory and carry off men and women and plunder. The Persians were in deadly fear of them. You have heard of the man-sellers?'

'Yes, my Lord. They were a terrible enemy, it is said, and had no pity.'

'They were only robbers, and never fought if they could help it, but they had good horses, and rode fifty or sixty miles in a day, and the Persians were never ready for them. I paid my men well and they became faithful, and soon they learnt not to be afraid of the man-sellers. We killed many of them, and I was made Mîm Bashi, Commander of a Thousand.'

'Then the Persians had peace and were grateful?'

'Listen, and you will know how grateful they were. After some time the man-sellers saw that they could no longer raid in small parties, and that Khurasán was being lost to them, so they assembled all their tribes and suddenly crossed the border with many thousand horsemen.'

'And you fell upon them and scattered them?'

'The Governor had not many troops, and did not know what to do, for the man-sellers were ravaging the country on all sides. He called a council of his officers, but they were Persians from the Court, like himself, and their livers had turned to water. They said it would be folly for him to leave the city unguarded, and that the country-people must show courage and defend themselves.'

'Cowards!'

'Yes. Cowards as always. Then I spoke to them. I was only a Mîm Bashi, and had no right to speak in the council, but I was angry, and I saw that for a brave man the door of opportunity was open.'

'Afrîn! And you spoke bold words?'

'I said the Turkomans were only robbers, and that if the Governor would give me command of five thousand men I would clear the country of them. The Persian officers objected, and said that if the troops moved out they would be eaten up, and the city would fall. But the Governor was frightened. He knew that if he did nothing he would be recalled by the Shah and would lose his head, so he listened to me and gave me the command, and promised me that if I were successful I should be made Deputy Governor of Khurasán.

'Then I made arrangements for the security of the city and marched out suddenly with my own men and some "tufangchis," musketeers. The man-sellers came on and met me, for they thought we were afraid, but many of their horsemen were scattered over the country, pillaging, and their chief had only six or seven thousand men together. They surrounded us, and the tufangchis were afraid. Then I spoke to them. I said, "Where can you run? For a man on foot surrounded by horsemen the road of flight is the road to Jehannum—Hell." When a Persian officer wept and reproached me, I killed him—with this, and I said I would kill any other who turned his face. My own men laughed out loud. After that the tufangchis stood and fired because they were afraid of me, and the Turkomans were beaten off. Then I attacked with the horsemen. I killed the chief of the man-sellers, and thousands more were sent to Hell by the juwáns and the country-people. Soon all the province was cleared of the man-sellers, and I returned to Meshed. It was my first great victory.'

'Then you became Deputy Governor?'

'Then I reminded the Governor of his promise, but the danger was over, and he began to delay, using fair words like a Persian, and doing nothing. The Persian officers whose faces I had blackened were all speaking against me, and the Governor feared they would do him harm at Court. At last, when I had eaten much wrath, I heard that a young Persian lord had been given the place, and that I was to have nothing. Then I became mad and spoke angrily in Durbar, saying that the Governor was faithless.'

Nadir stopped speaking, and the look of rage came over his face again. His fingers closed fiercely on the handle of his axe.

'Great God!' he broke out, 'that I should live to say it. He gave an order, and I was seized by the guards. I fought and nearly broke through, but they were many, and I was overpowered. Then they threw me on the ground and bound me to the "felek," the bastinado pole, and I was beaten on the feet till I was senseless.'

The girl sprang up with blazing eyes, her hands clenched, and her whole body quivering with fury.

'They dared! they dared!' she cried. 'Oh the cowards, the faithless cowards!'

She fell on her knees, covering Nadir's feet with her kisses.

'It is nothing, little one,' he said. 'It was many years ago, and by God I have paid my debts. Never think of it again. But you know now why I hate the Persians.'

'I shall always hate them, always, always, while I have breath in my body.'

Nadir laughed softly. 'You will do well, for they are dogs and sons of dogs; but it is long ago. Now forget it.'

Then he told her the rest of his story. How after his disgrace he had returned to his people at Kelát, and made another attempt to claim his rights, but in vain. 'So,' he said, 'I was driven out, with my brother Ibrahim and one or two more. We were hungry, and in the end we decided to live on the Persians by striking the road. It was a poor life after commanding an army, but what could we do?

'One day we heard that a caravan was leaving Meshed, and though we were very few, five or so, we agreed that we would attack them at night, and we hid ourselves among the rocks near a "tangi," a narrow place in the hills through which the road passed.'

'Had the caravan no escort?'

'Yes, but only a score of tufangchis, and we knew what sort of things tufangchis are.'

'Five to twenty! And then?'

'I was leader of the party, and I gave orders that all should get some sleep, for we were weary with a long march. We were to watch by turns, one at a time, and the man on watch was to wake the rest when he heard the mule bells. In the night one could hear them a mile away.'

Nadir stopped and hesitated.

'In India do your gods speak to men in dreams and tell them what is coming?'

'I have heard men tell strange tales of things made known in dreams.'

'Well, Ibrahim was to watch first, and I lay down and went to sleep. Then a messenger came and stood by me and told me to follow him, and I got up and followed.'

'Who was he?'

'God knows, but he said that the holy Ali had sent for me.'

'The holy Ali, whom the Persians call the Friend of God?'

'Yes. The messenger walked away across the plain, and I followed, until we came to a tree, and under it Ali was sitting, with a sword in his lap.'

'How did you know it was Ali?'

'I knew it. He said, "You are Nadir of the Afshar. God has called you to save my people, who are scattered like sheep without a shepherd. You are his sheep-dog to watch over them. If you are faithful He will make you great, and you will be ruler of Irán." Then he gave me a sword.'

'What did you say, my Lord?'

'I asked how I was to know that the vision was true, and Ali answered that he would give me a sign. He said that I was waiting to hear the bells of a "káfila," and that when Ibrahim woke me I was to restrain my people and let the káfila pass without attacking. If I had faith and did so, I should see within a few hours another káfila, much larger and richer than the first.

I was to attack this, and I would get much gold. Then I was to go on and become great.'

'And did you believe his words?'

'Yes. When Ibrahim woke me I told him of Ali's order. We woke the other men, lest they should be surprised by the caravan and do something foolish. They were angry at being held back, and began to murmur, but I had this by me, and I said I would kill any man who did not obey.'

Sitara laughed. 'As always,' she said. 'And you persuaded them, my Lord?'

'Yes, I persuaded them, and they remained quiet. Then after a few hours the second káfila came. It was large, and there were many tufangchis, but I had faith in the promise. We attacked suddenly with shouts, like the yells of the man-sellers, and the tufangchis fled without firing a shot. I heard afterwards that they ran all the way to Meshed. On the road, by the favour of God, they met a Persian who had been a slave among the Turkomans and had escaped as I did. He was dressed like a Turkoman, so they killed him and took his head to the Governor, with his horse. They said they had been attacked by a thousand men of the man-sellers, and had fought all day, killing many, among others the chief.'

'Cowards and liars!'

'Aye, cowards and liars as always. Were they not Persians? But the Governor said they had fought like Rustems, and he made the merchants in Meshed subscribe a large sum to reward them. But of course he ate the money himself. When the tufangchis came to his Durbar to get a present he was angry and gave them the felek. So they got what they deserved. Alhemdulillah! Praise be to God!'

'And afterwards, my Lord?'

'Afterwards, by the help of God and the holy Ali, I prospered greatly. I struck many caravans, and got money to pay more men, and soon I had a large band and did what I pleased.'

'Did not the Governor send troops against you?'

'Yes, often, but I cut up some of their parties, and when they were too strong I kept out of their way. The country-people hated the troops, who always robbed and ill-treated them. I was always kind to them, so they were friendly to me, and with their help it was easy to make fools of the troops.'

'But how did you get the Kingdom?'

'The Shah was in great misery. The Afghans had invaded the country and taken Ispahan. The Turks too had come across the border, and the Russians had taken Gilán and the silk country. Nothing was left but a few districts in the mountains. The Shah was a fool and a drunkard, thinking of nothing but wine and women. He was hiding in the jungles of Mazanderan.'

'But what could you do with a handful of road strikers?'

'When I was strong enough I went back to Kelát, and killed my uncle, and took possession of the fortress. Then I gathered more men, and soon I was master of a large district.'

'When was it, my Lord?'

'Ten or twelve years ago. At last, knowing the Shah had hardly any troops left, I offered my services to him if he would grant me a full pardon. He agreed, and I joined him.'

'And you gained his favour?'

'Yes. I showed him that his general had been

cheating him and not paying the troops, who were discontented and useless. Though he was a fool he saw that my troops were good because they were well paid. So he made me his Commander-in-Chief.

'Still you had little strength against Turks and Afghans and Russians?'

'At first, but I gathered strength quickly. The Afghans were very few. They had taken Ispahan only because the Persians were cowards and would not fight. I defeated one of their detachments and then another, and after each victory men came to take service with me. Soon they came in thousands, good men from the north, Uzbegs and Turkomans, and the Afghans themselves joined me when I had beaten them. Even some of the Persians learned to fight when they found they were well paid.'

'I shall always hate them.'

'You do well, little one. At the best they are vain and faithless. But I made them of some use. I got some European officers, who drilled them after the western fashion, till a thousand moved like one. Then I taught them to attack in silence, without any of their silly shooting and shouting. It astonished the enemy, and gave the Persians confidence, till they thought they were brave men. I had to kill some of them first—with this. But they learnt. They are not without understanding. When I had a great army well armed and disciplined, I fought the Turks. They were brave, and made me eat a defeat. I lost thousands of men. But more kept coming, and I won many battles. At last I drove out the Turks altogether.'

'Afrîn! And then you took the Kingdom?'

'First I made ready to attack the Russians in Gilán,

but they were afraid, and agreed to give up the provinces they had taken. Then all Irán was free.'

'When was that, my Lord?'

'It was only three years ago. I had been making war without ceasing for seven years.'

'It was not a long time to do so much. No one else in the world could have done it. There has never been such a conqueror.'

'I am nothing, but God is great. Then he put into my hands the reins of government. The people had seen that the Shah was a fool and worse than a fool, and had brought the country to ruin, so he had been deposed. The nobles and great men all met together and asked me to rule over the Kingdom, and seeing that it was the will of God, I accepted.'

Nadir was silent for a minute, and a grim smile came over his face.

'It was the will of Allah,' he said, 'and all the great men and troops agreed. The only people to give any trouble were the mullas, and I taught them not to meddle in such matters.'

'The mullas? What had they to do with it?'

'Nothing, but they were heretics—Shias—like all these dogs of Persians, and when I told them to compose their differences with the Sunnis and make one religion, they drew their heads from the collar of obedience. The Mulla Bashi, the head priest, was imprudent and spoke foolish words.'

'What did you do, my Lord? Priests are always self-willed, and they are strong.'

'The Mulla Bashi received pardon from God.'

'You punished him with death?'

'He was delivered from the miseries of this perishable world.

'After that I assembled the other mullas and asked them what they did with the revenues of the Faith. They said the money was spent according to ancient custom in salaries for priests, and in keeping up colleges and mosques, in which prayers were continually offered for the success of the Shah and the prosperity of the Empire.

'I told them it was as clear as the sun that their prayers had not been heard, since the country had been going to ruin for fifty years, until God's victorious instruments came to its relief, and I explained that these poor priests of God, the Kizlbash, were in want. So I took the Church revenues for the payment of the troops.'

Sitara laughed.

'Were they not very angry?'

'Chirá? Why not? And they tried to do "badi," to make mischief, but the soldiers mocked at them.

'Then I told the people they could do what they pleased, but that I had not much occasion for mullas, and would not tax my poor subjects to support them. Then the people mocked also. They do not love mullas —or taxes.

'After that the mullas were quiet. They hate me, of course, but what can they do?'

'Inshallah! they can do nothing. And since then you have won many victories?'

'God is great. Some of the Afghans raised the head of rebellion, and it became necessary for me to take Kandahar and Kábul. Then I saw that the reins of power had fallen from the hands of the Moghul. The infidels of India had beaten his armies and disgraced him, and as he was a Turkoman too and a Mussulman, I offered for the sake of Islam to come and drive them away. His own Ministers had written me letters inviting me to come. But misunderstanding my object he returned foolish answers, and would not send any money to pay my troops, who were ready to help him. Also his people killed one of my envoys.'

'I have heard that he was killed by some rebel Afghans.'

'God knows. Kings should not let their people rebel and bring a bad name upon them. He has acted like a fool, and now he has seen the consequences.'

'My Lord, it is all wonderful. There has never been any conqueror like you, never in the world. And you did it all with your own hand, from the beginning.'

'Balé. Yes. It is easy to be a king—unless a man is a fool like the Moghul. What is difficult is to become a king.'

Nadir ceased speaking. He sat for a time in silence, thinking over the past, with a quiet pride in his eyes. Then his look grew harder and more concentrated. The strong, thick underlip tightened up. India had still to be conquered, and the kingdoms of Tartary, and perhaps—God willing—the empire of Rûm—Constantinople—Why not that? And more?

CHAPTER VIII

While Nadir was telling Sitara the story of his life, another conversation was going on not far from the spot, a conversation of which she was the subject.

The Shirázi had seen during the march, with anger and mortification, that Nadir's visit to her had done nothing to turn him from the Indian girl. On the night of their arrival her women brought her word that he was again in Sitara's tent.

The Shirázi cursed them both with the eloquence which characterised her. Having done so she got leave from the Agha Bashi to visit her brother, and putting on the long cloak and veil which made all Persian women appear alike, she walked over to his quarters. Ali Akbar had had a hard day's work with a crowd of office-seekers, but by dint of vague promises, backed by his merry talk and charming manners, he had got rid of them at last. After that he had supped heartily in his Anderûn. When the Shirázi arrived at the door of his tent he was lying on his cushions in comfort, his coat unfastened to aid digestion, and the stem of his kalián in his hand. He had been drinking freely, and a flask of Shiráz was on the carpet beside him. As she stood at the doorway she heard his loud voice and jovial laugh, which stopped suddenly when she sent in her name.

To tell the truth, he was not greatly pleased at her

arrival, for he had been looking forward to a pleasant evening, and he knew from experience that her sharp tongue was likely to disturb his peace. But he was not an unkindly man, and she was useful to him, so with a sigh of resignation he told his servants to admit her.

She came in, and tossing aside her veil and cloak, disposed herself on the cushions in front of him. Her first words showed him that his fears were well founded. She pushed aside irritably the cup of wine he offered her. 'This is no time for drinking,' she said, with a look of contempt at his flushed face. 'Do you not see what dust has fallen on our heads? While you are soaking your brain with wine, the Shah is shut up again with that accursed black girl.'

Ali Akbar moved uneasily on his cushions. 'What does it matter, my sister?' he said. 'Let the Shah amuse himself. It will not last long.'

She made a gesture of impatience. 'Do you think I should trouble myself if it were only that? He is nothing but a Turkoman robber, and a dirty slave girl is good enough for him. But this is another matter.'

Ali Akbar looked round uneasily and held up his hand. 'Speak lower,' he said. 'Some one might hear.'

'What do I care? Cannot you understand? This time it is not one of the old fool's passing fancies. The girl has bewitched him with her Indian sorcery. For weeks they have been like Leila and Majnún. Is she to become the Banu, the chief Queen, and make us all eat dirt? Who knows what mischief she may do?'

'She is not likely to do badi. One of her women is in my pay. She says the Indian is as simple as a child, and more in love with the Shah than he is with her. He will soon tire of her, and she will be nothing.'

'Your woman is a fool. These black Indians are full of shaitáni—devilment. I tell you she has been sent by the Moghul to bewitch the Shah. How else but through sorcery could she have made a fool of him as she has? A black slave girl as ugly as the ghoul of the desert.'

Ali Akbar smiled a rather mischievous smile. 'She is not ugly. I have seen her. She is young and beautiful, as straight as a cypress, with eyes like a deer. What need has she of sorcery? That is all pooch—nonsense.'

The Shirázi's temper rose. 'Young and beautiful is she? And I am old and ugly; that is what you mean. But all do not think as you do. Praise be to God! You will see who wins in the end. You will see.'

Ali Akbar sighed wearily. 'For God's sake leave the girl alone. The Shah has never let a woman get the mastery over him, not even you. What harm can she do?'

'Are you wholly without understanding that you cannot see? Of course it is nothing to you that she should make me eat dirt. But if my face is blackened so is yours. Already your market is lessening. You have many enemies, and they are laughing at your beard.'

'Because the Shah takes a new slave girl, as he has done a thousand times! Soon he will want money for the troops, and will come to me, and who will laugh then?'

'Oh! my brother, truly wisdom will die with you. Is he not getting camel loads of gold and silver from these idol worshippers? He will soon want no more money, and then how will you keep your place?'

That arrow was well shot. Ali Akbar's face grew dark.

'It will not last for ever,' he said; but the Shirázi saw that she had touched him.

'Long enough to make him think he does not need you, and you have enemies. The Agha Bashi hates you, and he and the Indian girl are like two almonds in one shell. He will do you badi.'

Ali Akbar knew the Agha Bashi did not love him. The negro was too faithful to Nadir. He distrusted both the brother and sister, whose feelings towards his master he more than suspected.

Ali Akbar moved uneasily on his seat. 'Holy Allah,' he said, 'what can the black eunuch do to me? He is half a man at best.'

'He has power to do evil. Has not the wise man said, "Despise a small enemy—leave a little fire unheeded." And he is not a small enemy. He is always at the Shah's ear.'

Ali Akbar caught at the quotation. Brother and sister were both vain of their learning. 'Yes,' he answered, 'and did not the wise man say also, "To kindle a fire between two persons and be burnt in it oneself is not wisdom."'

But he was shaken. There came to him suddenly the remembrance of the night when he had seen Sitara draw her dagger. He had not distinguished himself then, and he recalled the look of contempt on her face. It was not a pleasant recollection.

His sister saw that her words had had their effect, and she pressed her advantage, now with stinging shafts of contempt and ridicule, now with appeals to his interest or his affection, for he was in a way fond of her. Gradually her more energetic nature, and keener feeling, prevailed over his indolence and caution. Before she left him he had promised to help her against the woman she hated. For the present it was agreed that they could do nothing, but he would watch his opportunity, and strike when he saw a chance. The chance was sure to come, and when it came, he would use it.

The Shirázi went at last, well pleased with her evening's work. She put on her cloak and veil again, and said good-bye.

'Where are you going now?' Ali Akbar said.

'Not to the Shah,' she answered. She was going to see one of the Persian officers of the Guard, with whom she was on friendly terms. Her brother knew about it, but had made no attempt to interfere. The man was a useful recruit to secure for his party, and the brother and sister understood one another. They had no scruples in such matters.

Ali Akbar shrugged his shoulders. 'Please yourself,' he said with a short laugh, 'but take care. The Shah is not a man to show mercy.'

'Trust me,' she answered. 'There is no danger'; and she went out with a confident air. Her vanity always led her to think she was more than a match for any one she chose to deceive.

Ali Akbar returned to his wine cups, but they brought him little peace of mind, and late into the night he sat pondering over his sister's words.

Yes, he decided at last, she was right. She was jealous and spiteful, but she was right—the girl was not of their kind. Her influence could never be on their side, and it might grow too strong for them.

Any man, even Nadir, might become a fool about a woman. She must, if possible, be got out of their way.

And so about Sitara's innocent head the plot began to weave.

CHAPTER IX

In the bright sunlight of a fine spring morning Nadir Shah made his triumphal entry into the historic capital of the Moghul Empire.

The captive Emperor and his troops, all who had not disbanded at Karnál, or deserted on the way, had been brought back to Delhi in the train of the conqueror. The Moghul had accepted the terms imposed upon him. He had surrendered his guns, his treasury, his elephants and horses, all the appanage of his power and state. A train of two hundred selected cannon was on its way to Persia, under charge of a body of Kizlbash horse, to show the full extent of the victory. The Moghul officials were busily collecting the enormous war indemnity which Nadir had demanded.

As Sitara had told Nadir, there were many brave men among the Indian soldiery. They burned with indignation at the disgrace of their arms, and at the savage contempt with which they were treated by the Persians, but what could they do? Their orders were to submit as their Emperor had submitted. Sadly and silently they endured the insults heaped upon them by the barbarians whom they loathed and despised.

Nevertheless, in spite of the submission of the Indian Emperor and his people, Nadir was too good a soldier to neglect any precautions. He knew that the great city was full of armed men—disbanded soldiery, the retainers of the nobles, the hangers-on of a dissolute Court. His troops would be at a disadvantage in the narrow streets, and any check to his arms at the capital might result in a flame of revolt all over the country. It behoved him to be careful.

The Moghul Emperor, therefore, was sent on in advance to occupy the fort, and to make all preparations for a peaceful entry on the part of his conqueror. He issued orders for all shops and houses to be shut up, and for the population of the city to remain at home. Backed by the fears of the inhabitants, who trembled at the sight of a Persian, his orders were obeyed, and when Nadir marched in with his Kurk, escorted by twenty thousand horsemen, the city seemed to be deserted.

Sitara, riding by the side of the Agha Bashi, was saddened by the change which had come over the capital since she had left it a few weeks before. A mournful silence brooded over the streets she had always seen swarming with noisy life. Not a sound was to be heard except the trampling of the cavalry, the clatter of their accoutrements, and an occasional word of command. The balconies and flat roofs, which used to be crowded with eager faces whenever anything was to be seen, were without a single occupant. She knew that thousands of men and women and children were gazing in the fascination of mingled curiosity and fear from behind every screen, and through every chink in the closed shutters, but they gazed unseen.

Nadir and his women were lodged by the Moghul Emperor in the 'Palace of Joy' within the fort. The troops camped all round the lofty walls. Their quarters had been carefully marked out for them in advance, and, trained by years of war, they moved into their lines in perfect order.

The fort and palace of Delhi were in the hands of the Persian conqueror; and outside the city, ready to move forward at any moment, lay the great army which had struck down the Empire of the Moghuls. Their standards, and the glitter of their arms, were plainly visible to the northward all along the historic ridge which dominated the city; and the plain beyond was full, as far as the eye could see, of tents and guns and horsemen.

The Moghul Emperor had prepared a feast for Nadir and his followers in the Palace of Joy, and the two monarchs spent the afternoon together, making all arrangements for the future control of the country. In the course of the day, at the request of the Moghul, Nadir issued a proclamation to his troops forbidding in the severest terms any injury or insult to the inhabitants, and ordering his 'Nasakchis,' or executioners, 'to spare no punishment, such as cutting off ears and noses, and bambooing to death' any soldier who disobeyed.

The troops, knowing well that Nadir never threatened in vain, were careful to avoid offence, and the night passed quietly.

While the Kings were together their Rajput wives had come together too. Nothing is long a secret in an oriental Court, and it had become known that the former dependant of the Rahtor Queen was now the favourite wife of the Persian conqueror.

It was a strange meeting. The two women had parted only a few weeks before, one still a Queen in spite of her lord's defeat and humiliation, the other a poor, dishonoured girl, handed over with others to become a slave in the Persian camp. Now the nameless girl shared the proudest throne in Asia, and her former mistress came to her as a suppliant, sent by the craven Emperor to entreat that she would use her influence to soften the Shah's heart towards his beaten enemy.

Sitara received the unhappy Queen with every mark of respect that she had been accustomed to show in the past. She had passionately resented the order which handed her over, in spite of her entreaties, to shame and lifelong exile. But now in the flush of her happy love all resentment had vanished, and to her the Rahtor Queen was still the representative of her race and country. She promised to do whatever she could, and sent her old mistress away full of gratitude.

That night Sitara told Nadir all that had passed between them. 'My Lord,' she said, 'I know that I am nothing. It is not for me to ask favours of the Shah; and God knows I have no love for the Moghuls. But I am a Rajputni, and my Lord is merciful. He will forgive my presumption if I speak for the people of Hind.'

Nadir showed no displeasure. It rather gratified him to feel how high he had raised her.

'You have become very great all at once,' he answered with a smile. 'Very great and powerful that the Moghul's Queen should come and present petitions to you. But let your heart be at rest. You have done no wrong. I wish to show the people of Hind nothing but kindness if they behave properly. Already I have given orders that they shall not be molested in any way'; and he told her of the proclamation he had issued.

She thanked him, and he laughed a rather grim

laugh. 'There is one who will remember my orders, and take care that they are made known to all,' he said. 'I entrusted that to a nephew of Ali Akbar, who recommended him for service. Like all these accursed Persians he is full of empty talk, a nut without a kernel. When I gave him his orders he thought his head was as high as the skies, and began to make protestations after their manner. So I told the guards to show him the felek, and make him eat a few sticks.'

'Why, my Lord?' Sitara said; 'what had he done?'

'He was talking too much, and not listening to what I said. Men who are given service should listen and not talk. It will do him good and make him remember.'

Sitara thought the measure a little hard. She did not say so, but he read her silence.

'It does them good,' Nadir said: 'with them it is all words.' He laughed again. 'Once a fool stopped me as I was riding, and said he had a petition. Then he read me one of their silly poems, full of flattery and lies. It ended with a verse saying his bosom was torn with the nails of affliction, and he had nothing to eat. I ordered him to eat sticks for delaying me, and he has done useful service since.'

Sitara laughed too. Her remembrance of Nadir's own story was still too vivid to let her feel much sympathy for any Persian who became acquainted with the felek. But, born of watchful love, an uneasy feeling came to her that Nadir's form of humour might end by becoming dangerous to him, and she ventured to say something of the kind.

'My Lord, forgive me,' she said; 'will not Ali Akbar resent his nephew being beaten, and is he not a man of consequence? I sometimes fear that the Persians may do badi.'

Nadir's face darkened at once. 'I know my business,' he said. 'Kings cannot be too tender. God knows I am not without pity. I am never hard because it pleases me. I am hard because without some hardness a king cannot be feared, and a king who is not feared is the worst of kings. Let your heart be at rest. You have seen what the Moghul has brought on his country by not keeping his people under control.'

CHAPTER X

SITARA was soon to learn that, pitiless or not, Nadir could be very terrible in his wrath.

She was awake next morning before dawn. It was a clear, cool morning, and she watched from her lattice of fretted marble the sun rise unclouded out of the eastern plain. Below her lay the great city, its domes and minárs breaking through the smoke and catching the early light. All seemed fair and peaceful.

The day passed quietly and the evening came. Towards sunset Sitara went out upon a balcony where she could enjoy the breeze, and looked down over the city, waiting for nightfall.

As she sat there, watching the colours fade from the sunset sky, and thinking of all the happiness that had come to her, she was startled by hearing some distant shots, followed by a sound of shouting and tumult. Her heart sank within her, for she knew what the Delhi mob was like.

She could see nothing through the haze of smoke which overhung the town, and after a few minutes she sent a servant to the Agha Bashi, asking him to come to her. He came at once, and she begged him to go out and make inquiries.

'It is nothing, Khánum,' he said; 'do not be troubled': but he went, and remained away an hour. While he was away there was some more firing, and Sitara awaited his return with growing anxiety.

When at last he came his face was grave. He said that a messenger sent by Nadir to bring news had come back bleeding from a sword cut. The man reported that he had been stopped by the mob, and narrowly escaped with his life. The Moghul Emperor was in great alarm, and had also sent out messengers. They had brought back news of a riot at the grain stores. The city population was much excited. There had been some fighting between the mob and small parties of the Kizlbash.

As the Agha Bashi spoke some musket-shots were fired from the fort, and then a gun or two. There was a roar in the town below, but it died away.

After nightfall the shots and tumult ceased, and Sitara hoped that all was over; but when Nadir came to her, later than usual, she knew that things were going badly.

Before he entered the Anderûn she heard him outside giving his final orders, and vowing vengeance if any of his people had been killed. There was a tone in his voice which was new to her, like the growl of an angry beast.

He lifted her curtain with a rough hand, and stood an instant looking at her, but with his thoughts evidently elsewhere. As she raised her eyes to his face she saw that it was dark and threatening. There was a flush on his cheek, and his eyes glowed with an angry light.

The sight of her seemed to calm him, and the frown faded from his face as he came forward. She stood before him in silence, but he needed no words to show him her anxiety.

'Do not be afraid,' he said, 'it is nothing. There has been some affray with the "lutis," the roughs, of the town, and I fear one or two of the Kizlbash have got into trouble, but they are able to take care of themselves. The mob has been making a noise down below. All is quiet now, and I do not want to send the troops into the narrow streets while it is dark. In the morning I shall move out and put things in order. The mob will be humble enough then.'

But in spite of his assurances he was evidently disturbed in mind. He called for wine and drank cup after cup of Shiráz. Sitara knelt by the side of his takht, her hands at work upon the muscles of his great limbs, and gradually his wrathful mood yielded to the influence of her touch and her soothing words, but more than once before he slept he broke into imprecations which boded ill for the morrow.

Even when he dropped off, his sleep was uneasy. He muttered and gripped the handle of his axe. Once there was a momentary alarm among the sentries on the walls of the fort, and a few shots were fired. He started up at once, with flushed face and angry eyes. It proved to be nothing, and he went to sleep again; but for Sitara it was a restless and anxious night. She hardly closed her eyes, and before the first glimmer of dawn she was broad awake, watching his face. He woke soon afterwards, and rose at once. He was irritable from want of sleep, and his first word was a curse.

Before he left her he controlled himself and regained his usual manner. He even laughed at her anxiety, and tried to reassure her. He took her face in his strong hands and looked into her eyes. 'What! a Rajputni and frightened?' he said. 'I thought the Rahtors were the best soldiers in India.'

His tone emboldened her. 'I am not frightened,' she

said. 'What are the badmâshes, the evil livers, of the Bazaar? But, my Lord, you will be careful? The streets are narrow, and matchlock men may be hiding in the houses.'

Nadir laughed again. 'Allah will protect me,' he said. 'It is not my fortune to be hurt in fight.'

She shook her head. 'You are too fearless, my Lord.' Then she thought of her countrymen. 'My Lord, you will be merciful? There are badmâshes in the city, but most of the people are Hindus, and mean no harm.'

Nadir's face hardened and he answered impatiently. 'I have promised,' he said; 'let your heart be at rest, but I must put down rebellion.'

Looking down from a window which commanded a view of the city, and of the ground under the walls of the fort, Sitara saw the troops move out. Some regiments had been dismounted to clear the way. Then came the cavalry, squadron after squadron. Finally, when several thousand men had been swallowed up by the streets, Nadir and his escort followed. Sitara watched him with trouble at her heart as he disappeared into the great maze below.

At first all seemed quiet, and she hoped for the best. But the morning was still young when she heard a shot, then one or two more, followed by a burst of shouting. Then the shouting was drowned by a rattle of musketry and the roar of guns, and smoke began to rise into the blue air in various quarters of the city.

The story of that terrible day has been told by many. Nadir had ridden out of the fort fully intending to avoid, if possible, any unnecessary fighting or slaughter. But as he went forward he learned that some small parties of his men had been cut off during the night, and the dead bodies of several Kizlbash were found in the streets, shockingly mutilated. Nadir's anger was roused, and as the actual murderers could not be found, he gave orders for the punishment of certain quarters of the town. He was giving those orders when from a neighbouring house there was fired a shot which narrowly missed him and killed one of his officers. At the same time the sound of firing in his front gave warning that some of the Persians were being attacked. Then his patience gave way, and reinforcements from his camp having joined him, he let loose his troops.

The fierce soldiery had been longing for a chance of sacking the Moghul capital, and they sprang forward to their work with a roar of joy. For several hours the city was given over to an awful vengeance, in which the innocent suffered far more than the guilty. As the wild Uzbegs and Turkomans rode to and fro, slaying and burning and ravishing, a madness of terror came upon the townspeople. Men stabbed themselves, or set fire to their houses and perished in the flames with all belonging to them. Women threw themselves into the wells, or leapt from the roofs and were dashed to pieces on the stones below. The long Tartar lances dripped with the blood of children who were hunted through the streets, and speared with shouts of devilish laughter.

A few score of Nadir's men were killed, for here and there, maddened by despair and rage, the wretched people sold their lives dearly. But resistance soon ceased, and it became evident to the master of those savage legions that all danger to his supremacy was over. At last, feeling that enough had been done for safety, he gave orders for the slaughter to stop; and when the troops, drunk with blood and rapine, could be brought under control, the sounds of firing and the yells of fury and terror gradually died away.

But when the sun set that night the flame and smoke of conflagration rose from every quarter of the great city, and thousands of Indians had been butchered.

CHAPTER XI

News of what was going on had come to the Anderûn, and with all its ghastly details. For the Rajput girl, watching hour after hour at her window in the fort, the day had been one of grief and horror. It is true that the people of Delhi were not her clansmen. A year or two before she would not even have understood their language. But they were largely of her faith—Hindus—and the bond was strong. She had tried with passionate entreaties to move the Agha Bashi to go out and intercede with Nadir. But he shook his head and refused. 'I know the Shah,' he said; 'whoever tries to interfere with him now is a dead man.'

Sitara had reproached him as heartless and a coward. At one time she had made up her mind to go herself, to send Nadir the seal he had given her, and claim his promise. But the negro had made her see that the attempt would be hopeless. 'You would never get to the Shah,' he said. 'The soldiers would stop you in the streets. The stone would mean nothing to them. They would ill-treat you or kill you.' And he had made her understand, respectfully but beyond the possibility of mistake, that if she made the attempt he would have her stopped himself. He was responsible for her safety, and he knew that Nadir would never forgive him if he let her go.

As the night came down, and the sound of slaughter

ceased, the Agha Bashi came to her again. He found her lying on the floor of her room, with unbound hair and tear-stained face, full of mingled sorrow and wrath. To all he said she gave no answer. At last, hoping to rouse her, and perhaps truly fearing for her, he spoke more roughly.

'God knows I am sorry for you, Khánum, but what has been done has been done by the Shah's order. It was necessary. The Shah's troops were being murdered. What will he say if he comes to-night and finds you like this? He is angry, and evil thoughts may come to him. For God's sake compose yourself and do not bring his anger upon you.'

Sitara's wailing ceased, and she turned upon him fiercely. 'Go,' she said, 'go and leave me in peace. If the Shah comes I will tell him he is no man, but faithless and a murderer—a murderer of women and children. Go and leave me.'

The Agha Bashi sighed. He was about to speak again, but checked himself and walked out of the room. 'The Shah must not see her,' he thought. 'If he does she will say all that is in her mind, and she will be lost. He will never forgive her.'

Happily Nadir did not come. His first outburst of rage had been succeeded as the day wore on by a stern determination to give the Indians a lesson which would prevent any general rising against him; but through it all there had come to him at times the remembrance of Sitara's face as she pleaded for mercy to her people. Far more than the entreaties of the Moghul Emperor that remembrance had stayed his hand.

She never knew it, but it was so; and when he had done what he thought necessary he turned away willingly enough from the work of punishment. But he understood to some extent what the day had been for her, and shrank from meeting her at once. Better, he thought, give her time to master her grief and see reason.

His instinct was not at fault. When he did come to her again a day or two later, she had thought over it all, and recognised that he had been provoked beyond endurance. She had recognised, too, that for the safety of his army it had been necessary to strike terror into the ill-disposed. And she knew that the massacre, awful as it was, had been stopped by him before the troops got thoroughly out of hand. She received him without reproach, as if the massacre had never been.

Yet each knew that the other had not forgotten, and a few days later they were reminded by a ghastly witness, for the stench of the rotting corpses invaded the fort.

Nearly two months longer Sitara remained in the Moghul capital. Nadir's cupidity had been stirred by the enormous treasure which he had taken from the fallen Emperor. The prospect of laying up a sum which would make him free thenceforward from all anxiety about the maintenance of his armies appealed to him with irresistible force. His treasury filled once for all by the plunder of India, he would march from conquest to conquest, perhaps to found a new empire, far from his hated Persians, on the shores of the Golden Horn. So during those long weeks his hand pressed with ever-increasing weight upon the Moghuls and their wretched people. None perhaps suffered more from his wrath and his exactions than the traitors who had invited him to attack their master. He made them responsible for the collection of colossal sums. They were supervised by Persian officers, who treated the highest of them with every sort of indignity. Many were flogged in public: many were forced to disgorge their own ill-gotten gains to make up the tale demanded of them. Some killed themselves in despair. All repented bitterly of their madness in exchanging the feeble rule of the Moghul for the merciless tyranny of the Turkoman conqueror.

The people suffered cruelly. No fresh massacre came to add to the miseries of the cowed and abject capital, but food rose to famine price in the crowded streets, and for scores of miles on every side the Tartar horsemen rode over the country collecting supplies and marauding. Their horses ruined the fields of grain, the villages were plundered, and any who resisted the seizing of their goods or the dishonour of their women were slain without mercy. Soon all resistance ceased. Far away in the provinces the local governors oppressed the people to make up the tribute demanded of them. It was a time of horror all over the land.

As if in mockery, Nadir took the opportunity to marry his son to an Indian princess, and the Moghul in his distress had to find money and jewels for her dower. Nadir himself gave the bride a great store of gems which he had taken from the Moghul's treasury. And the trembling citizens had to show their joy by fireworks and illuminations.

Throughout March and April the work of collection went on, and the great stream of treasure flowed steadily into his coffers. His troops received all their arrears of pay; a large gratuity was given in addition to every soldier and camp-follower; and recognising that the resources of the Persians had been drained to supply the needs of his army, Nadir, with politic care for his own interests, so far repressed his hatred that he sent to Persia an order remitting all taxes for three years.

Towards the end of April he had done all that could be done. The heat was beginning, and he had a long way to march before his troops could get back to the uplands of Central Asia. One night he told Sitara that the time had come, and that in a few days more he would set out on his return.

She heard the news with relief, if not with joy. The past two months had been a time of misery to her countrymen, and her heart had ached for them. In all the splendour of her new lot, in all the intoxication of her love, their sorrows had been her sorrows. And she had seen with ever-increasing regret that a change seemed to have come over Nadir himself. There was growing upon him a lust of gold, a fierce rapacity, which seemed unlike him. His former contempt for wealth, except as a means of supplying the needs of his armies, was giving place to something lower. She hated to see his eyes grow eager as he described the jewels and treasures he was amassing, and something of her feeling showed in her face. She was longing to get away from the great city. Once in the camp again, she thought, he would become again the Nadir of her first night, the soldier-king at whose feet she had fallen.

CHAPTER XII

On the first of May the Moghul Emperor and his chief officials were received by Nadir in farewell audience.

Soon after daybreak the officials were assembled and were honoured with khilats, and soon afterwards the Moghul himself came to take leave of his conqueror. The monarchs had breakfast together, and then Nadir as suzerain invested the fallen Emperor with the insignia of his restored royalty. The descendant of so many warriors and kings humbly accepted his crown from the hands of the Turkoman soldier, and even stooped to ask his suzerain to nominate his chief officers of state. Nadir refused, and bade him make his own appointments, but promised to chastise all who did not obey his orders. With a last refinement of contempt and irony he warned his feudatory to beware of the traitors who had betrayed him in the past, and especially of those who had invited the Persian armies to India. Then the Moghul went back to his Palace of Joy in the Delhi fort.

A day or two later Nadir Shah marched away from Delhi, bearing with him the priceless Peacock Throne, and an enormous booty in gold and jewels. In his turban glittered the great diamond of the Moghuls, the famous Koh-i-nûr, or Mountain of Light. It glitters now in the crown of the British King.

Before finally setting out on his return to the frontier

Nadir sent back to Delhi the Indian women whom his officers had married or taken to themselves, and having done so he came to Sitara's tent. She had not seen him for some days, and her face was alight with pleasure as he stepped in and dropped the curtain behind him. But his look was stern, and his first words made her heart stand still. Taking no notice of her salutation, he stood looking at her as if displeased.

'I have sent back all the Indian women from the camp,' he said, and she looked up startled at his tone and words. 'You too are an Indian.'

She fell on her knees and laid her hands on his feet. For a moment he was silent.

'You are free to do as you please. Why should I take you away against your will? I have been hard to your people. If you wish to remain with them you are forgiven, and I will see that you are received with all honour. Say all that is in your mind. There is nothing to fear.'

Nadir knew well enough what her answer would be, but he could not deny himself the pleasure of inflicting the trial upon her, and of saying at the same time the words of half apology which he was sure would bring him full forgiveness.

'Oh my Lord!' she said, 'I am yours. You can kill me and you can let me live. If you send me away it is death.'

'But your country and your people. Can you leave them for ever? You will never see them again.'

Nadir's axe was hanging from his wrist. With a swift movement she bent forward and kissed it. 'Better this,' she said, 'if you wish to kill me.'

He laid his hand on her head. 'As you will, little

one. You shall go with me.' He looked into the eyes that were raised to his own. 'You are not like other women,' he said; 'I believe you would give your life for me.'

A smile of pride, almost of scorn, passed over her face. 'My life,' she said; 'what is that to give? When have the women of the Rajputs thought of their lives?'

It was a proud speech, but the history of many ages has borne witness to its truth.

And so when the Persian host marched away from the fallen capital of the Moghuls, the Rajput girl went with the conqueror of her people, drawn by a love which was more to her than all the world.

The line of march lay across the Punjab, and as the country had already been devastated by the Persians in their advance, Nadir led back the main body of his troops by a fresh route further to the north, where supplies were more easily procured. It was a rugged country at best, and Sitara riding along in the Kurk saw with each day's march westward how the face of the land became harder and more sterile. The fertile districts about Delhi, with their flourishing towns and springing crops, gave place to barren plains and stony ravines, where the patches of cultivation were few and far between, and the flat-roofed, treeless villages on their little mounds were hardly to be distinguished from the earth around them. It was no new thing to her, for it reminded her of the sandy wastes she had known in her childhood, the Land of Death of the Rahtors; but still with every day it seemed to her that India was fading away into the past. The men and women she saw were of an unfamiliar type, taller and wilder, and even their language was strange.

The heat in the daytime was already great. Nadir's soldiery, accustomed to the colder climate of the Central Asian plateau, and clothed in heavy stuffs and sheepskins, sweated and murmured as they toiled across the sunburnt plains. One morning, as Sitara found herself by chance riding in Kurk not far from the Shirázi, that lady took advantage of the occasion to torment her rival. She had always been as insolent and contemptuous as she dared to be. Now, irritated by the heat and dust and discomfort of the slow march, she gave rein to her temper.

'Allah! what heat,' she said, as she drew up alongside Sitara. 'It dries up the marrow in my bones. And what a country! No wonder you are glad to leave it,' and she quoted a Persian couplet which was a favourite at the time, 'Oh God! when you had Hind, why did you make Hell?'

Sitara answered hotly: 'All Hind is not like this, and there are deserts in Persia too, they say. The real Hind is a country so beautiful with water and trees and crops that you have not seen the like of it even in a dream.'

'I have seen enough,' the Persian answered. 'If it is so fine a country, why did the men of Hind not fight for it? They fled like deer before the Kizlbash. They said with the poet:

'"Not worth that a blood-drop should fall on the ground."'

Sitara flushed to the temple with anger and shame. 'Who can stand against the Shah?' she answered. 'His horsemen are the same Afghans and Tartars before whom the Persians have been as the dust of the earth since man can remember. How many thousands of your men and women are slaves in the black tents, tending the sheep of the man-sellers?'

The Shirázi laughed an evil laugh. 'Aha! you are learning the lesson well,' she said, 'but we shall see. Irán has endured for thousands of years. It will not always be defiled by dogs.'

The Ágha Bashi had been riding close behind. He pushed his horse between the women. 'Peace, peace,' he said to the Shirázi. 'Let the Khánum be. Has she not eaten grief enough these two months?'

The Shirázi's eyes flashed as she reined back her horse. 'Ah, it is you,' she said contemptuously. 'Come, then. Your place has been empty. Like colour, like heart.'

The Agha Bashi hardly waited till she was out of hearing. 'Khánum,' he said to Sitara, 'why do you have anything to do with her? She has a tongue that stings like a scorpion, and she hates you. Keep out of her way.'

Sitara was glad of the interruption. She felt that she was no match for the Shirázi in a war of words, and she was smarting under the lash of the Persian's sneers.

'I will keep out of her way if she will let me. God knows I do not want to quarrel. It is always her doing. But what does it matter if the Shah understands? She is nothing to me.'

'The Shah understands well enough. You have nothing to fear. He knows those who are faithful to him.'

And in that thought she found comfort. 'I will not let her trouble me,' she said to herself. 'I will think only of the Shah. Perhaps some day I shall be able to do him a service. He knows I would give my life for him. He has said it himself. Perhaps some day I shall be able to show him his words were true.'

Her opportunity was to come sooner than she thought. A few days more and the long march to the frontier was over. The weary troops were resting on the banks of the Indus. Nadir had hoped to turn the defiles of the Khyber by the country of the Yusufzai, and was negotiating with their head-men for a passage. His tents were pitched not far from a branch of the river, which was guarded by his men, their posts extending along the eastern bank.

It was night, and Nadir had talked late with Sitara, to whose tent he had come. A little before midnight he fell asleep, and she lay close by him, thinking over all he had said. Ever covetous of men, he was trying to draw to his standards the wild tribesmen of the Yusufzai. He had spoken warmly of their courage and hardiness, and had wished he could recruit his army with a few thousands of such fearless soldiers. But they were fierce and independent, he said, owning allegiance to no king or chief, and paying little regard to the orders of their own council of greybeards. They might be difficult to manage if he got them.

The night was hot, and Sitara could not sleep. After lying quiet for a time her restlessness grew too strong for her, and she rose to her knees. Nadir was lying on his takht, his axe as ever by his hand. She got up without a sound and stole across the tent to the doorway. Putting aside the curtain, she stepped into the outer passage of the tent, and stood looking across the river at the Yusufzai hills, which lay dark and distant under the starlit sky. Everything was still in the camp, and she could hear no sound but the far-off tinkle of a mule bell, and the deep voice of the water as it flowed swiftly by in its narrow channel, hidden from sight, a hundred feet below, by rocky cliffs.

The tents of the Anderûn were pitched as usual in a circular enclosure, which was surrounded by a high wall of tent canvas, and an outer fence of network. The space between the two was constantly patrolled by armed eunuchs. Beyond the network fence, covering the main entrance of the enclosure, was a guard tent.

As Sitara stood at her doorway, looking out through the hanging mat which concealed her, she saw something move near the entrance; and her eyes having grown accustomed to the starlight, she felt sure that she could distinguish a dark shape on the ground under the shadow of the tent wall. At first she thought that a stray dog wandering in search of food had eluded the sentries and crept under the canvas; but the form, whatever it was, lay still for a full minute, and when it moved again it crept forward so slowly and stealthily that her interest was aroused. Gazing at it as it came out from the shadow of the tent wall into the open ground she saw that it was followed by another and another, and suddenly it came to her with a thrill of fear at her heart that the forms were those of men crawling across the enclosure straight for the door of her tent. Another instant and her doubt gave way to certainty, for as the leading man moved again there was a faint glimmer of steel in the starlight.

Sitara's first impulse was to call out and alarm the camp, but the crawling forms were hardly fifty paces from her, and she felt that if they meant evil, one rush would bring them to the tent door. By letting them come on slowly, thinking themselves unseen, she would gain time to wake Nadir. She turned and crept into the tent again, swiftly and silently, and laid her hand on his. Nadir's senses, trained by a life of constant watchfulness, served him well. He woke at once, and seeing by her face and gesture that something was wrong, he was on his feet in an instant, his axe in his hand, and his brain as clear as if he had not slept. She drew him to the doorway and pointed to the place where the danger was. The men lay on the ground, motionless. Perhaps the faint sound of her footfall had reached them and made them pause in their advance. Nadir stood for a second or two gazing intently at the spot, Sitara's guiding hand still holding his. Then the leading form began to crawl forward again.

Nadir was no coward, but he felt that if he gave the alarm or moved out he might be assailed at a disadvantage. He stepped into the tent again, and signing to Sitara to put on her cloak, passed out by the entrance at the back.

'The Agha Bashi,' he said in a whisper.

Sitara took him straight to the tent where the negro usually slept with his guard of armed eunuchs. One man was in it, seated on the floor awake. As Nadir raised the curtain he sprang to his feet. Nadir signed to him to be silent.

'Where is the Agha Bashi?'

'He went out a few minutes ago to visit the guards.'

'Show me the way to the guard tent in front of the Anderûn.'

The man led the way through a tangle of pegs and tent ropes, and in a minute they were out of the enclosure in the starlight. Nadir walked to the door of the guard tent and looked in. There was a lamp in the tent, and by its light he could see the men of the guard lying asleep.

A moment more and they were out of the tent, armed and ready, a dozen of them, men of the Shah's own tribe, Turkomans of the Afshar. Nadir sent some of them to warn the posts along the river-bank.

'Stay here,' he said to Sitara, and she stood by the door of the guard tent watching.

Nadir and the guard stepped across to the entrance of the Anderûn. Close to it they could see in the starlight the form of the sentry who should have been pacing in front of it. He was seated apparently asleep on a piece of rock, his back propped against it, and his head covered. His matchlock lay by his side. Nadir laid his hand on the man's shoulder, but he did not move. He was dead. His back was soaked with blood from a deep knife wound between the shoulders, and a rough woollen cloth had been wrapped round his head.

Nadir had hoped to surround the Anderûn quietly and capture the assassins, but their quick ears had caught the sound of the stir in the camp. As he was giving his orders he heard a warning cry from Sitara, and turning towards her saw three men running swiftly past the guard tent in the direction of the river. One of them as he ran struck savagely at the cloaked figure in his path. There was a shout and a rush of men from all sides, and a few shots; but as Nadir and his guards reached the edge of the almost perpendicular cliff which overhung the river they heard a clatter of stones below them, and a plunge. The bank was soon alight with torches, and a hot fire of matchlocks was poured upon the dark face of the river below, but it was useless. Nadir waited for a moment and went back to the guard tent. Sitara came out as he called to her.

'I am safe, my Lord,' she said. 'He thought I was a man and struck at me, but I sprang back, and he ran on. I am not touched.'

'Thank God,' Nadir said, 'Ján i ma—my life,' and he laid his hand on the girl's shoulder. 'But for you it might have gone hard with me.'

A distant shout came across the river from a point below where they were standing. The tribesmen had been carried far down by the current, but had landed in safety, and were sending back a farewell of triumph and defiance.

A grim example of their prowess lay near the riverbank. One soldier had been quick enough to get in their way as they ran. He lay on the ground dead. The heavy, straight 'chûra' of a tribesman had fallen fair on his shoulder, close to the neck, and had cloven its way through bone and flesh down to his heart.

'Afrîn!' Nadir said. 'That is a man's stroke. Our faces are blackened, but by Allah they are men!'

All was soon quiet again, and Nadir was back in Sitara's tent. The jewels she had taken off that night were gone. They were worn for many a year afterwards by three girls of the Yusufzai.

Nadir was soon asleep once more. He was too old a soldier to let such an incident disturb his peace of mind. But perhaps he slept the more quietly for knowing that he had by his side so quick and faithful a watcher.

A YUSUFZAI

From Elphinstone's 'Account of Caubul

CHAPTER XIII

THE unfortunate men who had been on guard during the night paid dearly for their negligence. Partly for his own safety, partly for the proper training of his troops, Nadir on such occasions was without pity. The sun had hardly risen next morning before he was at the river-bank, finding out where the Yusufzais had crossed. Then he took his seat in Durbar, and all concerned were brought before him. A few minutes sufficed for their trial. The men who had been in the guard tent at the entrance of the Anderûn were at once ordered out for execution. Of them no questions were asked. They were soon followed by those who had been on duty to right and left of the point where the tribesmen had landed and swarmed up the cliff. Almost all died without useless complaints or prayers. Nadir's face was set like a flint, and they knew that they might as well have asked for mercy of the rocks about them. One only, a youth of Nadir's own tribe, the Afshar—upon whose chin the down was still soft—cursed him wildly. Nadir's hand rose, and in an instant the boy had been dragged to the entrance of the Durbar tent, his head forced backward by the Nasakchis, and his throat cut.

The rest, all men of the Six Thousand, walked out proudly to their doom. They laid aside their white coats and cuirasses, and knelt down in a line, stripped to the waist. Each man as his turn came repeated the kalima, 'There is no God but God, and Mahomed is the prophet of God.' The next instant his head fell to the ground, shorn off by one dragging cut of the executioner's sword. The bodies lay for hours where they had fallen, a terrible warning to their comrades.

But towards the Yusufzai tribesmen Nadir's attitude was wholly different. Their exploit only whetted his desire to obtain Yusufzai recruits; and when by dint of promises he had induced a 'jirga' of the tribe to come into his camp, he spoke to them without anger.

Not a word was said about the attempt to murder him.

Standing among the tribesmen on the open ground, under the two great flagstaffs from which floated the Imperial standards, he showed them the ordered lines of his great host, the splendour of his retinue, glittering with the spoils of India, the innumerable cannon, always a terror to the imagination of wild men, and the long ranks of Indian elephants with which he could ford or swim their mountain rivers.

'Men of the Yusufzai,' he said, 'choose which you will. Your men are brave, but they are poor. If they will join me, they will have honourable service and pay, and such booty as they have never dreamed of. Your tribe will grow rich with the plunder of kingdoms. If you insist on doing me evil, on your heads be it. None have yet been able to stand against my victorious troops. You are brave, and I honour brave men, but you are few. Why should your tribe be blotted out of the book of existence?'

Little by little his words prevailed. Greed of plunder

perhaps, rather than fear, was the motive that acted upon the needy tribesmen; but when Nadir marched away, there was peace between him and the Yusufzai, and a large contingent of the mountaineers had enlisted under his banners.

Nadir dealt in a similar spirit with the tribes who held the Khyber, to which route he had reverted. With all his bold words, he was too good a soldier not to know that if he tried to force his way through their rugged mountains, he would lose time and men, and a fine recruiting ground. So he lavished freely on the wild tribesmen the wealth he had taken from the Moghul, and to this day they boast that the mighty conqueror paid them for a passage.

The heat was fierce when Sitara, riding with the Kurk, looked her last on the Indian plains, and saw in front of her the head of the column plunge into the mouth of the great defile. She was leaving behind her for ever the land of her birth, and those who know the Hindu know how the men and women of her race dread going out to a world of strange customs and strange beliefs. It was breaking with all that she had held dear and sacred. And she was doing it for the love of a man whose loves had been countless. She knew how precarious her position was, how his sudden passion might at any moment change into indifference or dislike. Then what would be before her but a life of misery, in a land of strangers who hated or despised her and her people? It was not without something of fear and sadness that she faced her unknown future. But her heart never faltered in its resolve. Full of the unmeasured devotion which marks the woman of the Rajputs, she had but one object—to serve, and if need be, to die for, the man she loved.

The long column wound through the pass, and to right and left the rock walls closed in until they towered a thousand feet sheer above her head. On a jutting point here and there, far out of reach, she saw the dark form and long matchlock of a tribesman, guarding the defile against marauders, and the girl thought of what might have been if the mountaineers had been enemies. But the column passed on its way in safety, not a shot fired to delay its march, until at last it descended the mountain slopes on the western side, and saw before it the comparatively open country of Afghanistán. There were mountainous tracts ahead still, but Nadir's innumerable horsemen covered the face of the land, and the tribes to which it belonged were his most trusted soldiery, the men on whose rugged faith and valour the great soldier relied to keep order among his own countrymen. They were a difficult people to manage too, wild and fierce and fickle like the Israelites from whom they claimed descent. The Persians hated and feared and despised them. 'Afghan be imán, the faithless Afghan,' was the word constantly in a Persian's mouth. But Nadir knew the 'Ban i Israil,' and for him they were faithful to the death.

The army marched on slowly now, with many halts, through the open valleys towards Kábul. After the heat of India, the air of the Central Asian uplands was fresh and exhilarating. Instead of the desolate, dust-coloured plains of the Punjab, Sitara saw around her the green of springing crops. The streams which poured down from the mountain-sides were clear and cold. The blue air was full of swallows. And as yet Nadir's love held true. It was a happy summer.

AN AFGHAN

From Elphinstone's 'Account of Caubul'

As the autumn closed in, Nadir's troops, who had been rested and strengthened by their leisurely advance, marched into Kábul. On the last day of the march Sitara, riding over a stony 'kotal,' or mountain pass, saw on a hillock by the roadside an iron cage raised on a post. Inside the cage was crouched something bearing the semblance of a man. She asked the Agha Bashi what it was.

'It is the justice of the Shah. When we marched down last year, there were two Ghilzai robbers who were striking the road. They held up one of the Shah's káfilas. It was not a great loss—a string of camels laden with Shiráz wine and melons from Ispahán; but the Shah was angry. Soon afterwards one of the Ghilzais was surprised in his sleep by men in the Shah's pay, who brought him in to camp, bound hand and foot. The Shah ordered that he should be put there for an example, where he had attacked the káfila.'

'He was killed?'

'No, Khánum. The Shah wished to teach the Ghilzais that they must not strike the road. The man was put in the cage where all who passed could see him, and left without food or water. He was a strong man, and lived for sixteen days they say.'

Sitara was silent. It seemed a horrible punishment.

'Being very thirsty, he asked the guards for the sake of God to kill him and put him out of his torment, and they would have done it, for he was a brave man and they felt sorry for him, but they knew the Shah would hear of it, and dared not. So he was long in dying, and the Ghilzais have never struck the road since.'

Sitara sighed.

'Khánum,' the Agha Bashi said, 'what would you have? These people are Shaitáns. Killing them is no use. They laugh at death. And the King's road must be made safe.

'Afsôs. It is a pity.'

'Yes, Khánum, it is a pity. But kings cannot show mercy to evil-doers. The Shah knows his business, and the country is quiet, though it is full of Shaitáns.'

They rode on over the pass and across the open plain, a long march, to where the citadel of Kábul lay against a stony hillside. Under it was the town, surrounded and half hidden by poplars and willow-trees. Near the gateway of the citadel they came upon another example of Nadir's justice. In a piece of open ground by the side of the moat, Sitara saw a man seated on the ground. An iron collar was round his neck, and was fastened by a chain to a stump. By his side was a basin of water, and a brass platter with some pieces of unleavened bread. The Agha Bashi reined in his horse and spoke to a sentry who was standing close by. He came back to Sitara with a grave face.

'What is it?' she said.

'Khánum, the man is an officer of the Kizlbash. He was left here with the garrison when we marched for India. They say he was jealous of an Afghan whom the Shah favoured. One day they went out for a ride together, and this man challenged the other to race him across the plain to a tree he pointed out. On the way there was a deep ravine, and in it he had placed two men with muskets. When the Afghan came to the ravine he had to ride down slowly, and they killed him and hid his body. But the Shah's spies know everything, and a report was sent to the Shah. He ordered that the murderer should be exposed as you see him. He has water and bread, but both are half salt, so that if he eats or drinks it is torment. He will die soon. He is nearly mad now.'

Sitara could not repress an exclamation of horror and pity. The Agha Bashi shook his head.

'Khánum, it is the Shah's order. Treachery like that must be punished. For God's sake be careful what you say.'

'I will be careful,' the girl answered, 'but these things frighten me. Is it good for the Shah's name that he should do them?'

Nadir's camp was pitched around a walled garden in the valley to the west of Kábul, amid lines of poplars and spreading plane-trees. The sky was without a cloud. In the pure dry air of the Central Asian plateau, some thousands of feet above the sea, the mountains stood out with exquisite clearness, their bare sides and summits taking the most delicate shades of colour. To the north, the distant ranges were already white with snow.

The troops, refreshed by their quiet summer, now feasted upon the good fare of the Afghan valleys. Grain and meat were plentiful, and fruit of every kind was almost too abundant. Grapes, apricots, peaches, apples, the pomegranates of which Asiatics are so fond, all poured into the camp.

Sitara, looking out from the window of a garden-house where the Agha Bashi had lodged her, the nights being already cold, used to see the villagers coming in with donkey loads of sweet little seedless grapes. A dozen men of the guard would pour out the contents of the panniers on the ground, and sit round in a circle, eating bread and grapes till they could eat no more. True, it was the month of Ramazán, when believers should fast, and some of the more faithful among them did so. As sunset approached and the hours of fasting were nearly over, Sitara would see a line of Kizlbash, each with his kalián in his hand, waiting for the evening gun. As the sound rang out, the pipe-stems went to their lips, and for a few seconds nothing was heard but the gurgle of the water in the bowls, and deep inhalations of the much-craved tobacco smoke, always the first thing taken. But most of the rough soldiery of Nadir recked little of Ramazán, and Nadir gave them free dispensation, both by precept and example. His first care was that his 'poor priests of God' should be well fed and fit for duty, and they took full advantage of the licence allowed them. In spite of their mullas the troops, as a rule, passed the time in feasting and comfort.

Yet amid all the rest and peace of that pleasant autumn Nadir himself worked unceasingly. From her window Sitara could see him sitting, hour after hour, in his tent of audience dispensing justice and transacting his manifold affairs. A constant stream of men came before him. Afghan chiefs or village head-men, charged with maintaining order in the country or finding supplies, would be brought in one by one; big bearded men in sheepskins, the wool inside and the leather roughly embroidered with yellow silk. Military commanders and civil officials came in scores to receive orders or write despatches at Nadir's dictation. Or his chamberlain, a tall, richly dressed officer bearing a silver-topped staff of office, would usher in a deputation of mullas and seyyids, descendants of the prophet, with voluminous turbans of white or dark green.

In spite of his contempt for the Shia priests of Persia, Nadir showed a politic respect for the orthodox mullas of Afghanistán, well knowing their power over the ignorant and fanatical tribesmen. Once they demanded from him the life of a man who had been guilty of blasphemy, and Sitara, looking from her window, saw the man taken out and stoned. He knelt on the ground, covering his face with his hands, and a circle of men standing round hurled masses of rock upon him till he was beaten down and hidden from sight.

Offenders of all classes were brought before Nadir, and received summary justice. Once a train of these poor wretches passed under Sitara's window, and she shuddered to see them. There were men who had suffered the felek, limping by in agony with bandaged feet; blinded men, with blood oozing from their empty sockets; men who had been mutilated in other ways, with their heads or arms swathed in bloody cloths. All were submissive and almost silent, save for a groan of irrepressible anguish, or a low heart-broken wail. The Tartar horsemen drove them mercilessly past, pricking with their long lances those who lagged, and laughing aloud if some poor wretch flinched at the sudden touch of steel. It was horrible, horrible, and as Sitara shrank from her window feeling faint and sick, she said to herself, in spite of the warning of the Agha Bashi, 'I will speak. I must speak to him. For his own sake I must speak to him.'

She tried that night. He came in to her rooms with a suddenness which startled her. As she sprang to her feet and made her salaam, he laughed. 'Frightened?' he said. 'What evil have you been doing?' and his eyes were so full of good-humour that it gave her courage. Soon she found her opportunity. There was a tray of fruit on the carpet where she had been lying. 'It is a fine country,' he said. 'There is no fruit like the fruit of Kábul. But my Afghans are a rough people. With all their grapes they make no good wine —nothing like the wine of Shiráz.'

Sitara smiled. 'Then the Persians are good for something, my Lord?'

'Yes. They can make wine, and drink it, but they are good for nothing else. An Afghan is worth ten Persians.'

'And yet, my Lord, you have to punish the Afghans very often. I saw many of them coming from the Presence to-day and . . . oh! my Lord, it was a sad sight.'

Nadir's face clouded over. 'You have a soft heart. But you should not eat grief for them. Offenders must be punished.'

'I know, my Lord. Who am I that I should speak? But, my Lord, forgive me. Is such "sakhti"—such hardness—necessary? Some were nearly dead from the felek, some had lost their eyes, and some their hands. And on the road I saw the cage where the Ghilzai robber had died, and the man in chains at the gate of the Bala Hissar. My Lord, it frightens me. They are a fierce people. Will they not do evil in revenge?'

Her voice shook as she finished, for Nadir's eyes were very stern.

'I will forgive you this time,' he said, 'for you mean no harm. But never let me hear you speak of such matters again. Affairs of state are not for women.

Kings cannot be merciful. Mercy to offenders is injustice to the good. I know my business, and I will have no interference. Remember that once for all.'

'My Lord, forgive me. I was wrong to speak. But I was thinking only of my Lord's service. I will never speak again.'

Nadir relented. 'I have forgiven,' he said. 'Remember for the future. God knows I do not wish to be angry with you.'

The lesson sank deep into Sitara's heart, and perhaps she loved him the more for knowing that she could not move him. Brave and impetuous as she was, she was glad to feel that he was her master.

CHAPTER XIV

NADIR'S stay in Kábul was short. His troops, their health restored, and their ranks swollen by many thousands of the hardiest fighting-men in Asia, were ready now for fresh fatigues and fresh victories. As usual, he was growing restless under inaction.

He had during that year done enough to satisfy most men. The great empire of the Moghuls had fallen before him, and he had returned in triumph with such wealth as he had never before dreamed of possessing. Gold and jewels and ivory, and the precious work of Indian looms, and elephants and horses and camels—all that an eastern monarch could desire—he had gathered in incalculable quantities. Even his rough spearmen had begun to wear rich stuffs, and to adorn their arms and bridles with silver and gems. He laughed at them, but encouraged them, for it all brought him recruits, and he meant to leave them no time to get soft. He had already made his plans for the conquest of the Central Asian Khanates of Bokhara and Khiva. He would end once for all the ancient rivalry of Irán and Turán, Persia and Tartary, and hunt down in their deserts the man-sellers who had so long ravaged the fairest provinces of Persia. Then perhaps he would turn his attention to the Caucasus and Constantinople. He had already sent to the Sultan an embassy with presents selected from the plunder of India—elephants and jewels and rich stuffs. The embassy was charged with demands which the Turk was very unlikely to grant, and the demands were backed by a threat of war. The dream of founding a new empire on the Bosphorus was ever before Nadir's eyes.

But before marching towards the north and west, Nadir had to make all secure behind him. When he was leaving India, the Moghul Emperor had formally ceded to him all the countries west of the Indus; and at the beginning of the winter Nadir set in motion his great host for a march to the south and east.

It was a toilsome march, and the troops suffered much from the cold. For those of the men who observed the fast of Ramazán, the suffering was intensified by hunger and weakness. It is no light thing to march all day without touching food or water, or drawing one whiff from the kalián. There was scanty provision for the animals, and toiling over the rough roads, crossing and recrossing the icy streams, chilled by cold blasts from the hills around them, many of the mules and camels perished, and much baggage was lost. In this respect, Nadir, like all great soldiers, was pitiless. Beforehand he made all the preparations he could; but once started he thought only of the object before him, and pressed on regardless of the losses and sufferings of his people. It was the only way of accomplishing great deeds, but the vast armies of Eastern conquerors, with their trains of artillery and animals, always suffered terribly on their marches through these sparsely inhabited and barren countries. The wonder was that they could subsist at all.

The mountains were left behind, and in the warmer country on the banks of the Indus the perishing force was once again in plenty. The buried grain stores of the deserted villages were unearthed and distributed among the troops, the baggage animals grew fat again on green wheat and barley, and the winter passed agreeably enough.

An old chronicler who accompanied Nadir on this march relates a characteristic story of the Shah's wild soldiery. 'During the whole of this march all the villages through which we passed were entirely deserted; and the only person that I saw was a fat Brahmin sitting upon the highway begging alms in the names of Har and Mahadeo. I did all I could to persuade him to save himself by flight from the fury of the soldiers, who were near at hand; but he was so infatuated that he would not stir, and even asked me if I envied him the alms which he should obtain? During our conversation a party of Bakhtiaris came up, and binding the poor wretch hand and foot, they cut him in pieces, to try the sharpness of their swords.'

Nadir remained on the banks of the Indus organising his new province, until the festival of the Persian New Year. Then large sums of Indian gold were distributed among his troops, and all was peace and rejoicing. A few days later the army marched for the north by way of Quetta and Kandahar, and in the month of May they arrived in Herát

Sitara had accompanied the army, and day after day, as she rode in the Kurk, she saw all around her the results of long warfare and misrule. Here and there on the road were ancient cities and mosques and tombs, the remnants of a bygone civilisation; but the cities were in ruins, the mosques were deserted. Even Herát itself, once a fine town, was now a scene of desolation. The population had shrunk to a half of what it had been, and the ground-floors of the houses were ploughed up and sown with grain.

'This is not like the cities of Hind,' Sitara remarked with pardonable malice to the Shirázi as they rode through the ruined streets; and the Shirázi answered with characteristic aptness:

'The spider is the chamberlain at the door of Khusrú, and the owl keeps watch in the tower of Afrasiáb.'

But, fallen as it was from its former greatness, Herát was still the best base from which Nadir could attack the Khanates of Tartary; and there he halted his great army while he completed the preparations for his new conquest.

He began by passing in review the plunder of the Indian Empire. Before he left the Moghul capital he had given orders for the manufacture of arms and harness of every kind, inlaid with precious stones, and for the preparation of a royal pavilion which was to be as splendid as wealth and art could make it. Hundreds of the best workmen of India had been impressed for the service, and throughout the year, while he was on the march, the work had been going on. When he arrived in Herát, all was ready for the great display. In the open space before the Diwan Khaneh, or place of audience, was pitched the royal pavilion. It was a vast tent, covered with fine scarlet cloth and lined with green satin. In it were displayed the Peacock Throne of the Moghuls, another throne which Nadir had used before his expedition to India, others again which had belonged to some of the rulers he had conquered. All were richly carved, and inlaid with gold and gems and ivory. Around them were displayed many other specimens of Indian jewel work, sets of harness, swords and sword sheaths, spears and maces, quivers and shields. The Englishman, Hanway, who visited Nadir's camp two or three years later, describes his 'horse furniture' in these words: 'He had four complete sets, one mounted with pearls, another with rubies, a third with emeralds, and the last with diamonds, most of which were of so prodigious a size as hardly to merit belief; for many of them appeared as big as a pigeon's egg.' The walls of the tent itself were adorned with representations of birds and beasts, and trees and flowers, all formed of pearls and gems. The poles which upheld the pavilion were encrusted with jewels, and even the tent pins were of massive gold. Proclamation was made by beat of drum throughout the city and the camp that this magnificent exhibition, 'such as had never before been seen in any age or country,' was open to all; and the people of Herát and the soldiery came in their thousands to gaze and wonder.

These priceless spoils, and Nadir's treasure of every kind, were to be sent to Persia when the expedition started. In charge of them, as Governor of the country, Nadir left his second son, who had accompanied him to India. His eldest son, Reza Kuli Khan, who had been Governor during his long absence, was to join him and share the triumphs of the expedition.

Soon all was in readiness. The baggage of the troops had been cut down, and everything that could be spared had been stored in Herát. Light marching tents had been distributed, one to every ten men. The baggage animals had been carefully inspected and equipped. Before the end of June Nadir's restless spirit was once more appeased by action, and the army which was to conquer Turán, great in numbers still, but selected and weeded with the utmost care, marched out upon the road to the Oxus.

With it went a few of Nadir's ladies, riding in Kurk, and among them Sitara.

CHAPTER XV

It was a bright summer morning when the Kurk marched out of Herát. The sun was hot, but the air was clear and pleasant, and Sitara rejoiced at finding herself again on the back of her Arab. She had caught some of the restlessness of her lord, and she knew that in camp he would be less occupied and more cheerful than in the city, where the work of preparation had kept him busy from morning to night.

When he rode into the Kurk, soon after they started, it was evident that he had left all care behind. He galloped up as usual at headlong speed, and drew rein close to the Agha Bashi, who had dismounted to receive him. His eyes were shining, and his face bright with good-humour. He raised his hand with a smile in reply to the salute of the veiled women.

'Mount, Agha Bashi,' he said, 'and ride with me. I have just received good news.'

'May the Shah always have good news,' the negro answered, as he sprang into the saddle.

'The Vali Ahd's[1] camp has arrived near Herát, and he is riding on in advance. He will catch us up this morning.'

'His place has long been empty. It is two years since our eyes have been rejoiced by the sight of him.'

The Agha Bashi honestly shared in the Shah's pleasure, for Reza Khan was a favourite with all in

[1] *Vali Ahd*, heir-apparent.

camp. He was like his father in many ways, with much of Nadir's soldierly frankness and charm of manner. Though young, he had proved his courage in the field, and won the hearts of the Kizlbash.

Sitara, riding behind the Shah, heard the words, and her curiosity was aroused. Nadir had spoken to her of Reza Khan more than once, and she knew that he was proud of his soldier son. In fact, Nadir made no concealment of the fact that Reza was his favourite. His second son was a different character altogether, a man of the pen rather than a man of the sword.

An hour later, Sitara saw the meeting. Nadir was still talking gaily with the Agha Bashi, his deep laugh thundering out at intervals, when a mounted eunuch rode up from the rear. He spoke to the Agha Bashi, and pointed to a body of horsemen on the plain, outside the lines of the Kurk. Nadir turned his horse and cantered towards them. When he was out of the Kurk he reined up, and the horsemen, who had dismounted, came towards him on foot. Striding out in front was a tall, straight figure in whose walk and carriage, even at that distance, Sitara thought she could see the likeness to the Shah. Nadir leant from his saddle, and laid his hand on his son's shoulder. They seemed to exchange a few words of greeting, and then Reza Khan mounted again, and the two rode on side by side.

'The Shah will be happy to-day,' the Agha Bashi said. 'The Vali Ahd is a son to be proud of. God grant that they may always be of one heart.'

He was riding by Sitara's side.

'Inshallah! Please God,' she answered, with a touch of surprise in her voice. 'Are they not father and son?'

The Agha Bashi looked at her, and hesitated. 'Khánum, they are very much alike,' he said, in a low voice, 'and the Vali Ahd has been alone for two years. Also there are people always ready to do badi for their own advantage.'

He saw the look of indignation in her eyes, and smiled. 'Nay, there is no cause for fear, Khánum. I should not have spoken. Inshallah! All will go well. The Vali Ahd is a fine youth, and the Shah's soul is big. Let your heart be at rest.'

That night Nadir came to her—the first time he had done so for some days, and she fancied that he did not look so cheerful as he had been in the morning. After a few minutes he introduced the subject.

'You have heard that my son has come from Persia?'

'Yes, my Lord. I saw you ride out from the Kurk to meet him.'

'He is a fine boy. It is well that he has come. Besides him I have only my brother's son in the camp. He will be of much service to me.'

'Inshallah! They say that the Vali Ahd is a brave soldier.'

A look of displeasure passed across Nadir's face.

'Why do you call him the Vali Ahd?'

'That is how I have heard him called, and my Lord has spoken of him so to me. Is it wrong?'

Nadir looked at her, and paused a second before he answered. 'No,' he said. 'You have done nothing wrong. He is brave and capable, and he is the eldest. But it is for me to name the Vali Ahd.'

'Without doubt, my Lord, In Irán there is none but you. Whatever you order all will obey.'

Nadir's displeasure seemed to pass off, and for an

hour he talked of his son in words of praise. As he spoke of the boy's courage his face lit up with pride, and his eyes shone.

'Aye,' he said at last, 'he is a soldier like me. His heart is brave, and his arm is strong. He is young yet, and hot-headed at times. He has not had to win his way up as I had, and has not learned caution. But he is a brave man. There is no other fit to be Vali Ahd.'

The force marched on to the north-east by the edge of the Turkoman desert, crossing at one place a three days' stretch of waterless sand, where some men and many horses perished. But on the whole the month's march was pleasant enough. There was abundance of game in the reed jungle which fringed the line of march—pheasants and deer and wild boars. In the words of an eye-witness, 'the soldiers killed such numbers of deer that no one would eat mutton.'

Nadir had been surprised, and not altogether pleased, at finding his son so much stronger and more manly than he had expected, but the feeling seemed to have passed away. Reza Khan knew the country, and had made himself really useful. Nadir had, in fact, been unusually merry—joining in his son's hunting parties, and roaring with laughter when a wild boar dashed out suddenly from a reed bed and unhorsed one of his chief officers, who was supposed to be rather like a boar himself. 'Your little brother used you very uncivilly,' Nadir said. If the description of an old chronicler is to be believed, he had some excuse for his mirth. The man 'was short in stature, corpulent and ill-formed, of dark complexion, with a most detestable countenance; his skin hung in plaits like the hide of a rhinoceros; and his head and neck were only fit to be cut asunder. On the contrary, Nadir Shah was tall, had a beautiful complexion of red and white, with a fine animated countenance.'

When the day's march was ended Reza Khan would share Nadir's supper, and the two would quaff deep draughts of Shiráz, and sit talking and laughing far into the night.

If Nadir was less with Sitara in consequence, she was unselfish enough to rejoice in his happiness, and when at last they reached the historic city of Balkh, ruined, of course, but beautiful in its ruins, all seemed to be going well.

CHAPTER XVI

THERE was a short halt at Balkh while Nadir completed his preparations for his conquest of the Tartar kingdoms.

While far away in India, he had thought over the campaign, and with the foresight which characterised him, had given his orders a year in advance.

There was one road into the heart of Tartary—the majestic river which flowed northward to the Aral Sea.

The Governor of Balkh had been directed to lay in stores of grain upon its banks, and skilled workmen had been sent from India to build a thousand boats, some for the construction of bridges, others for the transport of supplies. The grain boats were now loaded up, and placed in charge of Nadir's nephew, Ali Kuli, while Nadir marched with his army down the left bank of the Oxus to protect them from any attack on the part of the nomad Turkomans, the hated 'man-sellers,' whose deserts lay to the westward.

The women of the Anderûn were carried in comfort upon rafts made of inflated bullock skins. A fleet of these rafts, guarded by boats full of armed men, floated down the river, and from one of them, lying at her ease on a soft carpet, Sitara watched day after day the orderly advance of the great army.

Twelve days' march brought all safely to Charjui, the

nearest point to Bokhara. Here a bridge of boats was constructed under the orders of Nadir in person, and the army crossed to the right bank.

By this time it had been ascertained that the King of Bokhara had given up all hope of resisting the conqueror of India. Awed by the fame of Nadir, and the vast scale of his preparations for the invasion, the King's people urged him to submit; and after some negotiation, without a shot being fired, the Persian force took possession of his capital. The historic city, the greatest of the capitals of Turán, was spared the horrors of a sack, and indeed the plunder would have been small, for in spite of its fame, Bokhara was poor in everything but mosques and tombs. But though Nadir preserved the city from destruction, he remembered that the King had in the past sent him defiant messages. Like the Moghul, therefore, the King was ordered to present himself in person at the camp of his conqueror, and his reception was even more humiliating than the reception of the Moghul had been.

Sitara, watching from behind her screen in the window of a building hard by, saw the ruler of Turán dismount from his horse and advance on foot to the open place where Nadir was seated. To impress the people of the conquered country, Nadir had once more determined to show himself in all his splendour. He sat on his throne wearing his robes of state, and surrounded by his courtiers in their most magnificent attire.

As the King was led forward, bending low before his conqueror, Nadir did not even rise from his seat, but merely acknowledged with a gesture and a few words of welcome the homage of a ruler whose reputation throughout Asia had once been far greater than his own. And for thousands of miles, throughout all the teeming bazaars of the East, it was known that the pride of Turán had been humbled at the feet of the Persian soldier.

A day or two afterwards the King sent to Nadir the diadem he had worn, with some hundreds of camels and horses, and some exquisitely written Persian manuscripts. It was all he had to offer, and his gifts were accepted with something like contempt. The scoffing Persians quoted a verse of the Holy Work: 'Those who possess learning and do not practise what it teaches, are like asses loaded with books.'

Nadir forced the King to release all the Persian captives who had been sold to the Bokhariots by the Turkoman raiders in days gone by; and some thousands of Uzbegs were enlisted for service in the Persian army.

Then Sitara learned, with a pang at her heart, that a sister of the fallen King had been taken to wife by the man who was all the world to her. She heard the sounds of shouting and martial music which announced the Uzbeg Queen's arrival, and that night, lying alone in her tent, she tasted once more the bitterness which the Eastern woman has to know.

CHAPTER XVII

KHIVA—lone Khiva in the waste. What memories thronged around the name! How many armies had perished in the sands of the desert trying to reach its fabled towers!

But to Nadir the difficulties of the enterprise were only a spur. His ambition was aroused. He had sworn to enter the magic city in spite of her deserts, and the myriads of horsemen who peopled them. For generations past their devastating swarms had raided the Persian plains. Thousands of miserable captives had disappeared into the north at the stirrup of those fierce riders, lost for ever to their homes and their kindred. He would lift the veil, and lay once for all the terror which had so long daunted the hearts of his countrymen.

He was still halted at Bokhara when he received news that the army of Khiva was marching southward to meet him. The Turkomans had gathered in the desert to attack the troops he had left guarding his bridge and grain stores. Some of the Kizlbash, who had been foraging far to the north among the villages on the river, had been cut off. A few of them had escaped, and reported the enemy in strength within fifty miles of Charjui.

Nadir marched at once with the main body of the force which had taken Bokhara. To ensure the safety of the stores, upon which the existence of his army depended, he sent on his son, Reza Khan, with some thousands of chosen horse and a hundred 'Zambûraks,' or camel guns—Wasps, as they were called—to reinforce the river guards.

Reza Khan accepted the service with eagerness. Masterful by nature, and accustomed for two years past to a life of independence, he had chafed under the return to his father's control, and longed to be free once more. His fiery spirit rejoiced at the chance of battle and distinction. He received his orders with unconcealed delight.

'Ba chashm,' he said. 'On my eyes be it. The Shah does me much honour. What are these dogs of man-sellers before the horsemen of the Shah? Inshallah! we shall sweep them away as the wind sweeps the dust of the desert.'

Nadir listened with a father's pride. He saw in his son a kindred spirit, and the words warmed his heart. But before all he was a soldier of many wars, and he had learned not to despise his enemy.

'My son,' he said, 'the Turkomans are robbers, and there is no weight in their attack; but they are swift and cunning. God knows how many thousands of their horsemen are gathered in the desert. I have given you important service. Your business is to secure the boats and the grain stores. They are the life of the army. Take care that you deserve my trust, and are not drawn away into any rash fighting before I come.'

Reza Khan promised that he would be careful, but through all the respect of his manner there was an undertone of impatience. Hardly had he been dismissed before he was in the saddle, and pressing on with his horsemen and his 'Wasps' across the sixty miles which divided Bokhara from the river.

The sun had hardly risen on the third day when Nadir rode to the bridge head at Charjui. The bridge was intact, and the broad waters of the Oxus were covered with grain boats. The army of Khiva had made no attack. Nadir dismounted, and in sight of all laid his forehead on the ground and returned thanks to God.

Reza Khan had crossed the river the day before, and was out on the plain to the westward. He had left word that he would feel the strength of the enemy and send back news.

As the troops came in, fatigued with their long night march, Nadir sat in his tent awaiting the arrival of his son's messengers. He was now free from any anxiety for the safety of his supplies, and he wished to rest his men before the action which seemed to be impending; but he gave orders for them to cross the bridge and camp on the western bank. Some thousands of them had crossed, and more were still defiling over the bridge of boats, when he received news which made him mount and cross the river himself. Small bodies of horsemen were to be seen on the plain to the westward, and from their movements they were believed to be the enemy. If so, they had got behind Reza Khan's force, and there was reason to fear that he might be in difficulties.

Nadir rode to the top of a hillock on the western bank, and all the troops available were rapidly formed up to meet an attack. To his practised eye there was no doubt. He knew the Turkomans too well to make a mistake. Parties of their spearmen were on the plain within a mile or two of the river, advancing slowly towards the bridge head. Far away in the distance beyond them he could see a cloud of dust rising into the clear blue air of the desert. The dust was not rising in a long trail, as if made by a column on the march, but from one point.

Suddenly there was a commotion among the Turkomans, who turned their horses and began galloping. More dust rose as they moved, but through it he could see the glint of their spear-heads. Another moment and Nadir made out a single horseman riding straight for the bridge. He was coming on at full speed, and the Turkomans were closing in upon him from right and left.

The thing could only have one meaning. A messenger from Reza Khan was trying to reach the bridge, and the Turkomans were doing their best to cut him off. Nadir could see the colour of his horse, a grey, and the flash of his sword as it rose and fell. He was evidently hard pressed, riding for his life.

Nadir's deep voice thundered out a word of command. He raised his axe high over his head and pointed to the front. His horse sprang forward, and with a shout the long line of his Kizlbash was racing on his track. As they went they saw the single horseman swerve to avoid some Turkomans who had got in his path, and for a moment or two it seemed as if he were surrounded. Then from the galloping line there was a roar of triumph and applause. The grey horse burst from the cloud of dust and spear-heads, and came straight on. The Turkomans pursued for a few strides, then seeing they were too late, wheeled and cantered away across the plain.

Nadir reined in his horse, and the broken ranks of the Kizlbash came to a halt. As they did so, the man they had rescued galloped up to Nadir, and sprang to the ground. His turban had fallen, showing his huge shaven head. The blood was streaming from a gash across his cheek, and dripping from his beard. The long, straight 'chûra' he held in his hand was dripping too. The grey stood with hanging head and labouring flanks, his crimson nostrils wide open.

'Shávásh! shávásh!' Nadir said, seeing the man was an Afghan, 'you rode well. What news have you brought?'

The horseman saluted, recognising the Shah, and tried to speak.

'My Lord,' he said, his breath coming in gasps, 'my Lord, for God's sake move forward. The Vali Ahd is surrounded by the whole of the enemy's army, and cannot break through. The Kizlbash have fought like Shaitáns, and killed thousands of the man-sellers, but they are as thick as locusts all over the plain. The Kizlbash have been fighting since daybreak, and are weary and faint with thirst. Their last attack was beaten back, and the Vali Ahd hardly escaped with his life. He told a few of us who were well mounted to get through if we could while he tried another charge. He is holding some sand-hills, and the fire of the Wasps has kept off the enemy till now, but the ammunition is running low, and there is no water. Az baráe Khudá—for God's sake—order an advance.'

Nadir's face grew dark.

'Who are you?' he said, 'and can you show the way? You are wounded.'

'My Lord, it is nothing. Some of their spears touched me, but it is nothing. I can show the road. I am Nek Kadam, Yusufzai, of the Vali Ahd's body-guard.'

'Shávásh!' Nadir said. 'The Yusufzai are men. Get your wounds bound up.'

He turned to give his orders, and before long he was advancing across the plain with a considerable force.

He was angry at having to do it. Some of the troops had come with him from Bokhara, and were tired with the march. Nadir was loth to call upon them for fresh exertions. Moreover, he did not want to engage the Khivans in the plain, and with a portion only of his army, which he had meant to keep together close to the river. It was necessary to rescue Reza Khan, for the capture or destruction of the heir-apparent and several thousand Kizlbash would have elated the Khivans beyond measure, and discouraged his own troops. His hand had been forced. But he resented it deeply. By neglecting his warnings, Reza Khan had endangered the success of the whole expedition.

As he rode forward, carefully feeling his way, and guarding against any attack, his feelings showed themselves. He told Nek Kadam to ride alongside him, and questioned the man about all that had gone on the day before. It was as he supposed. On arrival at Charjui, Reza Khan had crossed the river, and pushed up northwards with his horsemen and his Wasps to feel for the enemy. So long as he kept to the river-bank among the canals and villages, he was safe enough. But the Turkomans had worked round his left in the desert, and suddenly threatened his rear with a force no larger than his own. He had attacked and driven them back with little difficulty, but had been tempted to pursue them across the plain. At nightfall they had drawn him some miles from the river, and his men and animals being tired, he had ordered a halt. When day broke, he had found himself surrounded, and his fiery attacks had been unsuccessful, the Turkomans meeting them with steadiness, and perpetually threatening his flanks and rear. The manœuvre was simple and obvious, but it had succeeded. Not all the Yusufzai's enthusiastic praise of Reza Khan's courage could make the angry father excuse him.

'He fought like a Rustem,' Nek Kadam said, 'riding in among the Turkoman spearmen, and striking them down with his own hand. They were like children before him.'

'That is the work of the Kizlbash,' Nadir said contemptuously, forgetting for the moment the axe in his hand. 'If I had not been here to help, how would it have ended? How will it end now? We may be too late.'

He checked himself, remembering that he was speaking of his son.

'How did you, a Yusufzai, come to be in the Vali Ahd's bodyguard?'

'My Lord, the Vali Ahd had heard——' The man hesitated.

'Yes, what had he heard?'

'My Lord, forgive me. He had heard that I swam the river when the army was in the Yusufzai country.'

Nadir did not answer. What Reza Khan had done was just what he would have done himself, but at the moment he was angry. 'So,' he thought, 'my son chooses his bodyguard from the men who would have murdered me.'

The road to the battlefield was easy to find. The plain was bare, without obstacles of any kind, except a sand-hill here and there. The cloud of dust was a good mark, and the sound of the camel guns was becoming audible. Evidently the Persians were still holding out. The force pushed on eagerly, forgetting their fatigue, and the enemy's outlying swarms fell back. Another half-hour's march, and the Turkomans were seen to draw off to right and left, leaving Reza Khan's position clear. When the two Persian forces were within a few hundred yards, Reza Khan himself rode out from the line of sand-hills with a small body of horsemen. Before meeting his father he dismounted, and came forward on foot. He was covered with dust and sweat. Nadir received him with a stern face.

'Is this the way you obey my orders?' Nadir said. 'How can I ever trust you again? It is the work of a fool.'

Reza Khan flushed up, but stood with bent head at his father's stirrup—silent.

The Turkomans were evidently in great numbers, and though they had allowed the Persians to make a junction unopposed, they were now seen to be drawn up on a long line of sand-hills to the westward, offering battle. Their backs were on the desert, a safe refuge for them, who were desert born, but a deadly foe to the Persian army. And it was already afternoon.

For a moment Nadir hesitated, knowing that he could not pursue them far. Then, as they seemed inclined to make a stand, he determined to attack them. For his own credit and safety, he must, if possible, inflict some punishment before retiring.

He formed up his troops as rapidly as he could, and meanwhile served out to Reza Khan's exhausted men some water from the skins he had brought with him on trotting camels. They had suffered heavily in their repeated attacks, and had seen their wounded comrades speared and beheaded by the exulting enemy. Their last onset had been half-hearted, and for the time they were incapable of further effort.

While Nadir's comparatively fresh troops were forming beyond them, leaving them in rear as a reserve, Nadir called up the water-carriers whom Reza Khan had taken with him. The supply of water camels had been small. Two officers who were responsible for this were stripped of their turbans in front of the troops, and their ears were shorn off. Then they were made to mount and ride down the lines bareheaded, the blood dripping upon their shoulders. Nadir felt that Reza Khan himself was in fault. But for that they would have lost their heads instead of their ears. The angry soldiers jeered and shouted.

One of the two officers, Mûsa Beg, was a fine-looking man, who had often distinguished himself in action. As he rode down the line, disgraced for life, he cursed Nadir under his breath. 'Son of a dog,' he muttered, 'I will not forget.'

Nadir's well-trained troops moved with swift precision, but the sun was already declining when the line was formed. There was no time for manœuvring, and against so mobile an enemy it would have been useless. The attack must be delivered straight to the front. The Turkomans swarming on their sand-hills awaited it with confidence. They were exhilarated by their partial success, and the darkness would soon come.

When all was ready, Nadir cantered down the front of his troops. The men forgot their fatigue in their eagerness, and a roar of cheering went with him down the line. The Turkomans answered with shouts of defiance, waving their spears. Then Nadir came back to the centre of the line, and raised his axe high above his head.

The fight was fierce while it lasted, but it did not last long. This was a different thing from Reza Khan's fiery onsets. On the right and left compact bodies of horsemen, riding at a slow canter stirrup to stirrup, drove back the Turkoman wings, and the main body of Nadir's troops fell in one long orderly array upon their swarming centre. The first shock was met steadily enough, but a second line came pouring in through the openings left in the first, and after the second came a third. It topped the sand-hills like a mighty wave, hung a moment on the crest, and then poured over with irresistible weight, and down the slopes to the westward a broken sea of horsemen went rolling into the plain.

The Turkomans for once had played their enemy's game. The pursuit was short, for in Nadir's force men and horses were weary, and directly the charge was over, the disordered squadrons were stopped and re-formed. But the work was done. As they rode back over the ground they had won, they found the line of sand-hills covered with dead and wounded men, of whom by far the greater number were Turkomans. The pitiless Kizlbash drove their long lances through every form that showed signs of life. A few of the Turkomans had worked round the flanks of the charging squadrons, but they had been repelled by Reza Khan's men.

The fight was over, and far away to the westward, across the sands reddened by the setting sun, the dark swarms of the broken enemy were seen in full retreat.

Slowly and wearily Nadir's victorious troops marched back through the gathering darkness towards the river. Reza rode by the side of his father, out of earshot of the escort. His heart was hot with humiliation and anger, for Nadir did not spare him. Once or twice, stung by some scathing word, he tried to defend himself.

'At least I am no coward,' he said. 'The men will tell you how I fought. My sword was red with the blood of the Turkoman leaders.'

'Afrîn!' Nadir answered. 'Boast like a Persian now that you have escaped. But for me you would be walking with bound hands at the stirrup of a man-seller.'

'Never! By God! I would have died first.'

'Better have died than come back with shame, out-witted and beaten by these dogs of the desert. A great thing truly that you fought—as a drunken Kizlbash would fight. If you had not done that at least, I would have killed you before them all.'

Nadir's pride had been wounded. He spoke fiercely, and said more than he meant. But the words sank deep, and that night, as Reza Khan took his leave at the door of his father's tent, there was mingled with his humiliation a deep resentment at what he conceived to be Nadir's harshness and injustice.

And unluckily, before the night was over, Sitara made matters worse. After Nadir had taken some food, he came to her tent.

'You are welcome, my Lord,' she said. 'They say you have gained a great victory. Thanks be to God.'

Nadir answered shortly. 'A victory over a horde of man-sellers?' he said. 'I am ashamed. They have killed many of the Kizlbash. If I had not come up in time, the whole of the force would have been taken. The Kizlbash had eaten defeat, and their livers had turned to water. My face has been blackened.'

'My Lord, it is said that you killed thousands of them, and that the Vali Ahd also slew many, that he fought like a Rustem.'

Nadir's wrath blazed up. 'Great God!' he said. 'Fought like a Rustem! He fought like the fool that he is—let himself be drawn into the desert by a trick that a child would have understood. What does a woman know of such things?'

CHAPTER XVIII

Reza Khan had gone to his tent sore from Nadir's words, and his soreness had been increased by some mischievous words on the part of others.

Ali Akbar had been present when Nadir returned to camp, and it had struck him that the opportunity might be a good one to advance his own interests. Suspecting that something was wrong between father and son, he bethought himself of paying a visit to Reza Khan, and gaining information as to what had passed. He sent a message over to Reza Khan's tent, and asked whether he could have the honour of kissing the Vali Ahd's feet. Reza Khan agreed, reluctantly enough.

As Ali Akbar came in, he saw that he had guessed right. Reza Khan had been comforting himself with a generous allowance of Shiráz. His face was flushed, and his eyes bright. But the wine had not brought him peace. The flushed face wore an ugly scowl.

Disregarding the ungracious reception accorded him, Ali Akbar broke into voluble congratulations.

'Forgive me for intruding,' he said, 'but I could not refrain from coming to kiss the feet of your Highness. Praise be to God that you have come back in safety. All the camp is talking about the battle to-day. The Kizlbash say your Highness was like a lion chasing deer, that from morning to night you rode through the man-sellers, smiting and slaying and scattering them. They were like dead leaves before the wind. I swear by Ali I have never heard of such valour. Praise be to God!'

Reza Khan's scowl soon gave way to a look of gratified vanity.

'It is your kindness that makes you say so. I did nothing. The Kizlbash fought like Shaitáns. If I killed five or six man-sellers, what is it? They are dogs, not men.'

'Your Highness is accustomed to victory. It seems nothing to you now. But the Kizlbash understand. They are all struck with wonder. They say no one has seen anything like it—even in a dream. Mashallah! They say that even the Shah was wondering too.'

Reza Khan's face darkened again. 'Many of the Kizlbash were killed. The Shah ate much grief on their account.'

'Without doubt. The Shah—may he live for ever—always grieves for the loss of his victorious soldiers. His heart is very kind. But in war men must die.'

Ali Akbar had the contempt of the bourgeois for the soldier who fights his battles,—the contempt which brings nations to ruin.

He remained talking for an hour, and before he took his leave, Reza Khan had told him all he wanted to know. He learned with much appearance of surprise that the Shah was not pleased with Reza Khan, and that Reza Khan thought himself unjustly treated. His sympathy was warm, and without saying anything definite, he let Reza Khan understand that he thought Nadir had been harsh. He even managed to convey in the most delicate manner the impression that perhaps Nadir thought his son had distinguished himself rather too much.

Reza Khan was not entirely deceived. At the bottom of his heart he knew that he had fallen into the trap against which Nadir had warned him. But he easily found excuses for his mistake, and when he presented himself in the morning at Nadir's tent of audience, his manner, though respectful, was cold and sullen. Nadir saw it at once, and resented it.

A day or two later, when Nadir, who thought he had been sufficiently punished, spoke to him in private about the advance on Khiva, Reza Khan was imprudent enough to betray his feelings still more clearly. He excused himself from expressing an opinion, and inquired whether the Shah wished him to accompany the expedition. That was fatal. Nadir felt that he required a lesson, and before long he found himself on the way back to Persia in charge of the wounded, and the superfluous baggage. He was to wait at Meshed until the expedition returned. The father and son parted without an open quarrel, but it was evident to all that Reza Khan was in disgrace.

After his departure, the force marched northwards, along the western bank of the Oxus. There were some villages on the way, watered by small canals drawn from the river, but most of the ground over which the advance was to be made was waste and broken—a wilderness of alternate sand and marsh and thicket. It offered good opportunities for an enterprising enemy, and the advance was made with caution. A strong body of cavalry rode far ahead on the left flank towards the desert. The main body was formed in a hollow square, the baggage in the centre. The artillery, with six thousand chosen horse, closely followed the river-bank, to protect the grain boats, and the flotilla of rafts which carried the Anderûn.

All the troops had orders to keep their close formation, and not to leave the line of march for any attack on bodies of the enemy who might threaten them. The marches were all made by day, starting after sunrise. The Turkomans did, in fact, show themselves at times. They hung upon the flanks of the invading force, on the watch for an opportunity of striking, or of picking up baggage and stragglers; but the discipline of Nadir's army was perfectly maintained, and no chance ever presented itself. Without losing a man in action, the force and its accompanying flotillas arrived on the borders of the Khivan oasis.

The troops had suffered some distress from the suffocating clouds of dust through which the great square had to march day after day, but they were otherwise in good health and spirits.

After their arrival in Khivan territory proper, there was a little fighting. The Khivans had some considerable forts, with mud walls of no great strength, but surrounded by reedy marshes which made attack difficult. These, however, offered no prolonged resistance; and the Turkoman raiders of the desert, shrinking from a second conflict with Nadir's veterans, kept aloof in their steppes. Before long the Khan and his Court were prisoners in the Persian camp. The stronghold of the man-sellers, the fabled city which could never be reached by an invader, had fallen almost without a blow. Forethought and organisation had triumphed, as they will always triumph, over difficulties of distance and ground.

Seven thousand Persian slaves, men and women, were surrendered by the Khivans and sent back to their own country. Many of them had been so long in slavery that they had no desire to return; many died on the march from cold and want; and those who reached Persia again found it so devastated by constant war, that they heartily regretted their liberation. But they were all sent off, and after them, as a warning for the future, Nadir sent an equal number of Khivans, men and women, to expiate as slaves in Persia the misdeeds of their countrymen. The long-standing insult to the majesty of Irán had been fully avenged.

Nadir knew that the mud-built towers of Khiva were not worth looting, and he had no wish to rouse the enmity of the population, which meant trouble in collecting supplies. He had therefore given orders that the inhabitants should not be molested. But in every eastern army there are some who cannot resist such a temptation; and a body of his troops, among them a number of Yusufzai recruits, who had left their barren mountains in the hope of enriching themselves, broke into the bazaar and began to plunder.

Nadir was away at some distance, and they thought themselves secure; but his spies were everywhere, and he soon got news that his orders had been disobeyed. The culprits were brought before him. Some were officers, and these he ordered to be beheaded. His executioners hated the work, for plunder seemed to them the legitimate reward of victory; but none dared to murmur. 'A father,' it is said, 'beheaded a son, and a brother a brother, and yet presumed not to complain.' For two days the headless trunks lay where they had fallen, an example to all of the results of disobedience.

But one brave man had dared to complain. Among the condemned was a brother of Nek Kadam, whom Nadir had detached from Reza Khan's bodyguard, and appointed to a better post, as a reward for his gallantry in the fight at Charjui. When the order was given, Ned Kadam was rash enough, or generous enough, to imperil his life in trying to save his brother. He made his way to Nadir's presence and asked to be heard.

'What is it?' Nadir said when the man appeared before him.

'My Lord, I have a petition. I want justice, 'insáf.' It is known to the Shah that the Yusufzai are poor. They have no horses, and have marched for a year on foot, bearing many fatigues and doing much service. Now winter has come, and they are perishing from cold. They have no money to buy clothes. My brother was tempted and took a postîn, a skin coat, and for this he has been condemned to death. I ask for justice. Let him live and go back to Yusufzai.'

Nadir heard the man to the end, and he answered without anger.

'What I have ordered I have ordered,' he said. 'The Yusufzai are men, but if they commit offences, they must suffer like the rest. That is justice.' He turned to the chief of his Nasakchis. 'Let the order be carried out.'

Nek Kadam's eyes flashed, and a fierce scowl came over his face. He laid his hand on the hilt of his chûra. 'Insáf nîst—it is not justice,' he said in a loud voice. The words were hardly out of his mouth when he was seized by a score of hands and held securely. He made no useless struggle.

'Now give the order to kill me,' he called out. 'Let all know how the Shah rewards those who serve him.'

Nadir paused a moment.

'You tried to murder me once, but it is true that you have done service. Though you have deserved death, I will spare you. You will be taken back to the Afghan border in chains and there released.'

As the guard removed him, Nek Kadam laughed aloud.

Nadir had less mercy on the fallen ruler of Khiva. The Khan had surrendered in the hope that his life would be spared. But until Nadir's army was surrounding his last fort, he had trusted in his deserts and marshes, and sent messages of defiance. Nadir kept him alive until he had witnessed the feasting and 'fire-play' with which the conquest of his country was celebrated in his own capital. Then he was strangled, and his wives and children were distributed as slaves among the Persians.

CHAPTER XIX

The conquest of Khiva had been completed only just in time. As Nadir marched back along the Oxus to Charjui the winter was setting in, and snow had begun to fall heavily.

He had determined to return to Persia, not by the long route through Balkh, but straight across the Turkoman desert. The oasis of Merv, afterwards the 'last home of the free lance,' was then in Persian hands, and Nadir rightly judged that the nomads of the steppes had been so cowed by their defeat, and the fall of Khiva, that they would not molest his march. Even before Khiva fell he had sent orders for the digging of wells in the desert, and for the collection of great numbers of water-skins.

These were now reported ready, and after a toilsome march of four days the force reached Merv. There was no opposition, but many of the Yusufzais, who had no horses, died of cold and fatigue, bitterly regretting that they had ever been tempted to leave their mountain homes for the hope of booty. By the time the survivors arrived on Persian soil they hated with the unforgiving hatred of their race the man who had deceived them.

It was intensely cold, and the ruined city of Merv offered little to tempt the suffering troops; so after a few days' halt Nadir pressed on again, and about the end of the year the army was once more in Khurasán. Here he was among his own tribesmen, who received him with every demonstration of joy.

He halted a few days, and deposited in the great natural fortress of Kelát, which was the home of his fathers, the bulk of his jewels and treasure. Ringed round by inaccessible mountains Kelát was a fit stronghold in which the robber King could store away the plunder of Empires, and there it remained untouched until his death.

Leaving it safe he marched away, and towards the end of January he was again in Meshed the Holy, where year by year thousands of pilgrims come to worship at the shrine of the great Imám. He had known Meshed all his life, and it was the chief city of his native province, the outwork of Persia. Nadir had determined to restore it to all its former grandeur, and had selected it for his own place of burial. While absent in India and Tartary he had caused his mausoleum to be built. It was here that his wrath was stirred by finding that even now, at the very zenith of his power and splendour, his name was beginning to be execrated by the Persians. He had hardly arrived in Meshed when one morning there was found carefully written upon the marble wall of the tomb a couplet which ran as follows :—

> 'There is not a song without your name,
> The world is full of you, while your proper place is empty.'

The lines were hastily erased by the man in charge of the building, but it was too late. Nadir's spies had brought him the news. He laughed and took no notice, but the jest rankled in his mind.

It was used with effect by Ali Akbar. He had pondered long and carefully upon the position of Reza

Khan, and had discussed the matter with the Shirázi. Eventually, after carefully weighing the arguments on both sides, the brother and sister had come to the conclusion that their interests would be best served by throwing the weight of their influence against Reza Khan, and fomenting as far as they could with safety to themselves the growing quarrel between him and his father. That it was growing they had little doubt. Since his return to Meshed in disgrace Reza Khan had more than once spoken imprudently, and his words were sure to have reached Nadir's ears.

True, Reza Khan might hereafter become ruler of the country, but Nadir was in robust health, so that such a contingency might without much danger be disregarded, while it would be fatal to let Nadir suspect that they had any sympathy for his son.

They saw, moreover, that Reza Khan might, if reconciled to his father, become a dangerous enemy to their party. He had taken to his father's habit of speaking contemptuously of the Persians, and this not only alarmed them but wounded their national vanity. Men will forgive injuries; they will not forgive contempt. Ali Akbar was no patriot. He would not have risked a drop of his blood for the sake of his country. But he was a Persian of the Persians, and he resented any attacks upon the character of his countrymen.

So did his sister. 'The Vali Ahd,' she said. 'What thing is the Vali Ahd? What is he but a Turkoman rider, with the brains of a camel? He has shown that he cannot even fight, and he is too great a fool to control his tongue. He is certain to come to trouble. Let us show him whether the Persians are fools like himself.'

So it was agreed that though they would have to act warily, they would do what they could to harm him with his father; and the couplet on the mausoleum was, if opportunity offered, to be attributed to him or his people, eager for his succession to his father's throne.

Reza Khan soon saw that Ali Akbar's attitude towards him had changed. There was no more seeking for interviews and enthusiastic flattery. Ali Akbar was civil enough, but only civil. Reza Khan, who had never liked or trusted him, began to suspect that the Persian's flatteries had been employed for a purpose, and that his own words had been carried to the ears of his father.

Since the army had returned to Meshed, Nadir had not humiliated him any further. At times Nadir had even seemed to be friendly enough, as indeed he was. His love for his son was not dead. But he looked for signs of penitence and affection, which he did not find, and his heart hardened. The fact was that they were too much alike. Both were proud and self-willed, and neither would make any real advance.

Matters were in this state when one evening Nadir invited Reza Khan and Ali Akbar to join him after he had dined. They had been talking pleasantly enough, when Nadir called for a cup of wine.

'I am thirsty to-night,' he said, 'as thirsty as if I were in the desert of the man-sellers.'

Ali Akbar laughed. 'I saw to-day Mûsa Beg, who was in charge of the water camels at Charjui. He wears his turban very low now.'

'Pidr sukhteh,' Nadir answered, 'son of a burnt father. He may thank God that he has his life. He was an ass, and his ears were too long.'

'Yes. The Shah was very merciful to him. He deserved death. They say the Kizlbash were hanging out their tongues like waterless dogs when the Shah came up.'

Reza Khan resented any reference to the fight at Charjui, as Ali Akbar was well aware.

'What do you know about it?' he said insolently. 'You were not there. I have never heard that you are to be seen when a fight is going on.'

Ali Akbar flushed up and laughed. 'This slave!' he said. 'Why should I be there? I am a man of the pen, not a man of the sword.'

'Then why do you speak? The Kizlbash were fighting like Rustems. It is not for men who keep out of the field to jeer at them.'

Nadir interposed. 'Ali Akbar is right enough,' he said. 'Your men were tired of fighting. Their hearts had burst. He says only what every one knows.'

Ali Akbar was silent, and sat with bowed head, hiding the triumph in his eyes. Reza was silent too, for he dared not answer Nadir, but he was white with rage, and Nadir saw it.

CHAPTER XX

WINTER had not yet given place to spring when Nadir, impatient to be once more in the field, marched away from Meshed towards the west.

During his expedition to India he had received news that the Lesghian mountaineers of the Caucasus had defeated and killed his brother Ibrahim, and he had vowed vengeance against them. Now that kingdom after kingdom had fallen before his arms, he had some ground for thinking that the same care and organisation which had triumphed over the mountains of Afghanistán and the deserts of the Turkomans would enable him to break down the resistance of the Caucasian tribesmen. His forces were assembling in the open country about Tehrán, and there he meant to join them.

His start was inauspicious, for as the Kurk marched away from the holy city a fierce snowstorm was raging; and Sitara, inured to cold as she had become during the long marches to Khiva and Merv, felt chilled to the heart as she rode with bent head into the cutting wind of the plain. She was out of spirits too, for during her stay in Meshed Nadir had been less with her, and when he came to her she had found him depressed and troubled. The attitude of Reza Khan was weighing upon his mind. Once or twice he spoke to her on the subject, and she could see that the conflict between his love for his son and his anger at Reza Khan's sullenness was depriving him of his peace.

> 'And to be wroth with one we love
> Doth work like madness in the brain.'

Sitara thought Reza Khan in the wrong, and she said so, but anxious not to make mischief, she did not say much in that sense. In fact she said too little, and gave Nadir the impression that she did not sympathise with him as warmly as he had a right to expect. No woman, he thought, had ever been loved by him as she had been. Surely her heart should have been wholly on his side? Surely she at least should have understood?

The snow ceased, but only to give place to the heavy spring rains, which flooded the rivers, and made the roads deep with clinging mire. Day after day Nadir rode on, moody and dissatisfied, and apparently regardless of the sufferings of his troops, many of whom fell by the way, exhausted with fatigue and exposure.

The Agha Bashi had watched with keen regret, but without surprise, the growing estrangement between father and son, and he had seen that some of Nadir's people, notably Ali Akbar and his sister, were fomenting it for purposes of their own. He had not dared to do much on the other side, for Nadir was in a dangerous temper. Moreover, in common with Sitara, he felt that Reza Khan was in the wrong. But the whole thing grieved and disturbed him. He saw that it was distressing Nadir, and doing him harm, for in spite of all, Reza Khan was a favourite with the troops, and the hardships of the march were beginning to cause discontent and murmuring among them.

And, what to the Agha Bashi's mind was a specially

bad sign, Nadir had of late been frequently spending his nights in the tent of the Shirázi. He feared that Sitara's influence was on the wane, and that the powers of evil were growing stronger.

They marched to the low-lying country south of the Caspian Sea, and were halted at Ashref, when one evening the Agha Bashi and Sitara found themselves together. She had been sitting alone, brooding over the change in Nadir's manner. The sun had set, and the garden in which the Anderûn had found quarters being some way from the town, all was quiet about her. As the night fell and the silence deepened she was aware of a faint, distant murmur which was new to her. When the Agha Bashi joined her she asked him whether he heard it.

'Yes, Khánum,' he said with a smile. 'The Persians would tell you it was the roaring of the demons. They say Mazanderán is the land of Divs and Jins. It is the sound of the sea. We are not far from the shore of the Caspian. In a few days more we shall be in Tehrán.'

'I do not like it. It makes my heart heavy.'

The Agha Bashi looked at her with a grave face.

'Khánum, the sound of the sea would not make your heart heavy if things were going well. They are not going well.'

Sitara flushed, and was silent.

'Khánum, I know what is going on. Ali Akbar and the Shirázi are doing badi. The Shah is angry about the Vali Ahd, and they are blowing the fire. Have you been defending him? It is dangerous for you.'

'I know it. I have said little. But it is bad that they should quarrel. It is bad for the Shah. It is making him unhappy.'

'Khánum, for God's sake leave that alone. You can do no good, and may do yourself harm. I think the Shah will come to-night. Try to make him forget it all.'

Sitara sighed. 'I will try,' she said. 'God knows I think only of him.'

Nadir came to her as the Agha Bashi had guessed, and she received him with a pathetic effort to please him. She tried hard to be bright and cheerful, and to avoid anything that could remind him of his trouble. But when he left her in the morning she was conscious that she had failed. He had been kind and gentle to her, but he had seemed silent and weary, and try as she would she could not rouse him and draw him out of himself. It had been a failure, and when he had gone she lay in her tent, with her face in her cushions, sobbing.

'It is no use,' she said to herself. 'I am not witty and bright like the Shirázi. She does not love him, but she can laugh and talk and amuse him, and he is going from me. It is all over. He is tired of me now. Soon he will come no more, and I shall die.'

She underrated her power over him, but it was true that for the time the Shirázi was doing mischief. Little as Nadir loved or trusted her, her flattery and her implied condemnation of Reza Khan were in accord with his mood.

The army marched on again through the jungle of Mazanderán, along the stone causeway built by the last of the great Shahs of a former time, and soon they were in the mountains of the Elburz.

One morning they entered a narrow pass where the rocks closed in on either side, until there was no room for flanking parties of troops. They were in Persia now, not in an enemy's country, and there seemed to be no need for special care. The flanking parties had closed in upon the road and passed on in advance. Nadir was riding without escort among his ladies. Immediately behind them came a body of musicians, all women, who were playing and singing to lighten the tedium of the march. Behind them again rode the Agha Bashi with some armed eunuchs, and then, some distance away, a detachment of troops bringing up the rear of the Kurk. The road wound through the rocky spurs, and at one specially narrow point there were two sharp turns in succession.

Nadir rode moodily along at a walk, his head bent, and his eyes on the ground before him. He had been talking at intervals to Sitara and the Shirázi, but had gradually become silent, and they had dropped back behind him. As the little party reached the narrowest part of the pass it was for the moment isolated. The soldiers in front were out of sight. Sitara had watched the spear-heads file round the corner and disappear. The armed eunuchs and the troops which followed them had not yet come into view behind.

At the foot of the steep mountain-side to the left was a small patch of broken ground, where some rocks had fallen from above, and had been overgrown with bushes. As Nadir's horse came nearly level with the rocks Sitara's eyes happened to rest upon them, and with a sudden thrill at her heart she caught among the bushes a glint of steel.

It was gone in an instant, but the Shirázi's quick eye had caught it too. 'What is that?' she said sharply. As she spoke Sitara, who was riding on the left, dashed the point of her stirrup into her horse's shoulder, and sprang forward with a cry of warning. Nadir started, but she was just too late. There was a puff of smoke among the rocks; a shot rang out; and Nadir's horse went down with a bullet through its withers. Nadir was on his feet in an instant, his axe in his hand. By his side, covering him from another shot, was the Rajput girl.

As the screams of the frightened women rang down the pass two men sprang from the bushes. They stood for a second in full view, then turned with a defiant wave of their swords, leapt from rock to rock, and disappeared up the broken hillside.

Nadir stood breathing hard on the spot where he had fallen. He was bareheaded, for the fall had dislodged his turban, and his left hand was streaming with blood, but he was evidently not much hurt. Before his assailants were out of sight the Agha Bashi and his armed eunuchs came galloping up through the throng of women, and a cluster of spear-heads showed round the point in front. A dozen men dismounted and dashed up the mountain-side in pursuit.

Nadir replaced his turban and watched them quietly, rolling a handkerchief round his wrist, which the bullet had grazed.

'It is useless,' he said. 'They are mountain men, and the Kizlbash will never get near them. They looked like Afghans.'

The matchlock found in the bushes told no tales.

The Kurk was soon on the march again, and Nadir called up Sitara to his side. 'Always ready, little one,' he said. 'This is the second time.' And for the moment the soreness against her passed away from his heart.

CHAPTER XXI

During the rest of the day Nadir, as he rode along towards his next camp, turned the matter over and over in his mind, trying to guess at the reasons for the crime, and to think who was most likely to be concerned in it. He felt that for such an offence an example must be made, or he would never be safe.

He was nearly at the end of the day's march, and had passed in review the names of a large number of men whom he had injured, when there flashed across his mind the recollection of the officers beheaded at Khiva, and of the Yusufzai who had defied him. He had spared Nek Kadam's life partly from an honest admiration for his courage, partly from a capricious desire to show his troops how magnanimous he could be; but even at the moment he had wondered at his own generosity, and felt that it would be wiser to put the man to death. Now it came to him with a sudden conviction that Nek Kadam's hand had fired the shot.

'The two men went up the rocks like wild-goats,' he thought. 'Even then I knew they were Afghans and hill-men. The Yusufzai tried to murder me before. Why should he not try again? He laughed and looked dangerous when I spared him, and with these hill-men it is always a life for a life. He is brave, and he has cause to hate me. And . . . Great God! he was of Reza Khan's bodyguard.'

As the horrible suspicion came into his mind Nadir repelled it fiercely; but, once there, it was not to be driven out. When he rode into camp that evening it had fastened upon him; and before morning, brooding over his son's behaviour during the last few months, he had almost come to believe that Reza Khan might be guilty of plotting his death.

In any case the Yusufzai must be found. Nadir's spies were everywhere, and they would be able to trace the man in any part of his vast dominions. Before mounting for another day's ride he had sent out the necessary orders.

It was already dark, a warm evening in May, when the Kurk reached camp before their last march. Next day they were to enter Tehrán, the northern town which Nadir Shah had practically made his capital instead of Ispahán, far away to the south, the royal city of former dynasties.

Ispahán was in the centre of Persia, nearly equidistant between the two seas, and had been well chosen for a national capital. In the course of time splendid palaces and mosques, adorned with exquisite tile-work and inlaid stone and carved wood, had arisen on the banks of its flowing river. Massive bridges spanned the broad channel of water and sand. Avenues of lofty plane-trees and beautiful gardens, watered by streams from the surrounding mountains, had made it a mass of verdure. The country round was fertile and well cultivated.

In the great central square the royal troops had held their parades, and the horse-loving Persians had assembled in thousands to watch the national game of 'chaugan,' polo, played by princes and nobles.

In Nadir's time Ispahán had fallen from its former

splendour. The tile-work had dropped in patches from its glittering domes; the palaces were some of them in ruins; and there were unsightly gaps in the vast avenues which made its pride. Still, even in its decay, Ispahán was a royal city.

But, for a soldier like Nadir, Ispahán was too far away from the frontiers where his armies were always at war. Tehrán, comparatively close to the Caspian, was better suited for his operations. From there he could march north or east or west by the great caravan routes which converged at this point, and could more easily bring together the northern recruits who filled his armies.

The town itself, compared with Ispahán, was a poor place. Its narrow-roofed bazaars, and mean houses of mud or sun-dried brick, were enclosed by a wall of no great height or strength. And around the town lay a tract of stony plain. But water was plentiful, and supplies could be got from the villages nestling under the slopes of the neighbouring mountains. Strategically the position was good. And Nadir the usurper preferred to live away from the ancient capital, with its traditions of the great days still cherished by a people whom he hated.

Nadir's formal entry into Tehrán was to take place in the morning, and the camp was astir soon after daybreak. The Anderûn had been given quarters in a garden a few miles from the city; and when Sitara had made herself ready for the short march which lay before her, she climbed up the steep brick stair which led to the flat roof of the house in which she had slept. A low parapet, topped with open blue tile-work, ran round the roof, and through this she could gaze unseen.

DEMAVEND

From a Sketch by James Morier

In spite of the barrenness of the surrounding country, an exclamation of wonder and delight broke from her lips. It was a cool, fresh morning, and the sky was without a cloud. The heat mist of the day had not yet formed, and in the pure crystalline air of that dry country everything stood out with exquisite clearness. To the southward lay the great plain, dotted here and there with villages or walled gardens, green oases in the waste. Ranges of rocky mountains broke the sky-line; some near, some far distant. Their treeless sides were beautiful with colour. To the north, beyond the stony glacis over which the army had marched the day before, stretched the long line of the Elburz, a chain of lofty summits crowned with snow. Fans of verdure pushed up into the folds at their base. Above them the great white cone of Demavend, topped by its fire-less crater, towered into the blue.

All about her were the tents of the army, teeming with picturesque life: marching horsemen, and lines of rising dust, and the glimmer of steel. At her feet was the walled garden. The cold mountain stream which watered it ran in by a covered way through the lower part of the house, and passed into the sunlight, glancing and murmuring in a channel of blue tile-work, from which it was drawn off in numberless rivulets through avenues of poplars and planes and fruit trees. The spring violets and white iris which had lined their banks a few weeks before, and made the whole air sweet, had given place to the rich colour and scent of innumerable roses. In the thicket under the wall the nightingales had built their nests, and laid their olive-coloured eggs; and even now, in the midst of the camp, they were singing as if all the world were at peace. A crested hoopoe sat on the parapet near its hole in the wall of the house, and its soft, fluty call mingled with the song of the nightingales. The air was full of swallows.

Sitara stood for a few minutes enjoying it all, her heart steeped in the sights and sounds of the delicious morning. Then the kettledrums of the Kurk rolled out the signal for the march, and with a sigh she turned towards the south-west, where a dim belt of smoke, pierced by a few domes and minárs, showed the place of the city. She knew how the reaction after a period of camp life always troubled Nadir; and she wished it had not come to an end.

It was near noon when the Kurk passed through the tawdry gateway of brick and tile-work which pierced the crenellated wall. The glory of the morning had faded. The short march had been dusty and wearisome. Lines of captured cannon were drawn up to right and left, and serried ranks of troops kept back the townspeople. Nadir had donned once more his golden helmet and gorgeous trappings, and he was greeted with enthusiasm by the gazing crowd; but when the closed takht i raváns, or mule litters, which hid from all eyes the ladies of the Court, followed him into the palace, Sitara felt tired and depressed.

Of course the main topics of conversation in the city were the late attempt on the Shah's life and the disgrace of Reza Khan, who was now virtually a prisoner. All sorts of rumours were afloat, and it was inevitable that in a country where jealousy between the monarch and his heir-apparent were the standing rule, the two things should be connected in men's minds. Who, in truth, had so much to gain by the Shah's death as the man who would step at once from his prison to the throne?

Nadir himself had failed to clear his mind of the suspicion. He still resisted it, for he had loved the boy and been proud of him; but there was no denying the fact that since Reza Khan had tasted the sweets of independence and power he had become headstrong and impatient of control. And of late he had met his father's advances, such as they were, with persistent sullenness. Nadir had, therefore, some excuse for thinking that Reza Khan might not be sorry to see him removed. It was a horrible suspicion, but in that age and country it was natural enough. And Nadir was not made less suspicious by the knowledge that Reza Khan was a favourite with the army and the people.

Nadir said nothing about the matter to Sitara, or indeed to any one; but in course of time the talk of the town came to her ears, and before long she felt sure from Nadir's manner that the idea had occurred to him. It distressed her, for she said that it was making him unhappy; and she could do nothing to help him. Until he spoke of his own accord she could only remain silent on the subject.

Nadir had brought with him from India a famous 'hakîm,' or physician, Alavi Khan, whom he had found in attendance on the Moghul Emperor. Alavi Khan was not an Indian, but a Persian from Shiráz, who had sought service in India, and married an Indian wife. He was an example of the best type of Persian, a man skilful in his profession, with old-fashioned, courteous manners, and a singular gentleness of character. With his gentleness were combined a firmness and independence not common among his countrymen. His great age and his reputation as a physician gave him exceptional weight, and it was soon found that he had gained much influence with Nadir, who always treated him with the highest consideration. On the march he was carried in Nadir's own 'takht i raván,' and it was noticed that while he was in Nadir's tent even the Shah's sons were kept standing outside in rain or snow.

The Hakîm had been robbed while the troops were in Tartary, and had earned the laughter and respect of all around him by refusing to move in the matter lest innocent men should be punished.

His influence was steadily exerted in favour of justice and mercy, and Nadir took the Hakîm's advice in such good part that in the words of one who accompanied him from India, 'for a fortnight together he would not order the discipline of the stick, much less command any one to be deprived of his eyes or life.'

During their two years of marching Sitara had made the acquaintance of the good Hakîm, whom Nadir had more than once sent to attend upon her when she had suffered from fatigue and exposure, and there had grown up between the two a feeling of friendship and sympathy. The Agha Bashi was the friend of both, and the three together had done much during those two years to soften Nadir's punishments.

When the attempt upon Nadir's life took place the Hakîm was in camp, and he had attended to the Shah's wounded hand. He had taken the opportunity of speaking a word in season.

'It is nothing, Hakîm Bashi,' Nadir said, 'a mere scratch. The scoundrels were too frightened to shoot straight. But, by God, they shall repent it. I know who my enemies are, and their punishment will be such as men remember. Even you would not spare treacherous murderers.'

'God forbid. Those who conspire against the Shah's

A TAKHT I RAVAN

From a Sketch by James Morier

life are deserving of death. But let the Shah forgive me if I represent for the service of the Shah what is in my mind. I hope the Shah will take care that punishment falls on the guilty alone.'

'You are too scrupulous, Hakîm Sahib. It is not always easy to prove such things, and the Shah's life must be made safe.'

'I pray the Shah to forgive me if I say again what I have said before. It is necessary for kings sometimes to show hardness. But hardness without justice causes hatred as well as fear. It may be that if there had been less hardness this thing would not have been done. The Shah knows best, but to this slave it seems that there is room for reflection.'

Nadir listened with the curious patience which he always showed under the old man's lectures.

'You are a good man, Hakîm Sahib,' he said at last, 'and I will be careful. But treachery and murder must be punished.'

Yet the Hakîm's words had their effect. A few days afterwards two Afghans were brought before Nadir charged with the deed. Nadir's people were afraid that if they failed to produce the criminals his anger would be turned upon them, and they were anxious to show their zeal and vigilance. The death of a couple of innocent men was nothing to them if it would avert danger from themselves. This time they made a mistake. Nadir went into the case thoroughly, and soon saw that there was nothing in it. He released the Afghans with a present, and turned fiercely on their accusers.

'Is this the way you serve the Shah?' he said. 'Am I a fool that you think to blacken my face and bring a bad name upon me with such lies as this? Go and find the real criminals. I know who my enemies are. If any more innocent men are accused your heads will pay for it.'

The weeks wore on, and the summer heat began. In the garden of the Tehrán palace, where Sitara was lodged, among the plane-trees and sheets of ornamental water, it was cool enough, but in the narrow streets around it the air was oppressive. The stench from the open sewers poisoned it. The snow and mud of spring had turned into a thick layer of dust, which rose in clouds as the feet of men and animals stirred it up. The pits where ice had been stored during the winter were opened, and the ice-sellers were driving a great trade.[1] Outside the walls the stony plain lay shimmering in the glare, and every line of marching men or string of camels raised a long trail of dust. The snow patches on the mountain-range to the north were shrinking daily. Soon there would be nothing left but little white triangles in the gullies, and then they too would fade away.

Nadir was impatient to be on the march again. Already the army with which he was about to attack the mountaineers of the Caucasus was assembled at Kasvin, a hundred miles away to the westward, beyond the long blue point where the mountain-range ran down into the plain. But he still had work to do, and above all he felt that he must not leave his capital before he had found the men who had attempted his life, and dealt out punishment.

As the weeks went on his impatience increased.

[1] In Tehrán the sun is hot, even in winter, and ice rarely lasts in the open. But by building very high mud walls, and digging a shallow trench along the northern side of them, the Persians get as much ice as they want.

He allayed it at times by spending a day or two in the camp, galloping impetuously over the flat road to Kasvin at a pace which tried his following, and left many horses to die by the wayside. But each time that he returned he seemed more impatient and irritable.

To Reza Khan in his prison quarters within the palace, and to Sitara, hardly less a prisoner, the time passed heavily. The girl was sad and anxious. After the attempt on Nadir's life she had for a time seemed to be as close to his heart as ever, but this had not lasted long. Now he came to her less and less often every week, and when he came his moods were changeable. Occasionally he was as he had been at first, and her spirits rose. Oftener the old gentleness seemed to have left him, and fits of fiery passion alternated with hours of silence and gloom.

Of Reza Khan he never spoke now. She more than once gave him an opening for doing so, and he said nothing, or said a word or two which were worse than nothing. His silence was eloquent. She knew that the shadow of his suspicion was darkening upon his soul, and yet he would not come to her for help. What could she think except that he no longer trusted her?

CHAPTER XXII

But though the shadow was gathering upon him, Nadir Shah was not always under its influence, and one night he walked suddenly into Sitara's room with a smile on his face. She had not expected him, for he had been away a day or two on one of his visits to the camp at Kasvin.

'My Lord!' she said, with a look of glad surprise, 'I thought you were with the army.'

'So I was, little one, but I was tired of being alone, and your face came to me when I was sitting in the Diwan Khaneh this morning. The horses are always ready on the road, and I came in.'

'In one day, and in this heat?'

'Yes, I wanted you, and I am not yet soft. I have been a soldier all my life. It is well that the troops should see that I can still ride a few score miles if need be.'

'And you came for me?'

'Yes, I came for you. But I was tired of the camp too.'

'It makes my heart warm again. But you have not been ill, my Lord? You always seem so well and happy in the camp.'

'I was tired of it. The army is ready to march, and there was nothing to be done, so I was discussing things with some mullas, and the pidr sukhtehs always tire me.'

'The mullas? What trouble are they making now?'

'No trouble, but one day when I was on the march to Bokhara there was some talk about a verse in the Korán, some silly little difference between Sunnis and Shias, and that fool Mirza Mehdi quoted the Heavenly books. So to get rid of him I told him to go to the Jews and Christians, and get copies of their Scriptures. He came into camp the other day from Ispahán with a camel load of books, and a swarm of mullas and Jews and Armenians, to prove that the heretic dogs of Shias are right.'

'Who is Mirza Mehdi?'

'He is an ass. "Khar ba tashdîd," a doubled ass.[1] He wants a place, and thinks he is wiser than Plato. He has done the pilgrimage to Mecca, and tries to talk like an Arab at the back of his throat. He comes to the Diwan Khaneh and quotes poetry and the Korán till I am sick and want to make him eat sticks. Some day I shall.'

Sitara smiled. 'My Lord has punished men for less.'

'Yes. He is a chattering fool, and the son of a burnt father. But sometimes he makes me laugh, and I have been merciful to him. Once he was talking about his sea-voyage to Mecca, so I told him to go and command the ships on the Caspian.'

'What does he know about commanding ships?'

'Nothing, but as much as any of these Persian dogs. And I thought he might get drowned.'

'It seems that he was not drowned.'

'No. The ways of God are past understanding. But he was very sick, and he wrote to Ali Akbar begging to

[1] Tashdîd is the mark over a letter which shows that it is double.

be recalled. He said the Caspian was not like other seas, but shallow and turbulent, and that it was taking his very soul from him. I remember he added that the comparison held good with regard to men, for he had observed that those of the deepest understanding were the least loquacious. Ali Akbar read out his letter and laughed till I thought he would die. He likes having the fool here to laugh at, and begged me to let him come.'

'And now what has he done?'

'He came with his mullas and his men learned in the Heavenly books, and talked all day till I was weary and put off the discussion. I said the Council of mullas was to take evidence and have the whole thing ready for me when I returned from the war.'

'But what is it all about?'

'God knows. Some silly little point between Sunnis and Shias. These things serve to keep the mullas amused. When they have done I shall decide in favour of the Sunnis, because it will please the Turks and Afghans and make the Persian dogs angry.'

'I have never understood what is the difference between Sunnis and Shias.'

'Why should women trouble about such things? Or men either. It is all pooch, nonsense. Priests always wrangle about trifles. All religions are good so long as the priests do not interfere in matters which do not concern them.'

'All religions good, my Lord? Are not Jews and Christians accursed?'

'So the mullas say, but God is great and the mullas are fools. Were there not holy men among your Brahmins? And are not the Jews and Christians people of the Book? There are no better subjects in Persia than the Armenians. They cultivate their fields and pay their taxes and give no trouble. Their old High Priest was a good man, much better than the mullas. I always conferred favours upon him, and asked him to pray for me. He was very old. He has now been delivered from the miseries of the world, and another has taken his place. This one has had disputes with the mullas in Ispahán, and the Vali Ahd decided in his favour. But yesterday I made him pay a heavy fine. I told him that priests had no occasion for riches, which only serve to perplex the mind and take it off from religious things. It is kings who require money, for the support of their armies and governments.'

'My Lord, I know nothing, but your words make me bold. My Lord has heard that your brother's son, Ali Kuli, has a Christian wife, a Georgian?'

'I know it. What of that?'

'My Lord, I have made her acquaintance, and she has spoken to me of such things. She speaks well, and much that she says seems to me very good.'

'We shall have you turning Christian soon. Well, you might do worse.'

'My Lord! Do you not believe that Islam is the true faith?'

'God knows. It is true, I suppose. I have seen the holy Ali in a dream. But the mullas invent many lies. I could make a better faith than theirs. Perhaps I shall some day. If a man is "but-parast," an idol worshipper, he is the grandfather of asses, but all who worship the one God are alike. He only knows what is truth. Be a Christian if you like, little one, and worship Hazrat i Isa. He was a holy man and a prophet. Or be a Guebr if it please you, and worship fire. The Guebrs are good subjects too. It is all the same to me. A woman should be beautiful and good-tempered and faithful to her lord. What does the rest matter?'

The discussion ended with a laugh, and left Sitara happy enough; but before Nadir slept she had lost the ground she seemed to have won. Emboldened by his mention of Reza Khan, and longing to regain his full confidence, Sitara ventured to touch the sore spot in his heart.

'My Lord,' she said, 'you spoke of the Shahzádeh. Does he too think well of the Christians?'

Nadir looked at her with a quick glance of suspicion, and his face clouded over at once. For a moment he did not answer. Then he spoke, slowly and deliberately.

'God knows,' he said, 'what is in the heart of Reza Khan. He is young and foolish.'

He turned to other things, but he seemed absent and thoughtful. His happier mood was gone.

During the next week Sitara never saw him, and then a bitter thing came upon her.

The Shirázi had been honoured during the week with more than one visit, and was proportionately elated. She had secured from a mulla a new love charm of peculiar potency, and it seemed to be working with success. In truth, Nadir came to her mainly to learn the gossip of the palace and town. But her vanity leading her astray she thought her time had come. She saw that he now spent less of his leisure with Sitara. The star of the black girl was paling. Now if she got a chance—now was the time to strike.

One night Nadir had been specially good-humoured. He had got on the subject of Mirza Mehdi and the mullas. It was a subject well suited for the play of her flippant wit, and she had been very merry about it all. She had fallen in with his humour and told him stories about the mullas, more or less indecent but all amusing, till he lay back on his cushions and roared with laughter. Her dark eyes were dancing, and for the moment she looked pretty.

'You little Shaitán,' he said, with a careless caress, 'you understand these pidr sukhtehs. I shall have you turning Christian next. It seems to be the fashion in the Anderûn.'

Her quick mind caught his meaning at once, and her heart leapt with joy. Surely the chance had come.

'I turn Isavi!' she said, 'walk about with my face bare, and eat the unclean flesh, and pray to a dead Jew? That may be good enough for an Indian idolater. Persians are not fools, and they have some sense of decency.'

'They are shameless enough, God knows—Shaitáns most of them. The women of Hind are faithful and modest.'

'Modest! Women who worship the Red Stone of lust! Did the Shah not see the images in their streets, and the carvings on their accursed temples, and hear the stories of their filthy rites? The very Kizlbash blushed with shame as they broke the images to pieces. And God knows,' she added with a laugh, 'it takes something to shame a Kizlbash.'

'I have seen and heard, yet the women of Hind are not like Persians.'

'God forbid! At least the women of Irán do not go out night after night to practise unholy rites, or worse.'

Nadir's face was dark as he turned upon her. 'More

than once you have spoken words with evil meanings. I am not a fool that I have not understood. Now I will have no more of it. If you have anything to say, say it plainly. And be careful. By Allah, you will repent it if you tell me lies.'

The Shirázi's courage nearly failed her. But she was committed now. Though her heart was beating fast, and her hands beginning to tremble, she resolved to stake all upon the cast.

'I have never lied to the Shah.'

A look of contempt came into Nadir's eyes. 'Does a Persian ever lie?'

'I swear I am not lying now. But I cannot bear to see the Shah's confidence betrayed. She goes out night after night across the garden to the quarters of Ali Kuli's Christian wife and meets Armenian women. Ali Kuli and the Vali Ahd are friends, and their quarters are not far apart. And the Shah knows that in Ispahán the Vali Ahd showed much favour to the Christian dogs. May the Shah forgive me if I am blinded by zeal for his service. Is it for nothing that she goes there so often? Let the Shah ask and see if I am lying. She is there night after night. She is out now. Let the Shah ask and see.'

Nadir listened to the end. He was not wholly deceived. He knew that the accusation was born of hatred; and he believed that Sitara's heart was true. But he had been brought up to distrust women, and from long brooding over his trouble about Reza Khan his mind was only too ready to admit suspicion. In any case Sitara should not give occasion for such speeches. She had at best been foolish and careless of his reputation. He answered with a laugh of contempt.

'So that is all,' he said. 'You are jealous. What do I care if the Indian goes to see the Christian women? She is not like a Persian, full of lying and intrigue. Because she is young and beautiful you hate her. Am I without eyes? Can I not see that your face is wrinkled, and that you are bearded like a Kizlbash? Is this your Persian cleverness, to lie like an angry child? Keep your lies for those who are fools enough to believe you, and never again say a word of the kind to me. By Allah, I could kill you like a snake.'

She crept to his feet, moaning out excuses and prayers for forgiveness, with fear at her heart and a blaze of hatred in her hidden eyes. He stood looking down for a moment in angry scorn, and then walked out of her room.

When he was gone the Shirázi rose and cursed him with all the curses her vocabulary supplied, and they were many and bitter. But in all her anger and fear there was mingled a sense of triumph. She had wit enough to see that she had touched him. 'He will not forget,' she muttered. 'I have sown the seed, and it will bear fruit in time. We will see who will win in the end. Low-born, thick-witted Turkoman fool. Son of a dog. You will have little peace to-night.'

A few minutes later she saw the Agha Bashi walk quickly over to Nadir's quarters, evidently in obedience to a summons, and she guessed the reason.

The Agha Bashi entered the Shah's presence. Nadir was standing with an angry frown on his face.

'The Shah sent for me?'

'Yes. Where is the Indian girl? I went to her rooms and did not find her.'

'May the Shah forgive me. I thought the Shah

would not honour her to-night. She has gone to visit the Anderûn of Ali Kuli Mirza.'

'Why does she go out at night, giving occasion to evil tongues? Has she not all the day to spend in chattering with these Christian dogs? Have you no sense that you let my face be blackened?'

'May I be the Shah's sacrifice. I thought there was no harm in it. She never leaves the palace, and she is always attended.'

'Fool. How do you know where she goes? Bring her here.'

The Agha Bashi went out in silence, and Nadir called for wine. He had waited some minutes when the eunuch returned with Sitara. Nadir dismissed him and turned to the girl.

'Raise your veil,' he said.

She did so, and he saw that her face was pale.

'Who are you that I should be kept waiting half the night when I send for you? Where have you been?'

'My Lord, I meant no harm. I was sitting with the wife of Ali Kuli Mirza.'

'Always with those accursed Christians. Have you no shame that you must go out at night? God knows where you go, blackening my face and making men talk evil of you. Am I nothing that you dare to be absent when I send for you?'

Sitara started and her head went up.

'My Lord knows I have done no wrong,' she said. 'I heard that the Shah had gone elsewhere, and I thought I should not be honoured to-night.'

The words angered Nadir. They seemed to savour of complaint.

'So you set spies on me. What is it to you where I go? Am I not the Shah?'

'My Lord. For God's sake do not be angry. I meant no harm.'

Nadir stood looking at her in silence. Even in his anger her beauty struck to his senses. He had not seen her for days, and there came over him a sudden longing to take her in his arms again, and let all be as it used to be. But his pride was too strong.

'Go to your rooms,' he said, 'and if ever I come to you again, take care that I find you. Go.'

Sitara looked at him for an instant with appeal in her eyes. Then she dropped her veil in silence, and turned and left him.

CHAPTER XXIII

During those miserable weeks Nadir had not mentioned to any one his suspicion that Reza Khan had been the real mover in the attempt to murder him. Although the idea was never out of his mind, he hoped his son was innocent of the crime. And he was too wary, too distrustful of all about him, to tell them what he was thinking. The Shirázi, like Sitara, saw through his reserve; and, unlike Sitara, did her best to foster his doubts. She and her brother found opportunities now and then, without committing themselves, to touch delicately upon the point. The Shirázi, with her 'damnable iteration,' would quote some apposite verse:

> 'The arrow seems to come from the bow, but wise men see that it is directed by the archer.'

Or Ali Akbar would stop in the midst of his laughter to say something about his own son, and to sigh over the little love that fathers could expect from their children. But Nadir took no notice of their hints.

Yet he had more reason than they knew to distrust his son. Only a few days after his arrival in Tehrán he had received from the Governor of Meshed an answer to his inquiries about Nek Kadam. The Governor reported that after the release of the Yusufzai, when the army struck across the desert to Merv, he had been seen in Meshed. Then he had disappeared. Nadir knew that at that time Reza Khan had also been in Meshed. The inference was clear. Nadir kept his own counsel, but sent back an autograph letter saying the man must be found at once.

The matter was now coming to a head.

Shortly before trouble came upon Sitara a special messenger brought Nadir the news that Nek Kadam had been found, and was being sent to Tehrán by forced marches.

Nadir received the messenger himself. He was a Kizlbash, and had ridden in from Meshed, six hundred miles, in six days. He bore a letter from the Governor saying that the Yusufzai had fought desperately when arrested, but had been overpowered. Since then he had been defiant and abusive, and openly cursed the Shah. Nadir warned the messenger to be silent about his errand, and sent him back at once.

But, carefully as Nadir had taken his precautions, the matter had come to the ears of Ali Akbar. He also had his informants, and it happened that the officer in command of the party which was bringing the Yusufzai to Tehrán was bound to him by ties of self-interest.

This officer, Huseyn Khan, was a Persian from Shiráz; and Ali Akbar had, for a consideration, got him a remission of land-tax on his estate. When put in charge of the Yusufzai he had guessed that Ali Akbar would be glad to know what was going on. The special messenger who brought the despatch for the Shah brought also a private letter for Ali Akbar, couched in the most innocent terms, which stated that Huseyn Khan was coming to Tehrán in charge of the prisoner, and that he hoped to have the honour before long of once more rejoicing his eyes with a sight of his benefactor.

Ali Akbar understood the whole thing at once, and sent word that he wished to see his sister. She came over to his quarters after dinner, and was received in his Anderûn. He told her what had happened.

'Now,' he said, 'what shall we do? If properly treated, the affair ought to work to our advantage.'

'Do you believe the Yusufzai fired the shot?'

'Chirá? Yes. Why not? But he has confessed nothing.'

'Then there is no proof against the Vali Ahd?'

'No, but it looks bad for him. The man was in his bodyguard.'

The Shirázi thought for a minute. Then her quick wit jumped to a conclusion.

'Write to the officer in charge,' she said, 'and tell him that the Yusufzai had better confess under promise of pardon. Then he can say he was employed by the Vali Ahd and the Indian girl.'

'The Indian girl! You are always thinking of her. That is childishness. The Shah would never believe she was in the plot. The little fool is in love with him still, and he knows it. It would spoil the whole thing to bring her in.'

'It is all I care about. The Vali Ahd is nothing to me.'

Ali Akbar repressed a gesture of impatience.

'You are mad about that. Listen. I will write as you suggest. That is a good idea. We will get the Yusufzai to believe that his best chance of saving his life is to denounce the Vali Ahd. Afterwards we can bring in the Indian girl somehow. But we must not bring her in now. It would spoil the whole thing.'

The Shirázi reflected. 'I suppose you are right,' she said. 'I will do all I can to help against the Vali Ahd. But promise me you will not forget the girl. She has blackened my face, and I hate her.'

'I will not forget. But one thing at a time. Let us settle the Vali Ahd's business first. Then I promise you I will find some way of doing what you want. Leave that to me.'

The letter went off the same day. It was guarded in its terms, but there was no doubt that Huseyn Khan would understand. The Yusufzai was to be persuaded that if he said nothing he would certainly be killed on suspicion, and that if he offered to tell Nadir the whole truth on promise of his life he would probably escape.

Huseyn Khan did his work well. He made no attempt to force the confidence of the suspicious tribesman, but he made it clear that every one believed the Vali Ahd to be the instigator of the crime, and that the Shah would do almost anything to get proof of it. Before the party had arrived in Tehrán the Yusufzai had made up his mind.

As a matter of fact, Reza Khan was innocent. The Yusufzai had come to him in Meshed, had told the story of the executions in Khiva, and had asked for service. Reza Khan had given him some money, but had refused to employ him. Angry as Reza was against his father, he was too much afraid of Nadir to take back into his service a man whom Nadir had punished and dismissed. It would have been madness. When Nek Kadam persisted he had answered roughly, and the Yusufzai had gone away burning with rage at the manner in which his services had been requited. He had remained in concealment until the army returned, and had then heard how his clansmen had suffered on the desert march. Among them was one whose rage was as fierce as his own, and the two had determined to take their revenge. The attempt had failed, but Nek Kadam now hated Reza Khan almost as much as he hated Nadir; and as he could not kill the father he was ready to fall in with any plan which would bring evil upon the son.

Nadir thoroughly distrusted all about the Court, and was determined, if possible, to examine Nek Kadam himself before any one else could get at him. When the party was a couple of marches from Tehrán he suddenly gave orders for some tents to be sent out to a point a few miles away on the Meshed road. A herd of wild asses had been seen on the plains close by, and he wanted a day or two of peace and hunting. He went off with a small escort, leaving the Court and officials behind.

As Nadir rode across the plain, and over the low, stony pass towards Meshed, his head was sunk on his breast, and he was thinking deeply over the coming interview. His old love for his son was not dead, and a few kindly words from Reza Khan might even yet have revived it. But Reza Khan had his father's imperious temper and his father's pride. He felt that he had been harshly and unjustly treated. He fiercely resented his disgrace. His manner showed his feelings only too clearly, and the few meetings between father and son had ended in making their estrangement worse. Each saw in the other, or fancied he saw, nothing but dislike and hostility. The son believed his father to be jealous of him. The father believed his son to be undutiful, and impatient for the coming of his inheritance. It needed little to fan their smouldering wrath into a blaze.

On the following morning Nadir made some pretence of hunting. The herd of wild asses was seen, but soon distanced their pursuers and disappeared over the desert plain. A few mountain partridges were killed with hawks, and there was a gallop after some gazelle. Then the dust of marching men was seen on the road to the eastward, and Nadir returned to his tent.

He had eaten his midday meal when the party rode in, and the officer in command was at once summoned to make his report. He informed Nadir that his prisoner was safe, but that he could say nothing more. Nek Kadam had been sullen and silent, and had volunteered no confidences.

'Do you know of what he is accused?' Nadir said.

'I know nothing. My orders were to bring the prisoner to Tehrán by forced marches and deliver him to the Presence. I swear by Ali, by my soul, that I know nothing more.'

Nadir looked at the man's expressionless face and downcast eyes, and disbelieved him. He was a Persian, and was backing his word by unnecessary oaths after the Persian fashion. But there was nothing to be gained by disputing his statements.

'Bring the prisoner here.'

The Yusufzai was led in by two soldiers. He had an iron collar on his neck and iron rings on his wrists and ankles, all fastened together by chains so tightly that he could hardly stand upright. In this state he had been made to ride fifty or sixty miles a day. He was worn and haggard, but in spite of all he bore himself like a man, looking Nadir full in the face with fearless eyes.

Nadir told the Persian officer to leave the tent. Then he turned to the Yusufzai.

'So you have come before me again. You were fool enough to think you could escape me by hiding in the Taimani country? I should have found you if you had gone to the ends of the earth.'

'The Shah's arm is long. Who doubts it? But I was not hiding. What have I done that I should hide myself?'

'You lie boldly, but I do not forget. You tried to murder me once before, and now you have tried again. Why should I give you your life a second time?'

'The Shah can kill me if he pleases. I am bound and helpless. But I have done no wrong. I did service to the Shah.'

'Yes, you did service. You are not a coward. Therefore I spared you when you behaved foolishly and deserved death. You owed me gratitude, and you know how you have shown it.'

Gratitude! The man's eyes flashed. But life is sweet. He answered quietly.

'What is the use of speaking? The Shah has power to do as he pleases. But I have done no wrong. I do not know of what I am accused.'

'Lies are for cowards. A brave man should not lie. When you fired at me from the rocks, I saw you. I do not forget men I have known.'

'The Shah's eyes deceived him. I fired no shot. Since the Shah dismissed me at Charjui I have been in Afghanistán, seeking service.'

'This is foolishness. My eyes do not deceive. But you are a brave man, and I have spared you once. I am obliged to punish at times, but I am merciful. You have seen it.'

The Yusufzai remained silent.

'Have you nothing to say before I give the order?

Have you no wish to see your village again? The hills of the Yusufzai are pleasant, and they say the maids of the Yusufzai are fair.'

The tribesman raised his eyes for an instant to Nadir's face. One hand was clenched hard on the other, and Nadir saw it. Still he was silent, thinking what words would serve him best.

'What good will it do you to die without speaking? Is life nothing? I am merciful, and would spare you if I could. Tell me the truth and you are free.'

The Yusufzai looked Nadir in the face again. 'I did not fire any shot. I have done no wrong. But I know something that might be of service to the Shah. If I speak, will the Shah swear by his head and by the Prophet that I shall have a safe conduct to my own country?'

'I swear by my head and by the Prophet. But it must be the whole truth.'

Ned Kadam felt little confidence in any such promises. It would be easy to find some excuse for killing him after all. But it was the only chance of life. Was he not already dead?

'Then I will speak. The Shah knows everything. Who has most to gain by the death of the Shah?'

So it had come. He had known it all along. God! that his own son, the son for whom he had felt such love and pride, should have plotted his death.

'Go on and speak plainly, not in riddles. And speak the whole truth, or, by Allah, you die this hour. First, you fired the shot?'

The Yusufzai hesitated, but what was the use of denying? It would not save him, and Nadir would be more likely to believe the rest of his story if he admitted it.

'The Shah knows everything. I will tell no more lies. I fired the shot. One of the Shah's ladies saw me, and I fired hastily. I do not often miss.'

'At last! And why did you do it?'

'When I was dismissed by the Shah I went to Meshed. I had been in the Vali Ahd's bodyguard, and at Charjui I had done him service. I thought he would help me.'

'Balé? Yes?'

'I saw the Vali Ahd, but he would not give me service. He was afraid the Shah would be angry.'

'Go on.'

'He said that I was a brave man, and that he had eaten much grief on my account. Then he gave me gold, and told me that if he ever became Shah, he would give me a good place under him.'

'How much did he give you?'

'Twenty gold tumáns. He told me to come and see him again after three months, and perhaps he would give me more.'

'That is nothing. The Vali Ahd meant no harm.'

'He said that the Shah had been hard to me, and my people, and that it was not justice, but that while the Shah lived he could do nothing.'

'Go on, and take care.'

'I said that twenty tumáns was very little, and asked what he would give me if I did him a great service; and he answered that he could do nothing while he was in disgrace, but that if he became Shah he would give me a thousand tumáns and a high post. Then I said plainly that I would kill the Shah and return in three months.'

'Afrîn! And then?'

'Then the Vali Ahd said that such words were not for

him to hear. I said Bisyar Khûb—very well. But if when I return you are Shah, you swear by God and the Prophet that you will give me the money and a post? And he swore he would.'

'If you are lying I shall know it, and you shall die a death that men will remember.'

'The Shah has power to do what he pleases. I am ready.'

'After you had failed to kill me, what did you do?'

'For a week I was hunted in the mountains. Then I got away to the Taimani country.'

'You did not return to the Vali Ahd?'

'What was the use? He would have given me nothing. Besides he was away in Tehrán.'

Nadir remained silent for a time, thinking it all over. Then he gave orders for the man to be removed, and sent in at once to the city. The guards and the officer in charge were strictly warned to keep the secret.

When this was done Nadir mounted and rode back to Tehrán. He rode alone, in deep gloom. He believed the Yusufzai's story, but he still had some faint hope that Reza Khan might be able to disprove it. The next thing was to see Reza Khan himself, and then, if necessary, confront him with the assassin.

CHAPTER XXIV

NEXT morning, after he had despatched some necessary business, Nadir summoned his son to his presence.

Reza Khan came into the room where his father was seated. His manner was respectful, but his face showed that he came to the interview without pleasure, and there was a touch of defiance in his carriage. He looked pale from his long confinement in the palace. Nadir had determined to make one appeal to his son's feelings, and he hoped against hope even now. But as usual Reza Khan's manner hurt him, and his eyes looked cold and hard as he returned his son's salute.

When they were alone, Nadir remained for a minute in silence, his gaze fixed on the face of Reza Khan, who sat with downcast eyes, motionless and expectant. Then, with something like a sigh, Nadir spoke.

'You remember that when I was returning to Tehrán an attempt was made to murder me?'

'I know it,' Reza Khan answered, without raising his eyes. 'Alhemdulillah! Praise be to God that the attempt failed.'

Nadir was watching his face.

'The man who shot at me has been found, and has confessed.'

Reza Khan looked up in surprise, and found his father's eyes fixed upon him with an expression which brought a sudden fear to his heart.

'Who was the man? What made him do such villainy?'

'The man was Nek Kadam, Yusufzai. He was once in your bodyguard.'

Reza Khan felt a hot flush mounting to his cheek, but he faced Nadir boldly.

'Nek Kadam,' he said, 'the man who behaved so well at Charjui. I have heard that he was foolish afterwards, and that the Shah dismissed him.'

'It is true. He was so foolish that he deserved death, but I spared him. Then he went to Meshed, and saw you.'

'Yes. He came and asked me for service, but of course I refused, and he was angry with me.'

'You knew when you appointed him to your bodyguard that he was one of the men who tried to kill me when the camp was on the Indus?'

'Yes, I knew it.' A sudden recognition of his folly struck cold to Reza Khan's heart. 'I knew,' he said, 'but the Shah had forgiven him, and taken him into service. He was not a murderer. He was fighting as these hill-men always fight, and the Shah had praised the bravery of the men of Yusufzai. I did not think the Shah would disapprove.'

'Yet you never told me you had done it.'

'God knows whether I spoke of it. The man had served in the army for a year, and showed much courage. He was recommended to me as a brave man, and faithful. I never doubted that the Shah knew.'

'You never spoke of it. I did not know until the fight at Charjui.'

'I see now that I should have asked the Shah's permission, but I swear by my soul that I never thought of it.'

'You swear like a Persian. At best it was the act of a fool.'

Reza coloured, but remained silent.

'When he came to you in Meshed you gave him money.'

'Yes. He had done me service, and he was hungry. I could not employ him, so I gave him a few tumáns.'

'And then he went away and hid in the mountains, and tried to murder me.'

Nadir's meaning was clear, and the full horror of his position rushed upon Reza Khan's mind. But he was innocent of the crime, and he fiercely resented Nadir's suspicion.

'Great God!' he said. 'Is it possible that the Shah thinks I knew of it? I will not believe that such a thought could darken his mind.'

Nadir was not sure what to think. Reza Khan's indignation seemed genuine, but circumstances were very much against him. Nadir would have liked to believe, but could not. He did what was perhaps the worst thing he could do.

'Listen,' he said. 'I examined the man myself, and he told me all. He said that you promised to reward him with money and place if he killed me. Be quiet and listen. You were angry when he came to you, and the young do not think before they speak. You have been in power while I was away in India, and you have become impatient of control. It is not strange that you should want to be a king. I have thought over it all and made excuses for you. Although you have done wrong, you are my son. Tell me the whole truth. Before God I am not merciless. No one knows what has happened. If you will trust me and show that you are penitent, all will be well. There is nothing to fear. But for your own sake do not persist in telling me lies. What more shall I say?'

Reza Khan had begun more than once to break in, but Nadir had stopped him. He spoke now, angrily and unwisely.

'What use is it for me to say anything? The Shah has condemned me already. Is this the Shah's justice? I have done nothing. I am blameless. The Shah has disgraced me in the sight of all, and I have been made to eat such dirt that I can never hold up my head again. And now the Shah listens to a lying Afghan who wants to do me evil. What justice is this? You offer me mercy if I will betray myself. What mercy have you ever shown? You are not my father. You have always hated me, and now you want to take my life.'

And in his passion he laid his hands on the hilt of his sword.

Nadir seized the axe by his side.

'Hah! You dare to threaten me? I have heard enough. Now I know what you are.'

He called, and the Agha Bashi came in to the room. Nadir pointed to his son. 'Remove him and let him be kept under guard till I send for him.'

A look of pain came over the negro's face. He saluted Reza Khan respectfully.

'Tashrîf biyárid,' he said. 'Let your Honour come.'

Reza Khan looked at his father. 'I did not mean to threaten the Shah,' he said, 'and I have spoken foolishly. I have been mad. But I am without guilt.'

Nadir made no answer beyond a slight gesture of dismissal, and Reza Khan walked out with death in his face.

For a full hour Nadir sat alone, pondering over the

scene through which he had passed, and gradually his anger gave way to a tormenting sense of doubt. What if the boy were innocent after all? But no, it could not be. He called for the Agha Bashi again.

'Have they brought in the prisoner from Meshed?'

'Yes, your Majesty. He came in last night.'

'Bring him here.'

The Yusufzai was brought in, and Nadir went over the whole story again, trying to entrap the man into falsehood, carefully testing every link of the chain. It was useless. The Yusufzai was perfectly steady. Neither threats nor promises could shake him.

That evening Nadir made one more effort to save himself from the horror which was coming upon his life. He was little given to consulting those about him, but at times the most self-reliant of men will feel the need of counsel, and Nadir resolved that before finally condemning his son he would hear all that could be said. He ate little that night, but drank cup after cup of wine. After his meal was over he summoned to his room an informal council of three. They were the Agha Bashi, the good Hakîm, and Ali Akbar.

The council was well chosen. Nadir knew that the Agha Bashi had always been a friend of Reza Khan, and yet was perfectly faithful. Ali Akbar was hostile to Reza Khan, and was the cleverest man he had about him. The Hakîm's honesty and scrupulous sense of justice were known to all, and Nadir also knew that he would speak his mind with entire fearlessness.

The relations between the Hakîm and Ali Akbar were outwardly good enough, but they were not friends at heart. Ali Akbar was extremely cordial to the Hakîm in his jovial, merry way, and the two might be seen walking in the Shah's garden hand in hand like children. But though he did not repel Ali Akbar's advances, the Hakîm thoroughly distrusted him, and Ali Akbar was very jealous of the Hakîm's influence. Seeing Nadir daily in private, the Hakîm had innumerable opportunities of saying whatever he chose, and Ali Akbar believed that some of his pet schemes had been crossed by arguments which he had no chance of meeting. There was no love between the two.

Slowly and carefully Nadir put the whole case before the council, and asked for their opinion. He turned to Ali Akbar first.

Ali Akbar answered much as Nadir had expected him to answer. He dwelt on the enormity of the crime, and the necessity for making an example in order that the life of the Shah might be secured from such attempts in future. He reluctantly admitted that the case against Reza Khan was very strong, but he urged that the Vali Ahd was young, and had perhaps said in a moment of anger more than he had really intended. If he now confessed, and said he was penitent, Ali Akbar thought that the Shah might indulge the inclination of his fatherly heart, and show mercy.

Nadir listened in silence and turned to the Hakîm. 'Your Majesty,' the Hakîm said, 'there is no doubt that an example is necessary, and that the guilty should be punished. But as the Centre of the Universe has deigned to ask for the opinion of this slave, I can only say that in my judgment the Vali Ahd is without guilt. He has perhaps been imprudent, but there is no proof that he has meant to do any harm to the Shah. The Holy Book says it is wicked to punish any man on mere suspicion. It is evident that the Yusufzai is guilty. He has confessed it. Who is he that his word should be taken against the son of the Shah? In my judgment he is lying to save his own life. What more likely? And if the Vali Ahd has enemies, or if there is any one whose interests would be advanced by his death, they would use the Yusufzai to serve their own ends. The Shah knows best, but in my judgment it would be for the service of the Shah that those who are known to be guilty should suffer, and that no importance should be attached to the statement of a man who has everything to gain and nothing to lose by accusing others.'

The Agha Bashi rather timidly supported the Hakîm, but suggested that before deciding the Shah should confront Reza Khan with his accuser.

When all had spoken, Nadir Shah pointed out that the Yusufzai had no motive for accusing Reza Khan, who had shown him nothing but kindness; and as to any mischief on the part of others, he said he felt sure there had been no opportunity for getting at the man.

Ali Akbar entirely agreed in this view. He said that he did not know the officer in charge of the prisoner, but that doubtless he had been chosen as a trustworthy person, and moreover the prisoner had been examined by the Shah before he came to Tehrán. It was practically impossible that any enemy of the Vali Ahd's could have obtained access to him. But perhaps the Yusufzai had mistaken the Vali Ahd's meaning. That was possible, and he hoped it was so.

The Hakîm listened quietly, his hand on the stem of his kalián. Nadir turned to him again.

'The Shah knows best,' he said in his gentle, deliberate way. 'Who am I that I should speak again? But in the judgment of this slave, the Vali Ahd is innocent.'

Nadir did not reply. He remained silent for a minute or two, and then dismissed his advisers. In the morning he would decide.

Meanwhile he gave orders for Reza Khan to be brought to a room adjoining his own, and kept under close guard.

CHAPTER XXV

THE morning found Nadir still doubtful. The Hakîm's words had produced considerable effect upon him, but he did not believe any one would have dared to tamper with the prisoner. To make sure he sent for Nek Kadam again.

'Listen,' he said, when the Yusufzai was before him. 'I have thought over all you have said. I told you I would spare your life if you told me the whole truth, and I will do so, but until now you have been lying. It has come to my knowledge that an enemy of the Vali Ahd has persuaded you to accuse him, and that you, being in fear of your life, have made a false charge. Now tell me the truth, or I give the order. The executioners are waiting.'

The Yusufzai never wavered. He had been warned beforehand to be prepared for such a contingency, and he met it with perfect steadiness.

'Bisyar Khûb,' he said, 'very well. The Shah has power to do as he pleases. I am weary of life, and if the Shah does not believe me, let him give the order. I have no more to say.'

And to that he resolutely adhered. Nothing that Nadir said could move him. He shook his head and refused to speak any more.

'What is the use?' he said.

Nadir dismissed Nek Kadam and sent for Reza Khan,

only to find him equally stubborn. His words were the same.

'What is the use? I have spoken the truth, and the Shah does not believe. I have nothing more to say. I am without fault. Whatever the Shah wills let him do. I am tired of life.'

Then Nadir confronted the two, and made the Yusufzai tell his story again. Reza Khan listened quietly at first, and admitted the truth of much that Nek Kadam said. Here and there he interrupted, but without heat.

'Darûgh. A lie,' he said quietly, two or three times.

When the Yusufzai had finished, Nadir turned to him.

'What have you got to say?'

'Of what use is it for me to speak? What he has said is partly true. I have told the Shah so already. When he says I offered him a bribe to do evil to the Shah, he is lying. I am wholly without fault. But what is the use of my saying anything? If the Shah chooses to believe it, he can do so.'

Reza Khan spoke as if he had no hope, and hardly cared to defend himself, but he spoke with dignity. To Nadir it seemed defiance.

Nadir asked one more question.

'If you made no promises of giving a reward when you became Shah, where are the people who were with you when you saw the Yusufzai? There must be many who remember.'

'There was no one present,' Reza Khan said. 'We were alone.'

'You were alone, and you gave him money, and he went away and did what we know. Do you receive alone men who come to ask for service?'

'No, but he came in the evening when I was alone in my tent, and I did not think of any harm, and let him come in.'

Nadir laughed — a short, contemptuous laugh. Reza Khan looked at his father's face, and felt that the toils had closed round him. A sudden storm of fury and despair swept over his heart, and a fierce cry broke from his lips.

'Aye—laugh—laugh. May the curse of God be on you! Now give the order to kill me. You have killed thousands of innocent men. Who am I that I should escape? Would to God that the liar had shot straight, and rid the world of you and your bloody tyranny. Now kill me.'

Nadir's hand closed on the handle of his axe, and the veins swelled on his temples. He mastered himself with an effort.

'You shall not die,' he said. 'You shall live to repent of your crime and thank me for my mercy, but you shall thank me in darkness. I have spoken.'

Reza Khan mocked aloud.

'Shukr! Shukr!' he cried. 'Thanks! thanks! my father. Your heart was always soft and merciful. I know the two who have brought you to this, making you their plaything, as always. Tear out my eyes and lay them in the lap of the Shirázi. How she will laugh with her lovers — the juwáns of the Kizlbash!'

Nadir started with fury at the insult, but said nothing. He pointed with his axe to the doorway. Reza Khan walked out erect and defiant.

CHAPTER XXVI

NADIR'S decision was soon known to the Shirázi, and late that evening, when there was no longer any chance of Nadir coming to her room, she made her way to her brother's quarters. She found him awaiting her, and not in the best of spirits. To do him justice, Ali Akbar was not cruel. He was quite ready to bring about Reza Khan's disgrace by any false accusation: that was fair fighting: but he did not like the thought of the horrible punishment which was about to be inflicted. When his sister came in he said so, with a flush and an uneasy laugh. The Shirázi's face took a look of contempt.

'You are as bad as that old fool of a Hakîm,' she said. 'What does it matter how these Turkoman hogs rend each other? You have got what you wanted. He will be out of your way for the future. Now for my share. How are we to bring in the Indian?'

'Always the Indian. Why can't you let her be? She is losing favour, and will soon be harmless too.'

'If she is losing favour, now is the time to strike. Who knows what her sorceries may do? Who can wash the black from an Ethiop?'

'She is not black. She has no sorcery but her beauty. And what do I care? She is nothing to me. I am sick of the whole thing. I wish I were a dervîsh, and free from all this devilment.'

The Shirázi turned on him impatiently. 'For God's sake don't be a fool,' she said. 'This is no time for child's talk.'

'It is the truth. I was not made to serve these bloody tyrants. I hate it all. "Better to eat barley bread and sit on the ground than to put on a golden belt and stand in waiting."'

'Oh yes, I know. And "a poor man with contentment is better than a rich man with substance." And so on, and so on. Have I not heard it all a hundred times?'

'This time it is no talk. I swear by the mother that bore me, that I will be a dervîsh.'

An unpleasant look came into the Shirázi's eyes.

'You promised,' she said. 'And what would happen if the Shah were to hear of a certain letter that went down the Meshed road?'

Ali Akbar started. 'God's power!' he said, and his face grew pale at the thought. 'You are the mother of devils!'

The Shirázi laughed. 'Then talk sense, and remember your promise.'

Ali Akbar knew his sister. If he offended her she was capable of anything.

He sighed and helped himself from the flask of Shiráz.

'Let me think for a minute. I will do what I promised, but it is not easy to see a way.'

He called for his kalián and took a few deep draughts of smoke. Then he blew it out from his lungs, and passed the pipe to his sister.

'Listen,' he said. 'If you must do badi to the girl, there is a way. You know what this blood-drinker is. While he is making up his mind he will hear all that you have to say, but once he has given an order, woe betide any one who says a word. To interfere in favour of a man he has condemned is like taking the prey from the mouth of a lion. The girl is soft-hearted and a fool. Get her to speak for the Vali Ahd.'

'Shukrullah! Thanks be to God! By thè beard of the Prophet, you have hit it. When you are not in one of your childish fits you have more brains than all the rest of them put together. But how is it to be done? Fool as she is she would suspect if I said anything. Balé? Yes?'

'Of course you must say nothing. It must come from outside. We must have nothing to do with it.'

His vanity was flattered by his sister's words, and his professional pride was roused.

'If she were like other women I would get at her through a mulla, but that is no use. She is not a Mussulman. I have found it! She is always with those dogs of Christians. And the Vali Ahd showed them favour in Ispahán. The Armenian high priest will want to save him.'

'Wonderful! Your intellect is as keen as a tempered sword. But how are we to get at the Catolicos? We have no time to lose. To-morrow it may be too late.'

'Leave that to me. I will see him to-night. I will set him to work on the girl through that Christian wife of Ali Kuli's. They are friends, and Ali Kuli was always hand in hand with the Vali Ahd.'

'Good. By all the Imáms, you are cleverer than King Sulieman.'

'Ah! and I was a child just now, and the grandfather of asses.'

'Báshad, báshad. Let that be. When you choose you can laugh at any man's beard. There is no one like you.'

'You are a Shaitán, but listen.' He was playing the game now *con amore*. 'There is another arrow to this bow, and that is for you to shoot. You know the Vali Ahd's mother. She is old, and the Shah never sees her. She knows she can do nothing herself. Get her to go to the Indian girl.'

'Alas! alas! I saw her a week ago, and laughed at her. She hates me now.'

'What short-sight is this? Why will you always make enemies for nothing? Have I not told you a thousand times that if you scatter the seed of sweet words, some of it will bear fruit in time of need? But the old woman will catch at any chance. Get one of your women to speak to one of hers.'

'I was a fool. I am not far-seeing, like you. But it is true our women know each other.'

'Go, then, and do what you can. Without doubt we shall have this bird in the net. We will show them what Persians are.'

'Inshallah! Please God.'

The brother and sister said good-night.

'Khudá Háfiz—the Lord be your protector'; and parted affectionately.

So it came to pass that before noon the next day, Sitara found herself in sore trouble. First, Ali Kuli's Georgian wife came to her, and pressed her to intercede with Nadir. The Georgian pictured Reza Khan's horrible fate—blinded for life in the first flush of his youth and strength. 'And he was always kind to us Christians. Shall we not do something to help him? Would Hazrat i Isa have stood by and let this thing be? If you are not a Christian, you are very near it. Help us now, and the God of the Christians will protect you.'

Her words were the words of the Catolicos, whom Ali Akbar had ensnared. Her woman's wit taught her a better argument.

'It is for the good of the Shah. He is angry now, but if he does it he will repent it all his life, as Abbas the Great repented it, and every one will condemn him. Save him from himself. Only you can do it. I know it is a hard thing to ask of you, but you are brave. It will soon be over, and he will love you all the better for it hereafter.'

In vain Sitara pleaded the hopelessness of the attempt, and the cruelty of forcing it upon her.

'I know him. I know him,' she said. 'He will think I do not care that his life should be in danger. He will never forgive me or trust me again. I shall lose his love, and it will kill me. Oh! I cannot. I cannot.'

The Georgian left her in deep distress. She had hardly been alone a minute when Reza Khan's mother came to her. If her interview with the Georgian had been painful, this was a thousand times worse. The stricken woman was tall and upright still, with the remains of a beauty which had once been the delight of Nadir's eyes. She had been the wife of his youth. But now she was old, as age goes in the East. Her hair was grey, and the once beautiful face was worn and faded. Forgetful of all but the boy she had nursed at her breast, she threw herself at Sitara's feet.

'Az baráe Khudá!—for God's sake, Khánum, save him, save him. Have mercy and save him. I swear that he is innocent. You are young and beautiful, and the Shah loves you. Say one word. Oh! I know the

Shah; I know how terrible he is; but they say you are brave and kind-hearted. Have pity, have pity.' And she clung to the feet of the woman who had won her husband's love, covering them with kisses and tears. Sitara tried to raise her.

'O Khánum!' she said, 'do not kneel to me. What am I that I should speak? You are the mother of his children. Surely he will listen to you.'

But the woman would not rise.

'No,' she said, 'he will not listen to me. I tried to go to him before, but he would not see me. I am old, and his love has long gone from me. But he is generous. He was never hard to me in old days. You are young and beautiful, and he loves you. He will listen to you.'

'Oh! I cannot. I cannot. You do not know what you ask. It is more than my life.'

'Ai wahi! wahi! Have pity, have pity. I will not let you go till you promise. I will not.'

What was it to the mother that she was asking another woman to peril her happiness and her life? All thought of herself and her pride had gone, and now there was no room in her heart for thought of another. 'Have pity, have pity,' she wailed. 'He is so young and strong and beautiful. Do not leave him to blindness and misery for all his life. Have pity, have pity.'

It was more than Sitara could bear. The grey head at her feet maddened her. She threw up her hands in despair. 'He will never forgive me,' she said—'never, never, and I shall die. But I will go. Now for God's sake leave me.'

'You will go? You promise? Swear to me that you will go to-day, now, this hour, or it may be too late. Swear.'

'I will go directly the Shah returns from the Diwan Khaneh. I swear it. Now leave me. O Khánum! have a little pity, you who ask for pity.'

The old woman rose from her knees, her face alight with hope, and poured out blessings upon the girl's head. But Sitara made no answer.

The Shirázi was standing at the curtain of her doorway when Reza Khan's mother passed. The elder woman's veil was down, but her walk and manner showed that she had succeeded. A smile of triumph came over the Shirázi's face.

'Praise be to God! Now, black girl, we shall see who wins. Inshallah, it will be the last time you will see his face.'

Sitara lay on her cushions sobbing. The scene she had passed through had broken her down, and for a few moments she felt as if she could not go on. But soon she controlled herself and rose to her feet. She had promised, and she would not break her word. There was no time to lose. She sent a woman to ask the Agha Bashi to come to her. By the time he came she was quiet and resolute.

The negro had guessed something of what was passing, and his face showed his concern. She told him in a few words what she had done, and he broke into angry protest.

'Khánum,' he said, 'it is madness. The Shah has made up his mind. Nothing enrages him so much as interference when he has given his orders. For God's sake do not go. They should never have asked you. It is playing with your life.'

'I know,' Sitara said, 'but I have promised. When his mother came I could not bear it, and I promised.'

'It is a shame and wickedness. Khánum, what is

the use of it? You have no proof of his innocence. It looks as if he had been guilty. What can you say?'

'I know. There is nothing to be said for him. Perhaps it is better so. I will only say his mother came to me, and asked for mercy.'

'It will be useless. It will only make him mad with rage. Khánum, give it up. Do not go.'

Sitara laid her hand on the negro's arm. 'Agha Sahib,' she said, 'you have always been kind to me, and I know you are right. It is madness. But I have promised, and who can say what may happen? The Shah used to love the Vali Ahd, and the hearts of kings are in the hand of God. I must go. You can only do one thing for me now. Take the stone to the Shah and ask him to see me.'

For a time the negro refused. 'If you will go, I cannot prevent you,' he said, 'but I will have no hand in it.'

His refusal was useless. He saw that it only distressed her without shaking her resolve. At last he gave way. Evidently she meant to go, and perhaps if he prepared Nadir for her coming, he might do some good. He took the seal and went to Nadir's room. Nadir was still in the Diwan Khaneh, and was not expected until sunset.

That morning Nadir had sent the Hakîm to Reza Khan asking 'for the last time' whether his son had anything to say. When Nadir returned, hoping against hope, the Hakîm was summoned. He reported that Reza Khan had answered, 'I have done no wrong—I have nothing else to say.' As a matter of fact, the old man had done his utmost to induce Reza Khan to send a different message—at least an apology for his words of the night before, but he had failed.

THE BRITISH SHIP *EMPRESS OF RUSSIA* IN ASTRABAD BAY, 1743

From Hanway's 'Travels

'It is no use,' Reza Khan said. 'I am doomed. For God's sake go and torment me no more.'

Before taking leave of Nadir, the Hakîm spoke out boldly.

'The Vali Ahd is without hope,' he said, 'and he is too proud and sore to ask for mercy. But let the Shah consider that he is young, and that he thinks he has been unjustly condemned. May the King of Kings forgive me, but I must speak once more. I am old, and shall soon seek the pardon of God. I cannot stand before Him if I remain silent now. In my judgment the Vali Ahd is innocent. Some enemy has induced the Yusufzai to accuse him falsely.'

Nadir answered, 'It is enough. You are dismissed.'

The Hakîm looked in his face and knew that all was over.

As he walked away from the door he heard Nadir call for the head nasakchi, the man who inflicted his punishments. The fatal order was given.

When the Agha Bashi entered, Nadir was sitting alone. His face wore a look of the deepest gloom. He looked up slowly. 'What, you too? What have you to say? Be careful.'

The negro's heart sank, and he hesitated.

'May I be your sacrifice,' he said, his head bowed, and his eyes on the ground. 'Sitara Khánum begs leave to kiss the Shah's feet. She told me to show this stone to the Shah.'

Nadir started.

'Are you mad,' he said, 'that you all conspire against me? By God! you are playing with your lives. You should not have allowed her to send the message.'

'May the Shah forgive me. I did all I could to prevent her, but she would not listen. She did not ask of her own accord. The Vali Ahd's mother was with her and made her promise.'

'Let her come.'

But Nadir's heart was sore against the woman he had loved. Surely she at least might have spared him in his misery.

CHAPTER XXVII

A FEW minutes later Sitara entered the room and dropped the curtain behind her. After one glance at Nadir's face she stood before him with her head bowed. Never before had she seen such a look in his eyes—a look of mingled pain and wrath which almost broke her resolve. Her heart was beating wildly, and a mist seemed to be gathering about her. His voice recalled her to herself.

'So you have come—you too. What have you to say?'

For a moment she could not speak. She longed to throw herself at his feet, and to pour out all the devotion that was in her heart. What was the Vali Ahd to her? But she thought of the grey-haired mother pleading for her first-born, and made a desperate effort to be true to her trust.

'My Lord,' she said, 'I am not worthy to be forgiven. I have no right to speak. I am nothing, and you have given me all. My life is yours.'

'Words, words. You came to ask for something. What is it?'

'My Lord,' she said, with a voice that trembled in spite of her, 'they say that the Prince has fallen under your displeasure and been condemned to punishment.'

'He tried to murder me and deserved death. I have

spared his life, but he must not be able to do evil any more.'

He spoke in a level voice which gave her courage.

'My Lord, I know nothing. What can I know? But they say he is innocent.'

'You know nothing, and yet you take advantage of my promise to come and thrust your hand into an affair which is not for a woman.'

'Oh! my Lord, forgive me for presuming. It is true that I know nothing. If my Lord says he is guilty, he is guilty and deserves death. But my Lord——'

'But what?'

'My Lord, he is your son. Have pity. Do not darken his life for ever. He has been foolish, if not worse; but he will never forget if you have mercy.'

Nadir laughed.

'Oh! my Lord, let me say a word for your service. His mother came to me. It is killing her, and she came to me. Have pity. They say he is innocent, and innocent or guilty, what can he do? If you spare him, all men will praise you. If not, your heart is great and generous; it will be a grief to you in time to come, and you will have no peace. My Lord, for your own sake, spare him. He is so young, and he is your son.'

Till then Nadir had remained master of himself. Now a wave of wrath surged over him. So this was the meaning of it all? Reza Khan was young, like herself, and he was old. Compared with the suffering of a boy, a traitor and murderer, his life was nothing to the woman he had loved and trusted. His deep voice was hoarse and broken now.

'Go,' he said. 'If anything were wanting to make me punish him, your words would be enough. I have given the order, and it is being carried out. Now he shall die.'

She threw herself on the ground before him.

'Oh! my Lord, have pity! Do not let me feel I have killed him.'

Nadir dragged her roughly to her feet.

As he did so there came from his son's room the muffled sound of a struggle, and of men's voices.

'Go!' he cried, 'and never let me see your face again. Go! Faithless and shameless that you are.'

The words wrung from her a passionate cry.

'No! No! Hear me. Only hear me!'

She was pleading for herself now.

She clung to his arm with a last desperate effort.

'Hear me, my Lord. Only hear me!'

He tried to fling her from him, but could not. What but a guilty love could give her such strength?

'Hear me. Only hear me!' and through it all there came to his ears a dreadful sound, a shuddering gasp and moan of agony which told him all was over. A fierce oath broke from him, and his axe rose in the air.

She saw it, and threw up her arm with a cry, but the blow fell, beating down the feeble guard.

Nadir stood for a moment, dazed with horror, looking at the girl who lay at his feet, a stream of blood welling from her temple across the floor.

Then, with madness in his eyes, he turned away.

CHAPTER XXVIII

NADIR sought relief in a night of reckless drinking. At last the tumult in his brain was dulled, and he slept heavily.

He woke to a sudden horror of remembrance. He heard again the moan of agony which burst from the lips of his son, the son who would live henceforth to hate him and curse him in darkness. He saw at his feet the woman he had loved beyond all women, lying in her blood, stricken down by his own hand. Then, fierce with drink and misery, he rose to face the life he had made for himself.

As he took his seat in his hall of audience and looked about him with angry bloodshot eyes, it seemed to him that all shrank from before him. The punishments he inflicted that morning were swift and horrible. A score of maimed wretches went wailing into the streets from the palace gateway, and as he left the Diwan Khaneh to return to his own quarters, the people about him were silent and terror-stricken. It seemed to him that he saw reproach in their faces as well as fear, and he hated them for it.

As he entered his quarters, the sunlight was overcast. A storm had come up from the Caspian, and heavy clouds had gathered upon the mountain-range to the north. Now they broke over the crest of the range, and swept down upon the plain.

Nadir passed to a room overlooking the palace

garden, and took his seat on his takht near an open window. A few minutes later the sky was the colour of lead, the thunder was rolling among the hills, and the ponds in the garden were bristling with rain-drops. Nadir gazed out with a gloomy face.

A servant came into the room, stepping noiselessly in his woollen socks upon the thick carpets that covered the floor. He coughed slightly to attract attention, and startled Nadir, who turned upon him savagely.

'The curse of God be on you! What is it now?'

'May I be the Shah's sacrifice. The Hakîm Bashi asks if he may kiss the Shah's feet.'

Nadir frowned. He guessed why the Hakîm had come. When he left India, the Hakîm had been starting upon the Haj, the pilgrimage to Mecca, and Nadir had detained him. Ever since then the Hakîm had been anxious to get away, and of late he had shown signs of impatience. Nadir had put him off on one pretext or another. He trusted no other physician as he did Alavi Khan, and was reluctant to lose him. Finally he had told the Hakîm to speak to him again in a week.

'Let the Hakîm Bashi come,' he said.

The old man walked into the room, saluted deeply, and remained standing some paces off. His face was grave, and his eyes cast down.

'What is it, Hakîm Sahib?'

'May I be forgiven for troubling the Shah. The last time I presented my request, the Shah ordered me to wait a week. The week is over.'

'Is it really necessary for you to go? I have always treated you as a friend. Cannot you stay until I return from Daghestán?'

'The Shah's favours have been much more than I deserve, but my going is necessary.'

The Hakîm paused, looked up, and added slowly, 'I no longer feel that I am safe in the Shah's service.'

'Not safe? Who would dare to do you evil while you are under my protection?'

'No one among the Shah's people would dare to do me evil, but I might incur the Shah's displeasure, as many others have done. The Shah himself might slay me, as he slew the Indian Khánum yesterday.'

It was a bold speech, so bold that it might have cost any other man his life, but the Hakîm knew his power over Nadir, and had weighed his words. He was determined to go, and determined also that before he went he would speak plainly. Sitara was not dead, and would probably not die. For her sake, and for the sake of Nadir himself, he would risk something. If Nadir had deliberately intended to kill her, he would get the girl away, and save her life at least. If, as he hoped, Nadir showed any sign of regret, all might even now be put right. Nadir had never been known to strike a woman. Whatever he might have done now in a moment of madness, he would surely be ashamed of such an act. And he had seemed to love the girl.

The Hakîm was right. At that moment Nadir had been thinking of her with passionate regret and longing, and there had been growing in his heart a faint hope that she was not dead. The reproach in the old man's words passed unheeded, or at least unreproved.

'Ah, she is dead,' Nadir said carelessly. 'She deserved death.'

'Has the King's arm grown weak that he should smite in vain, and a woman?'

'What have they done with her?'

'It was said that she had become a Christian. The Armenians took her body away—to bury her.'

Nadir sat silent, and the Hakîm searched his face with a quick glance. He fancied that he had caught in Nadir's voice a tone of anxiety. His face showed no signs of it. After a moment Nadir spoke again, and his words put an end to any hope. His accursed pride made him conceal all that was good in him.

'It is well. She was disloyal and faithless, and her death was necessary.'

'As for you, I will not detain you any longer. For six months you may be absent. Go and do your Haj. While you are in other countries you will see how needful it is for kings to punish treason. Have you not seen it in Hindustan? I know that you are faithful yourself, but you are too scrupulous. Go and think of it all, and when you return, do not forget. Interference on behalf of traitors is not wise or prudent. You may go; you have permission.'

The Hakîm laid his hand on his breast and bent low. A deep indignation was in his heart, but with it was something of sorrow for his master.

'I am grateful to the Shah for his kindness to me. Let the Shah forgive me if I speak one word for the service of the Shah. I have been faithful. I have never wished to interfere on behalf of traitors. But it may be that the Shah is sometimes deceived by those who are serving their own interests. To punish the innocent is not for the good of the Shah. It makes the heart of the people hot. The Shah is great and powerful. Who can do anything against him? Better that the guilty should escape than that innocent men should suffer.'

Nadir frowned and moved impatiently on his seat.

'Hakîm Sahib, you are a good man, but you do not understand. I know my business. A king cannot uphold his power without some hardness. You are dismissed. Go, and God protect you.'

The words were a command, and the Hakîm saw that it was useless to say more. With another deep reverence he passed from the room.

When he was gone, Nadir remained for an hour alone, thinking over all that had passed. It was an hour of torment, for reason as he would he could not dismiss from his mind some lingering doubt as to the guilt of his son. And as to Sitara he had no doubt. She had been faithful and had loved him. How she had loved him! And how beautiful she was! Never again would he find a woman who would be to him what she had been. And in a moment of fury he had thrown it all away. Fool, fool that he had been. And the shame of it. All men would know. The life of a woman, and a foreigner, was nothing to them, but that men should say he had slain her with his own hand! Even the Kizlbash would speak shame of him.

He turned for relief to the work before him. Once on the march against the Lesghis he would forget it all. By God! they should pay dearly for their insolence. Their men should be hunted down in their mountain fastnesses, and their women given over to his soldiery. The blood of his brother would be fearfully avenged.

He worked hard all day, issuing the final orders. At night, when all was ready for the start, he went to the tent of the Shirázi. She would help him to forget. In her eyes at least he would find no reproach.

She responded well to the call. Never had she been

so bright and pleasant. Not a word was said about the horrors of the day before. She saw clearly enough the feelings that underlay his reckless manner, and she carefully avoided anything that could stir them up. Instead she plied him with wine and merry stories till he laughed loud and long. Her eyes were shining and her wit was keen. At times she looked almost beautiful, and her lascivious caresses stirred his blood. For a moment at least the past was forgotten.

CHAPTER XXIX

THE next morning, soon after daybreak, Nadir marched away with his Court to join the army at Kasvin. The storm had rolled back among the mountains, leaving the sky without a cloud. After the rain the air was clear and cool. A sprinkling of fresh snow lay upon the summits of the range.

He felt happier as he rode out of the Kasvin gate, towards the long blue point where the mountain-range seemed to sink into the western plain. He was once more in the saddle, with war and excitement before him; and the Kizlbash rejoiced to see him again looking like the Nadir of old, his tall figure erect, his hand resting lightly on his axe, his eyes bright with pleasure as his Turkoman charger broke into a gallop.

But he rode no more with the Kurk. Since the attempt on his life he had determined that for the future he would remain surrounded by his troops. In truth, he had no desire to face the Kurk just now. The Agha Bashi's sorrowful face troubled him, and he shrank from the sight of the cavalcade in which he would never again set eyes on the graceful form of the woman he had loved. He galloped forward along the broad flat track worn by the feet of innumerable camels and horses and men, and close behind him rode a hundred of his bodyguard.

In the dreary palace at Tehrán, deserted now by the swarms of troops and attendants of the Court which

NADIR SHAH

From Hanway's 'Travels' (the royal plume is incorrectly shown on the left instead of the right side of the turban)

had peopled it, the blind Prince lay with bandaged face, still tortured by the pain of the red-hot iron which had burnt out the sight from his eyeballs, cursing the day he was born, and cursing above all the man who had given him birth. Not far away, in the Anderûn of the Hakîm, lay Nadir's other victim, the woman who loved him, unconscious and tormented by the phantoms of fever and delirium.

When Nadir struck, he had not meant to kill her. His one desire in the sudden frenzy of the moment had been to shake off the grip of her clinging hands, and put an end to the importunity which was maddening him. He had struck with the back of his weapon, and even in the act, when her arm went up, he had tried to check the blow. But it was too late. The axe had fallen, driving into her temple the jewelled bracelet which she wore upon her wrist.

When the Agha Bashi lifted her from the ground, she seemed to be dead; and the kind-hearted negro, who really loved the girl, carried her away in his arms with the tears pouring down his beardless face. But he sent at once for the Hakîm, and a moment's examination was enough to show that, though stunned and sorely wounded, she was alive. A hasty consultation followed, and they decided to remove her to the Hakîm's own Anderûn, where she would be safe from all eyes. They gave out that she was dead, and her women were transferred by the Agha Bashi to another of Nadir's ladies. The women helped themselves before going to some of Sitara's clothes and money, but the Agha Bashi took over 'for the Shah' her jewels and a box of gold which Nadir had given her during one of his fits of generosity. Before he marched away with the Kurk the Agha Bashi handed these over to the Hakîm, sure they would be safe with him. He handed over also Sitara's emerald seal, which Nadir had not taken from him.

The only man who was told of their action was the Catolicos. He had been instrumental in sending her to Nadir, and he was distressed at the result. It seemed to the Hakîm that she would for the future be safer among the Armenians. The Catolicos at once fell in with the plan, and promised to take charge of her when she was well enough.

It was fortunate that they acted so promptly, for before many hours had passed, Sitara had partly recovered from the shock and had begun to moan and cry out.

She was unconscious, and some days passed before her brain awoke to full remembrance. Meanwhile, she was incessantly going over the scene, pleading for mercy to Reza Khan, or throwing up her arm with a look of terror in her face.

When she did return to consciousness, she found herself in a strange room, and the face of the woman who was watching by her bedside was unknown to her. She lay for a few moments collecting her thoughts, and gradually the remembrance of what had passed came back to her mind. She put up her hand to her head and found that it was swathed in bandages. She felt weak and confused.

'Where am I?' she said. 'Please call my women.'

'You have been ill, Khánum,' the woman answered, 'but you are better now, and safe in the Anderûn of the Hakîm Bashi. I will call him.'

A few minutes later the Hakîm was standing by her. A look of pleasure came over his face as he met her eyes.

'Thanks be to God,' he said. 'Now, Inshallah, you will soon be well again, but you must lie still and not talk.'

'Have you been taking care of me, Hakîm Sahib? There was an accident. I fell and hurt myself. It is very good of the Shah to send you to me. How long have I been here? Why am I not in my own rooms?'

'Khánum, you have been very ill. You have been here some days. Now you will soon be well if you will rest and be quiet.'

But she could not rest till she knew more. Her eyes grew bright with eagerness, and her face flushed.

'Hakîm Sahib, tell the Shah it is nothing, and that I am well again. He was always kind to me. He will be anxious. Go and tell him it is nothing. You will go, and bring me his answer?'

A look of pain and pity came into the old man's face, and Sitara saw that he knew. She turned away her eyes.

'You will go, Hakîm Sahib,' she said again. 'Say my heart is burning because I troubled the Shah, and that I cannot rest till he has forgiven me. You will go now, at once?'

The Hakîm tried to quiet her, but in vain. Her one desire was for a word of kindness from the man she loved.

'Khánum,' he said at last, 'I cannot go to the Shah now. He is with the camp at Kasvin.'

A cry broke from her.

'And they have left me behind! Oh! I must go. I cannot stay here. I am well now, Hakîm Sahib. I am quite fit to travel in a takht i raván. Let the arrangements be made at once.'

Then he saw that it was useless to attempt any further concealment, and well as he knew the risk, he told her all—even to the bitter words the Shah had spoken about her.

'You see, Khánum,' he said, 'your going now would be madness, even if you were fit to travel. You must wait. In time, please God, the Shah's anger will pass away. But now, if he knew you were alive, he would give the order, and you would die a dreadful death. You must wait.'

But she would not be persuaded.

'Better so,' she said. 'Even if it means death I will go. It is better for me to die than be cast away. What is life to me? But I know the Shah. He was always kind to women, and he loved me. He never meant to hurt me, whatever he may have said. He will be grieving for it now. I must go to him. I must go.'

Then the Hakîm tried his last argument. It would have been better if he had tried it before.

'Khánum,' he said, 'if you do not care for your own life, you must think of others. The Agha Bashi and the Catolicos were always your friends. At the risk of their lives they saved you and sent you here. If the Shah learns that they have deceived him they will suffer death. Will you sacrifice them too?'

Sitara made a gesture of despair.

'Oh! why did they not let me die? Why did they deceive the Shah? They were faithless and deserve death.'

Then she broke into a storm of tears, and the Hakîm knew that he had prevailed. As she lay with her face buried in her arms he turned and left her.

A few hours later she sent for him again. She was

calm and clear-headed now in spite of the excitement of his first visit.

'Hakîm Sahib,' she said, 'I have been mad and ungrateful. I see that you are right. I will wait. But it is not for myself. God knows I would sooner die. You will let me know as soon as you think it safe for them, and I will go. You promise me that?'

The Hakîm gave his promise, though he had little hope it would ever be fulfilled.

From that time Sitara did all he told her.

The sooner she was strong again, the sooner she would be able to obey the summons which she felt sure would not be long delayed.

CHAPTER XXX

A FEW days later Sitara was taken over in a closed takht i rávan to the house of an Armenian family with whom she was to remain. When she was set down and drew aside her curtains, she found herself in a room close to an open window which looked out upon a garden full of trees and flowers. The good Hakîm himself helped her from her litter. By his side was standing a tall, elderly woman in Armenian dress, whose sweet face brought her a sudden sense of comfort. The two of them moved her to a couch by the window, and made her lie down.

'Khánum,' the Hakîm said, 'you are now among friends. The lady Miriam is well known to the Catolicos, and will show you every kindness. I know I can safely leave you in her care.'

The Armenian knelt down by Sitara's side, and took one of the girl's hands in both her own.

'The Khánum will be like a daughter to me,' she said in a gentle, well-bred voice.

The Hakîm smiled. 'Khudá Háfiz Khánum,' he said, 'God protect you. I shall be able to tell the Agha Bashi that I have left you well and in good hands.'

Sitara tried to thank him for all his goodness, but he stopped her.

'It is nothing, Khánum. I am a Hakîm. What I have done any one else would have done. It is nothing.'

Sitara said only one word more:

'You will remember, Hakîm Sahib? You will not forget what you promised me?'

'No, Khánum, I will not forget. Khudá Háfiz,' and with a salutation to the Armenian he left the two women alone.

Miriam sat for a time by Sitara's side, comforting her with gentle words. She told the girl she knew all, and that Sitara need never be afraid of speaking to her quite freely. 'As to the Shah,' she said, 'every one knows that he was always kind and gentle to women. It was all a mistake, and in time all will come right. You will stay with us a little while, and then, please God, the way will open and you will be happy again. Keep up your heart and get strong and well, and all will come right.'

Then she told Sitara about herself. Her husband was a merchant, and was absent with the camp. Her only son was dead, and for the present she was alone, but her husband came back at intervals, and would not be long away. Besides the house in the city he owned part of the village of Verawa, some miles off, where Miriam usually went in the summer. All in the village were her own people, and Sitara would be quiet there and in safety. They would start as soon as she felt well enough to stand the journey.

Before the Armenian went away, leaving Sitara to rest for an hour or two, the girl knew that she had found a friend.

She lay by the open window and looked out upon the garden below. It was full of beautiful sights and sounds. Although it lay in the heart of the town, and the Persian summer was upon them, the air was cool and pleasant. A light breeze stirred the leaves of the chinárs, and brought a silvery shimmer to the poplars. Rivulets of running water washed the roots of the trees, and murmured through the garden. Along their edges the tiger lilies blazed like flame; and the scent of numberless roses filled the air. From the thicket under the wall the nightingales were singing deliciously. A blackbird's slow rich whistle sounded from the summit of a sycamore. A pair of blue jays had built in the wall near the window, and a friendly hoopoe lit on the window-sill with its crest erect, and a soft 'Wu hu' of greeting. Among the green of the trees were one or two scarlet spots where the pomegranate was in blossom. Beyond, above the garden wall and the flat roofs of the houses, Sitara could see, a few miles away to the north, the long range of the Elburz, its summits still white with snow, the mighty cone of Demavend towering out above the rest. And to her wounded heart there came a sense of wonder and peace.

She remained there a week, and then one morning she and Miriam seated themselves in closed 'Kejavehs' on the back of a sturdy mule, and started for their summer home. With them were some other Armenian women and a guard of servants. As they wound through the narrow streets of the town there was much noise and dust, the camels and mules and donkeys jostling one another amid the shouts and blows of their drivers. These were rough, powerful-looking men, who cursed the Armenians for Christian dogs. The air was heavy and foul. But the streets were soon left behind, and the little caravan, passing through a gateway in the earthen wall which enclosed the town, came out into the open country. Looking through the curtains of her kejaveh, Sitara saw before

PERSIAN KEJAVEHS

From a Photograph

her a stony plain rising gently to the foot of the mountains which lay across the northern sky. Straight in front was the rounded summit of the great Tuchal, where patches of snow still lay among the grass and rocks. In the morning air every fold and wrinkle on its flanks stood out as clearly as if they had been a mile away.

As the mules with their tinkling bells picked their way along the narrow track through the stones, rising almost insensibly for an hour or two, the air grew cooler and keener. At last, before the heat of the sun had begun to tell, the caravan reached the foot of the mountain, and Sitara saw before them her future home. It was a little Armenian village surrounded by an earthen wall, with towers at the corners. About it were some corn-fields, beginning to turn yellow. The road wound through them. They were full of corn-flowers and scarlet poppies, and along their edges shone the delicate blue stars of the chicory. Before the gateway of the village were a few white mulberry-trees, into which some Armenian boys were throwing up stones. Beyond the village a little fan of cultivation pushed up into a fold in the stony flank of the mountain. A cold stream, fed from the snows above, came foaming down through a channel of rough boulders, and on both sides of it grew apple orchards and poplars and plane-trees.

Hidden away in its little valley, with no human habitation within miles of it, the village looked strangely calm and peaceful.

Sitara stepped from her kejaveh in the courtyard of one of the village houses, where Miriam was standing ready to receive her.

'Khush Amadîd, Khánum,' she said, her sweet face

bright with pleasure, 'welcome to your own house. May the blessing of God be on you.'

There, surrounded by kindly faces, health and strength coming back to her daily in the pure mountain air, Sitara began her new life.

The thoughtful care of the Agha Bashi had placed her beyond the reach of want. In the metal-bound chest which the Hakîm had handed over to her when he left Tehrán, was a store of gold pieces sufficient to support her for years if need be, and prevent her becoming a burden on her Armenian friends.

Sadly enough, but with hope in her heart, she settled down to face her future.

PERSIAN HOUSE IN A MOUNTAIN VILLAGE

From a Sketch by James Morier

CHAPTER XXXI

Nadir had marched with his army to the Caucasus, and had entered upon his long-deferred campaign against the Lesghis.

He had undertaken a difficult task. The Lesghis occupied a rugged tract of mountain and forest into which it was almost impossible for troops to penetrate. The grassy valleys in which they pastured their flocks were hardly free from snow even in summer. The inaccessible crags above them were the home of the eagle and the wild goat. In winter, rain and mist, snow and ice, made the country impassable. Safe in these fastnesses, a hardy race of mountaineers had maintained their freedom for ages. It was a Persian proverb: 'If any King of Irán is a fool, let him march against the Lesghis.'

Blinded by a course of unbroken success, and enraged at the defeat and death of his brother, Nadir had long ago determined to break down the mountain barrier and to subdue once for all the fierce tribesmen who had dared to defy the greatest conqueror of the age.

Now that he had arrived on their borders his wrath against them had become a consuming passion. During the march from Tehrán he had thought long and deeply upon the events of the past few months, and the scales had fallen from his eyes. Day after day as he rode on to the westward, remorse had fastened more fiercely upon him, until at last he seemed half maddened by it. The only thing which relieved him was the thought of his coming revenge. He turned upon the Lesghis with a rage born of unendurable misery, and the punishment which he vowed to inflict on them was so savage that even his soldiers wondered at his words. Never before had he shown such a spirit of hate towards an enemy in the field.

At first it seemed as if his boasts might be fulfilled. A contingent of Afghans sent on in advance, men trained from their birth to mountain warfare, had obtained some partial success against the tribes; and when Nadir arrived with his great army, a portion of the southern Lesghis came in with offers of submission.

They were deported, with all their families and possessions, to make a new home for themselves in a distant part of Persia; and their clansmen, fearing a like fate, resolved to die rather than surrender.

The early autumn of the mountains had already begun when Nadir crossed the border. He was met by a skilful enemy defending every cliff and forest pass with desperate courage. It was a warfare of ambuscades and night surprises. Entangled in wooded defiles where they could rarely see and never reach their enemy, his troops were harassed and shot down in mist and rain and snow, nntil they became completely disheartened. The main body eventually succeeded in piercing a portion of the range and establishing themselves at the town of Derbend in the open country beyond. But they had suffered very severely, and it soon became clear that for the moment further advance was impossible. The army was withdrawn into winter-quarters, losing heavily at every step of the retreat.

In the spring they advanced again, led by Nadir in person, and hewing a broad road through the wooded glens, they gained some measure of success. But again their losses were very heavy. One large detachment was hemmed in between snowy mountains and cut to pieces. The force left in the rear to maintain Nadir's communications was fiercely attacked, and hardly succeeded in repulsing the enemy. Even the main body under Nadir's command narrowly escaped disaster. Gathering round it unseen, the mountaineers suddenly fell upon it at night, and threw it into the greatest confusion. They were eventually beaten off, but they succeeded in carrying away a considerable quantity of treasure, and almost penetrated to Nadir's own tent.

It was with a force sorely reduced in numbers, and discouraged by constant defeats, that Nadir extricated himself at the close of his second campaign.

He had now fully realised the fact that it was useless to attack the mountaineers in front, and drive them back from one almost inaccessible fastness to another. The only course which seemed to hold out hopes of success was to occupy the country in their rear, and enclose their mountains by a chain of troops. For this purpose the mastery of the Caspian Sea was of great importance, as Nadir would thus be able to turn the Caucasus, and land troops and supplies at Derbend.

It happened that at this time an English company was endeavouring to open up a trade with the northern provinces of Persia through Russian territory. Among its servants was an English sailor of the name of Elton, a man of courage and resource, who had been recommended to Nadir by George II. of England. Some small armed vessels had already been built for the company. One of its merchants, Hanway, who visited Persia at this time, describes how he and his companions arrived at Yerkie and embarked 'in the British ship *Empress of Russia*, much delighted to find ourselves in a vessel of good oak, regularly built, well fitted, and probably the only complete ship which till that time had appeared on the Caspian. It was no less a pleasure to see the English flag hoisted, and some satisfaction to receive those common marks of esteem which masters of ships usually pay their merchants when they have any guns.' Elton was now received into Nadir's service, and dignified with the Persian title of Jemál Beg. He was given a considerable salary, and set to work to build, under infinite difficulties, a squadron of ships which was to turn the Caspian into a Persian lake. One of these vessels was completed, and carried twenty guns.

But the ambitious project was not given time to succeed. The Russians had abandoned some years before, at Nadir's demand, all their conquests in Northern Persia. Now, alarmed by his preparations, and anxious for the security of their own frontier, they moved up troops, practically in support of the Lesghis, and naturally enough did all they could to thwart Elton. At the same time Nadir's old enemies the Turks, also fearing for their own safety, showed signs of an intention to cast their sword into the scale. Nadir, enraged as he was at his want of success, was too shrewd a soldier not to see that the position was hopeless. He withdrew his troops from the mountains to Persian territory, and abandoned for the moment at least all hope of crushing the Lesghis.

It was the first real failure of his life, but it was complete. His troops fought their way back bravely enough, but they were followed and harassed at every step by the exulting tribesmen; and when they were encamped once more on the open plains, they had learned that even their mighty leader was not invincible.

It was the turning-point of Nadir's career. Like the great conqueror who devastated Europe half a century later, he had been foiled rather by the forces of nature than the prowess of his enemies, but he had 'eaten defeat.'

CHAPTER XXXII

MEANWHILE, in the little Armenian village which had given her shelter, Sitara was passing away the long months, always hoping against hope that some good news would come to her. At first she had waited with impatience, expecting every day that some of the many couriers who rode through Tehrán, bearing Nadir's orders to his outlying provinces, would bring her a letter from the Agha Bashi telling her all was well, and summoning her to return. But week after week and month after month passed by, and still no message came.

She saw the crops round the village ripen and fall under the sickle. Then on the smooth earthen floors where the sheaves were spread, the oxen went round and round treading out the corn. The villagers tossed the grain into the air from their broad fans, and the chaff floated away on the southerly breeze. The fields all about were alive with grasshoppers, and in the sandy patches the sunken cones of the ant lions were to be found in countless numbers. The great purple balls of the Persian thistle rose from the ground. The nightingales and blackbirds ceased to sing. Soft young blue jays and hoopoes sat solemnly on the earthen walls, or flitted in and out of the trees. Overhead, flocks of bronze-winged bee-eaters fluttered and hung in the air, with their sweet, chuckling call. The patches of snow on the mountain above grew fewer and fewer. The stream which had been so full and strong died away with the melting of the snows until its voice was silent, and its boulders almost dry.

When the wind turned after sunset and came down from the mountains, and the swift night fell, the little 'Hek Hek' owls called to one another with a pretty single note, but as summer wore on they too became silent.

In September, the snow on the Tuchal was almost gone, only a couple of little V-shaped patches clinging to the eastern ravines. A few days more, and the first fresh snow fell on the summit of the range. There was rain below, and the air turned cold, and the poplars began to get yellow.

The hawks came down at sunset from their hunting-places on the mountain-side, until at times many scores were wheeling in the air together.

Soon the range was covered with snow half-way down, and the duck and snipe and woodcock came flying over at night, and the great cranes. The sky was cloudless, and the trees blazing with colour, green and yellow and red.

And then the winter came, the beautiful wintor of Tehrán. Occasional heavy falls of snow nearly buried the village, drifting in piles in the courtyards of the houses; but there were long weeks of delicious cloudless weather, with hard frost at night, and a bright warm sun, when the snow lay glittering like diamonds under the clear blue sky.

It was dreary enough at times too, when the snow was gathering and the sky was grey, and all colour died out of hill and plain with the sunlight. Then

Sitara, born and bred in India, shivered with cold and sat close by the charcoal brazier in the middle of the floor, or nestled into the quilted coverings which were spread over it.

At last she received the message for which she had waited so many months. The morning had been fine, and Miriam had ridden away on her mule soon after sunrise to see her house in Tehrán. Sitara had walked with her a little way, and then stopped and watched her riding on down the lonely hillside. There had been no snow for some time. The last fall had melted, and the air was cloudless. A patch of haze and smoke far below showed the place of the town, the top of a mosque or gateway shining out faintly here and there. Beyond lay the great plain, streaked with lines of wall and tree. Out of it rose some rocky ranges. One was deep blue, with a Guebr tower standing out white near its centre, the funeral tower of the ancient Persians, where the birds of the air devoured the dead. Other more distant ranges could be seen to the south and south-west. The furthest were white with snow.

But as the day wore on, heavy clouds gathered on the Tuchal overhead. The sunlight faded, and the air grew chill. Then a cold sleety rain began to fall, and Sitara, looking from her window, became anxious lest Miriam should be caught by a snowstorm. A few flakes had fallen, and all looked unutterably dreary, when she heard the clatter of the mule's hoofs outside, and the Armenian dismounted.

Sitara received her with pleasure, but her eyes were sad.

'What is it?' Sitara said. 'Have you received any news?'

FUNERAL TOWER OF THE GUEBRS, NEAR TEHRAN

From a Photograph

'Yes,' she said. 'I have received a letter from the camp, and the news is not good.'

An Armenian servant had come from her husband, who was carrying out a contract for supplies, and could not leave the army. He wrote that the country all about had been exhausted, and supplies were difficult to obtain. The troops had suffered severely in the mountain fighting. The Persians were discontented and murmuring against the Shah, and even the Afghans and Tartars were disheartened. All said the Shah was strangely altered. In his former campaigns he had always prostrated himself in prayer before a fight, and given God thanks after every victory. Now he was fighting without prayer, like an infidel, loading them with reproaches if they failed, and inflicting upon them the fiercest punishments. Their superstitious fears were aroused, and they were weary of the campaign. The Armenian added on his own account that Nadir had returned to camp in a mood which terrified all about him. The Lesghian prisoners had been executed, and a great pyramid of heads had been erected near the camp. Even his most trusted officers were afraid to approach him. His anger fell upon all alike, and every day men were blinded or strangled for the smallest offence.

Finally, the Armenian wrote a few words about Sitara. He had seen the Agha Bashi, who had told him she must not think of returning to the camp. It would, in the Shah's present mood, be certain death to her and himself and the Catolicos. Please God, when the Lesghis had been subdued, things would go better and he might get a chance. Till then he dared not speak about her. He begged her, as she valued their lives, to remain in the closest hiding. If any of the Shah's spies got knowledge of her escape, it would be all over with them.

Sitara listened in silence as Miriam read and translated the letter, and her heart sank within her. She had been waiting month after month for a message, and this was the end. She was to wait indefinitely while the man she loved forgot her. She thought of the Shirázi, bright and triumphant in Nadir's favour. The thought tortured her, and for a moment she refused to accept her fate. She would go and risk all. Better die at once by Nadir's hand than face such a prospect.

But she soon realised the impossibility of reaching the camp. No one would dare to help her, and a woman alone could not make her way for hundreds of miles across a country teeming with robbers and lawless soldiery. To write to Nadir, even if a letter would reach him, might be to throw away all chance. She must see him herself. Miriam's entreaties and her own good sense soon prevailed, and she gave up the hasty resolve.

Through the winter months she remained in the village. Her first confidence was gone, and at times the waiting seemed more than she could bear, but she was young, and hope soon returned to her. Surely a few weeks or months at the outside would suffice for Nadir to beat down his insignificant enemy; and when his wrath had been replaced by the joy of victory the Agha Bashi would find courage to speak. In the spring or early summer, when the roads were open, the summons would come, and her long suspense would be at an end.

The winter passed away and the spring was upon them, but no summons came.

The west wind, the Bâd i Shahryar, drove away the clouds, and there were exquisite clear days when the sun was warm and the sky a deep blue. About the village, the soft earth came up in patches through the snow. Before February was over, the garden was full of violets which made the whole air sweet. In March, the weeping willows, always the first to come and the last to go, were waving in the wind their long streamers knotted with tiny leaves. A few round white buds appeared on a thorn-tree near the village gate. A faint green flush came over the stony plain. A blackbird began to sing. And still no summons came.

The March winds were over, and the village gardens were green with foliage. Lilac and laburnum and white acacia one after another broke into blossom. In place of the violets, forget-me-nots and sweet white iris lined the sides of the rivulets. The bee-eaters shimmered in the sunlight, and the soft cry of the hoopoes was heard again, and the pink-breasted blue jays were nesting in the walls. The snows were melting fast on the Tuchal, and brown torrents poured from the mountain-sides, carving their course through the plain. Here and there was a vivid patch of emerald—the springing wheat. And still no summons came.

April was gone. The garden was full of roses, and the nightingales were singing. The roads were lined with sweet-scented white may; and the little yellow 'Persian rose,' with its purple-brown centre, covered the stony plains. And still no summons came.

And then Sitara learned that Nadir and his army had marched away into the Lesghian mountains again, and that another summer of waiting was before her.

CHAPTER XXXIII

It was a long, hot summer, and Sitara often found the time hang heavy on her hands. She did what she could to help Miriam in her household work, and she became acquainted with one or two of the younger women in the village. But, kind as they were to her, she was a stranger among them, and she had little heart for making new friends.

She was much alone. Day after day, when the heat was over, she would wander away by herself to some quiet spot, and sit for hours looking down upon the plains at her feet, watching the distant life from which she seemed to be for ever cut off.

She saw the towers and mosques of the town shining dimly through the haze. Or her eyes followed the long lines of dust which showed where troops were marching westward along the road to Kasvin, perhaps to join the army on the frontier. She longed to be with them. Or a string of camels, laden with supplies for the town, would come slowly in to the Hamadán gate. It was all so silent, and so far away, that she seemed to be looking on from another world.

Often enough she would sit till dark, brooding over her sorrow. But there were times when her youth and health asserted themselves, and a restless desire for movement came upon her. Then she would roam about round the village, never going very far, but exploring the lonely hillside within a safe distance, and finding something to occupy her mind. She gathered bunches of wild flowers; or watched the ants threading their way between the cones of the ant lions in the sand; or the field-mice playing in the stubble where the wheat had been; or the sparrow-hawks quartering the sandhills.

Tehrán and the villages and gardens around were supplied with water by 'kenáts,' underground channels, which brought it down for miles from some point in the flank of the mountains, where a wise man with his wand had detected its presence. When a kenát was being made, shafts were sunk at distances of thirty or forty yards to keep the channel straight, and to let the men in charge clear it of weeds and silt. The earth thrown up from each of these shafts by a rude windlass and bucket formed a circular mound about it. The sloping plain was seamed with lines of these mounds, looking like rows of flat-topped molehills; and a small army of 'Mugannis,' water miners, was employed in keeping the kenáts in repair. It was hard work, and dangerous at times, for the channels were narrow and rough, mere burrows in the gravelly soil, and some of the shafts were deep, three hundred feet and more.

A line of kenát ran down past Verawa to a garden near Tehrán, and the mound by one of the shafts was Sitara's favourite seat. It commanded a wide view to the southward, and as the sun sank she was generally to be found there, looking down upon the plains.

During the long period of disorder from which Persia had suffered, many of the kenáts had been deserted and fallen into disrepair. This was one of them. The mugannis in charge had left it. Hares and foxes had found shelter in the mounds, and the shafts had become a home for colonies of wild pigeons.

One evening Sitara had been sitting alone as usual, when she grew restless and weary of brooding. She got up and wandered listlessly along the line from shaft to shaft.

By chance it occurred to her to look down one of them, where she had seen some pigeons settle. As she climbed over the little bank, most of the birds flew out with a great clatter of wings, but a few remained; and she watched them sitting below her at the entrance to their nesting-places.

As she stood looking down, she saw sticking out from one side of the shaft a stout wooden post, and below it another and another. They had apparently been put in with considerable labour, and seemed to form a rough ladder leading down to the water. They disappeared into the darkness, but Sitara knew that the stream was not more than twenty feet below the surface. Her curiosity was aroused, and a desire came upon her to see what the ladder meant. Ordinarily, the mugannis lowered each other with rope and windlass.

She tried the first two posts, which were within reach of her. Both were solid and firm. Then carefully, and with some trepidation, she lowered herself into the shaft. After the first few seconds she found that the descent was easy; and within a minute or two she was at the bottom. Then she understood why the ladder had been made.

The mugannis had dug out a little room, two or three feet above the level of the stream. It had evidently been occupied. Some light came down the shaft, and as her eyes became accustomed to the semi-darkness, she saw that several niches had been hollowed out of the wall, as in the mud walls of a Persian house. One had been used for a 'chirágh,' or oil lamp; the earthenware saucer was still there. In another was an old pack of playing-cards. The room had, no doubt, formed a cool retreat for the mugannis in the heat of summer, and a comfortable sleeping-place in winter, warmer than their little wind-blown tents on the ground above. The walls were in perfect preservation, as if they had just been dug out.

Sitara climbed back to the upper air, pleased with her adventure; and that night Miriam rejoiced to hear her for the first time talking brightly, with real interest and enjoyment. They decided to keep the secret to themselves. 'Who knows?' Miriam said, with a laugh. 'Some day you may find it of real use.'

The next day Sitara went back to the shaft, taking with her a piece of stout rope, which she fastened to the top post of her ladder. Easy as the descent had been, she had gone down the first time with a beating heart, and in truth a slip might have been fatal, for if unable to climb back, she would hardly have been found. Many a life has been lost by a fall into one of these shafts. With the rope to hold by, she felt she would be safe.

Often during the rest of the summer, the girl went down to her underground chamber, until the descent became as easy to her as going down an ordinary stair. In the worst of the heat the room was always cool, and the pure water of the stream was close by her.

She made arrangements for lighting the room, and took down a piece of felt and some cushions, to make it comfortable.

The entrance to the shaft was in a hollow between the two low sand-hills, which enabled her to come and go unseen, and none but Miriam ever knew where it was.

Finally, Sitara decided to make use of the room in earnest. Hiding treasure in the ground is a common practice all over the East. Miriam had more than once spoken to Sitara about the box of gold and jewelry which the Agha Bashi had handed over to her. It was probably safe enough in the house at Verawa, but it was an anxiety to the Armenian, who disliked to see it lying unconcealed in Sitara's room.

One day Sitara emptied it of almost all its contents, which she tied up in a handkerchief, and took away with her. The packet was small enough, and was easily concealed under her cloak. With a rough knife which she got in the village she dug out a hole in the floor of her hiding-place, and there deposited her treasures, carefully covering over the place, and stamping it down until the floor showed no sign of having been disturbed.

When she came back she told Miriam what she had done.

CHAPTER XXXIV

AT the close of the summer Miriam's husband, Ovanes, returned from the camp.

He was a fine old man, with white hair and a handsome, kindly face. His manners were courteous and well bred. Sitara liked him from the first, and felt she could trust him.

The news that he brought was not good. There had been fierce fighting in the Lesghian mountains, and serious losses. The troops were disheartened, and weary of a war which entailed constant exposure and hardship without apparent chance of a decisive victory. The Shah was imposing heavy taxes to meet the expenses of the campaign, and calling for fresh levies of recruits. There was discontent and murmuring in the camp, and in the country through which Ovanes had passed.

But what to Sitara was worst of all, Ovanes told her that her return was out of the question. He spoke to her very gently, and touched as lightly as possible upon the change which had come over Nadir himself, but he made it clear to her that until the Lesghis were subdued the Agha Bashi could make no attempt to help her. She must trust him and have patience. Directly he saw a hope of speaking to Nadir without fatal consequences for all of them, he would speak. Till then she must wait.

Sitara said to the Armenian what she had said from the beginning, that the whole thing had been a mistake; that if the truth had been told at first, Nadir would have rejoiced to know of her being alive, and her long concealment would have been unnecessary. If she could see him again now, she knew he would receive her gladly, and forgive all concerned. But the old man shook his head.

'You may be right, Khánum,' he said, 'but the Agha Bashi and the Catolicos are of one mind. They say it would mean death to all. God knows I feel for you, and so do they, but it is impossible for you to go now. You must trust them and wait.'

And with deep disappointment she resigned herself to the inevitable.

Ovanes went away again a few days later. In spite of all, his coming had done her good. The campaign, he said, must be over before long. In a few months the cold and snow must put an end to the fighting. The troops would be brought back to the plains, and during the winter the state of things might change altogether. In the spring, please God, she might be able to come. He left her with hope in her heart.

One thing he told her which gave her special comfort. The Shah, he said, had evidently begun to repent of his conduct towards Reza Khan, and had become incensed against all who had fomented the quarrel between them. It was said in the camp that Ali Akbar in particular had lost ground, and that the Shirázi was altogether out of favour.

In truth, if Sitara had only known, she need not have envied her rival at the moment.

Nadir was in Derbend, concerting with the Englishman Jemál Beg measures for the building of his fleet; and a force of his troops convoying some of his treasure and women, among them the Shirázi, had marched to join him.

This force was surprised at night and fiercely attacked by the mountaineers. The attack was so sudden and so impetuous that at first there was great confusion. Nadir's veterans soon rallied, and fighting steadily, drove off the tribesmen, but not until they had penetrated into the heart of the camp and carried off some of the treasure and several women. A day or two later the advancing troops found on their route a woman bound to a tree, on the trunk of which, above her head, was nailed an open letter in very bad Persian. It ran as follows:—

'To the commander of the defeated troops of Irán.

'Greetings. Inform your master, Nadir Kuli, the Turkoman robber, who has sworn to carry off our women, that we return one of his, who is bearded, and does not please us. The rest of them, and the treasure, we will keep until he comes to seek them. We hope he will come soon. It is also hoped that any other women whom he may provide for us will be more beautiful and less bad tempered.'

The torrent of railing which burst from the Shirázi's lips when she found herself free but unveiled and dishevelled among the laughing Kizlbash, justified the taunts of the Lesghis. And the worst of it was that, in spite of his wrath, perhaps because of it, Nadir showed her little sympathy. The troops responsible for the surprise were punished with ruthless severity; but when that night Nadir came to the lady's tent he came with a smile on his face and words of bitter sarcasm.

AN ENGLISH MERCHANT AMONG THE KIZLBASH

From Hanway's 'Travels

He condoled with her on her want of success with the mountaineers, and laughed at the fury which she could not conceal. When he left her she hated him worse than ever.

Nor had her brother been much more fortunate. It was true that he seemed to have become more indispensable than ever, as Nadir had of late found much difficulty in raising money for the needs of the army. But his vanity and impulsive nature had carried him too far. The night before the Shirázi's arrival he had been dining with some companions, and under the influence of the golden Shiráz he had spoken unadvisedly. One of them had praised him to his face after the Persian manner.

'It is wonderful,' the man said. 'I swear by the beard of the Prophet that, except your Honour, there is no one who can meet the wants of the Shah. Twice in the last month you have made the Jew and Christian dogs find large sums. I swear by Allah there is no other like your Honour.'

Ali Akbar's vanity was tickled. He had a way of abusing Nadir in private.

'The Shah is a fool,' he said, 'a pig-headed Turkoman fool. He can do nothing but fight, and even at that these ragged hill-men can beat him. As to governing the country, without us Persians he can do nothing.'

'It is true. I swear by Ali that in comparison with your Honour he is nothing at all. Khák ast. He is dirt.'

'Listen,' Ali Akbar said; 'I told him it was impossible to get another tumán now, and the fool believed me. All the time I knew where I could get a hundred thousand tumáns. I shall not give it him, but it is there. I could find it to-morrow if I chose.'

'It is wonderful.'

'Yes. I have it in my hand,' and Ali Akbar sat back on his cushions and laughed his jovial laugh.

He had forgotten the verse of the holy book, 'Curse not the King, no, not in thy thoughts, for a bird of the air shall carry the voice.'

Next day Nadir sent for him. When he presented himself he found his master alone.

'The Shah sent for me?' Ali Akbar said, with his hand on his breast.

'Yes. I want more money to pay the troops. I must have a hundred thousand tumáns at once.'

'A hundred thousand tumáns! Where is this slave to get such a sum? Only last week I sent for all the money-lenders and squeezed them dry for the Shah's service. I swear by God and his Prophet that I took the last tumán from them. They went away weeping. I had even to tie the Tajir Bashi, the Head Merchant, to the felek before he would find a gold piece. He had to sell his women's jewels to raise the sum the Shah wanted. I swear they cannot find any more for weeks.'

Nadir knew it was all a lie. Ali Akbar was not cruel. He had never in his life had a man tortured. But Nadir pretended to believe it.

'So,' he said with a stern face, 'you commit oppression on these poor subjects of mine, and order the felek as if you were a king.'

He made a sign and Ali Akbar was seized by the Nasakchis. There was always a felek outside Nadir's tent, and in a few seconds the great minister, in spite of his tears and entreaties, was lying on his face with his feet tied up to the bar, soles in air. He continued to scream out prayers and promises as the long canes came whistling down, but Nadir looked on with a grim smile until his cries and his writhings ceased. When his feet had been beaten into a shapeless mass, and he had fainted with the pain, he was untied.

After lying on the ground for a few minutes he recovered consciousness. His turban had fallen off, showing his shaven head, and his face and beard were covered with dirt. Nadir was standing by, leaning on the handle of his axe, laughing gently.

'Well, your majesty,' Nadir said, 'will you send innocent men to the felek any more? Go away now and come back at sunset with a hundred thousand tumáns, or you will eat sticks again.'

Ali Akbar moaned out a few words of protest and entreaty.

'Tie him up again,' Nadir said.

'No, no! Az baráe khudá, for God's sake! I will do all I can. Mercy, mercy! I will find the money.'

'I thought so. You Persians are very clever, not like Turkoman fools who can do nothing but fight. Without you Persians I could do nothing. Praise be to God, that I have got some of you.'

Nadir went back into his tent, and Ali Akbar was carried away to his own quarters, moaning and cursing. When his wounded feet had been dressed and wrapped in fresh lambskins, he had to set about raising the sum required. The money-lenders were summoned. There was about the man a charm which even money-lenders found it hard to resist. Coward as he was in the face of danger, he bore pain well and cheerily.

'Welcome,' he said, with a laugh and a twitching face. 'Forgive me for remaining seated. The Shah, who is always kind to his servants, thinks I need a little rest, and has forbidden me to stand up just now.' He laughed again in his half-shy, fascinating way, a slight flush in his cheeks.

Every one knew of his disgrace, which was nothing strange for Nadir's highest officials, and there was no use in trying to be dignified.

The money-lenders were sorry for him, and admired his courage. At first they said it was impossible to get a tumán; but by dint of coaxing and promises and oaths on the Korán, mingled with jests at his own expense, Ali Akbar got his way in the end, as he generally did. Before sunset he limped into Nadir's presence and handed over the money.

Nadir kept him standing in agony while the gold pieces were counted. When the counting was over, and Ali Akbar's white face showed that he could not bear much more, Nadir let him go.

'Afrîn!' Nadir said. 'The Persians are very clever. I thank God that I have such a servant as you. Go in peace. I will send my Hakîm to attend you. May your sleep be good.'

Ali Akbar returned to his quarters, and before midnight his sister came over to see him. Nadir had just left her, and she was boiling with fury at his taunts. She found Ali Akbar lying on his cushions, with his feet swathed in his lambskins, and a flask of Shiráz by his side. He had drunk a fair allowance of wine already, and for the moment was feeling more comfortable. After a few perfunctory words of sympathy the Shirázi turned to her own grievances, and told him, with many curses upon Nadir and the Lesghis, of all the indignities she had suffered. Ali Akbar condoled with her, and joined heartily in her remarks upon Nadir; but running through all his condolences was a certain vein of amusement.

'He is a dog and the son of a dog,' Ali Akbar said in a low voice, with a look round to see that they were safe, 'but after all it is over, and they have done you no great harm. Why eat any more grief about it? We will burn his father some day. Meanwhile take a cup of wine and forget it all. Balé?'

'Forget it!' she said. 'May Shaitán seize you and your wine cups. Have you no shame that you drink wine in Ramazán? And is it nothing to you that my face has been blackened in the sight of the whole camp? All the "luti putis," the riff-raff, in the bazaar are singing songs about it.'

Ali Akbar laughed. 'Ramazán! Those who serve the Shah night and day as I do cannot fast. The mullas have absolved me. And has my face not been blackened too? By all the Imáms, I am black from the soles of my feet to the crown of my head. If I can bear my troubles surely you can bear yours?'

His tone enraged her. 'Your troubles!' she said contemptuously. 'A few strokes of the stick, which all you clumsy fools get sooner or later. What is that to talk about? It was your own fault. Another time, "If you cannot endure the sting, do not put your hand on the scorpion's hole."'

Ali Akbar sighed. 'I was a fool,' he said, 'a fool to trust any one, and a fool from the beginning to take service with the Shah. I swear I will give it up and be a dervîsh.'

The Shirázi sprang to her feet with flashing eyes. 'Then be a dervîsh. God knows it is all you are fit for. If I were a man no Shah on earth would give me the felek and live.'

She flung aside the curtain and walked out.

'Wouf!' he said, 'she is like a wild cat. I will be a dervîsh, I swear it. And meanwhile——'

He filled himself a cup of Shiráz and tossed it off. 'Shukrullah. Thanks be to God. There are good things in this perishable world.'

CHAPTER XXXV

Although the reports of defeat and disaffection which reached Tehrán were exaggerated, and many of them false, there was yet too much truth in them.

The fact was that like other conquerors Nadir had been lured by ambition to push his conquests too far. He had, it is true, wisely refrained from adding India and Bokhara and Khiva to his territories, but even so his empire was greater than his resources. It is one thing to conquer, and another thing to hold. As it was, his dominions stretched from the Tigris to the Indus, from the Caucasus to the Arabian Sea. In those days of slow communication a large standing army was needed to hold together such a tract of country, inhabited by many turbulent nationalities; and for the expenses of such an army he required a great revenue. He did not possess it, for in the main his empire was poor.

The wear and tear of thirteen years of incessant war had caused a drain of men and money. Recruits were becoming harder to get, and his richest provinces were being impoverished. Some thousands of hardy Tartars and Afghans still flocked yearly to his standards, and he had in reserve the treasure plundered from the Moghul Emperor. But the supply of men barely filled up the gaps in his ranks caused by wounds and disease, and he shrank from drawing upon his hoards. His demands for recruits became more and more urgent, and heavy taxes were imposed. And as the pressure grew more severe the mutterings of discontent began to be heard. 'It is we,' the Persians said, 'who won him his throne, and now he oppresses us with an army of Tartars and Afghans.'

Even his army was weary of war. Officers and men were becoming worn out with constant fighting, and more and more reluctant to engage in fresh expeditions. They wanted to rest for a while, and to enjoy the plunder they had gathered. At the first touch of serious defeat they began to murmur, and to curse under their breath the man who had hitherto led them from victory to victory.

A change seemed to have come over Nadir himself. He was losing to some extent the old care and patience to which his wonderful successes had been largely due, and beginning to trust too much in the fear of his name. He was more rash in attack. Nor was this all. When he was only Nadir the General he had been even greater in defeat than in victory. His veterans remembered that when his army had been crushed by the Turks ten years before, he had borne his apparently irreparable defeat with patience and cheerfulness. He had lavished upon them praises and rewards instead of reproaches, and had risen from his fall stronger than ever. Now he seemed incapable of enduring the smallest opposition. Defeat enraged him to the verge of madness, and made him urge them on to attempt things which they knew to be impossible. And if they failed he loaded them with taunts and curses, or inflicted upon them the most savage punishments. In a hopeless attempt to storm one of the Lesghian peaks, a soldier had seen that Nadir himself was in great danger from the fire of the enemy, and had covered the Shah with his body. Nadir had turned on him with a furious oath. 'Do you dare to take me for a coward?' he had cried, and the man had been strangled on the spot.

Those about Nadir's person felt that he was no longer the same man. At times he seemed like the Nadir of old days. At times he was sunk in apathy and gloom, from which he would suddenly wake to bursts of ungoverned rage. His old sense of humour seemed to be leaving him. At times, too, he was ill. He had suffered when in India from the beginning of a dropsical complaint of which the Hakîm Alavi had cured him. Since the Hakîm's departure the complaint had returned upon him, and made him doubly fierce and irritable. The Agha Bashi and Ahmed Khan, and others who were really true to him, watched the change with sorrow and alarm.

He had become more suspicious too. Since the attempt on his life he had seemed to trust hardly any one. His most faithful servants had begun to be afraid of him, and to shun being seen together. One of his generals, looking up by chance in Durbar to find Nadir's eyes fixed upon him, had left the camp during the night and fled to the Turkish border.

It was said, and with truth, that the fate of his son was preying upon his mind; and that remorse and misery had done more to bring about the change in his character than all his defeats and sufferings.

Matters were in this state when Nadir abandoned his Lesghian expedition, and returned to his headquarters in Persian territory. The winter was over, and he intended to make a great effort to recover his strength in order to meet the coming trouble with Turkey.

His first step was to levy an extraordinary contribution on this account. The demand was exorbitant, and his tax-gatherers pressed it with such merciless cruelty, that the Persians, already suffering from over-taxation, were driven to despair. Traders and cultivators alike began to desert their homes, and take refuge in other countries. Great tracts of land fell out of cultivation, and his revenues dried up at their source. It was the beginning of the end.

The end was not yet, for with infinite exertion Nadir succeeded during the spring in gathering together a great army for the invasion of the Turkish provinces; and when in June the horse-tail standards were hung out from the palace at Constantinople, as a signal for war, the Persian army crossed the border.

The troops had rested from the fatigue of the Lesghian campaign; their ranks were swollen by fresh contingents; and Nadir held before their eyes the prospect of plundering Bagdad, and wintering on the Golden Horn. He hoped to dazzle the world by the splendour of fresh victories, and to wipe out from his banners the stain of the Lesghian failure.

He was in fact victorious, but not so easily nor so decisively as in the former war. He had taught his enemies to fight. He found that the Turks opposed him with a stubbornness and skill which they had not shown before. His victories were hardly won.

And such as they were they came too late. The news of the defeats in the Lesghian mountains, exaggerated by rumour, had spread all over the empire; and before he could make them forgotten by news of fresh triumphs, he learned that his own dominions were in a flame of revolt behind him. The belief that he was no longer invincible, coupled with the suffering inflicted by his exactions, had fired the train.

Far away to the south, his fleet was beaten in the waters of the Persian Gulf, and a force of his troops was destroyed at Muscat.

Then a large colony of Bakhtiari tribesmen, whom he had transplanted from the centre to the north-east of Persia, broke away from their allegiance. They had pined in exile for the cool, sweet air of their mountains, for their oak forests, and the breezy uplands where their flocks used to graze by the deep blue waters of the Karûn. They marched back to their homes and set the Shah at defiance.

To the eastward the Beluchis, in their sun-beaten deserts, refused to supply any more recruits, and pouring out from their miserable villages, defeated a body of troops sent to coerce them.

From Ispahán, the very centre of Persia, the old capital of the dynasty he had supplanted, news came that the people of the neighbouring districts were resisting his tax-collectors, or migrating in thousands to India and Turkey.

In the great southern city of Shiráz one of his ablest and most trusted lieutenants, Taki Khan, raised a force and declared against him.

In the north, near the Caspian, the Kajars revolted at Astrabad, and were joined by the nomad Turkomans. And the Lesghians, incited by the Turks, set up a Pretender, and invaded the Persian provinces near the Caucasus.

All Persia seemed to have blazed into insurrection at once, and Nadir felt that until he had stamped out the flame he must desist from his campaign against the

Turks. He recrossed the border, and established his camp in a central position at Hamadán, whence he could strike in all directions, and at the same time watch the Ottoman armies.

His vengeance upon the rebels was swift and terrible. Disregarding for a time the more distant of them, he turned fiercely upon those within his reach. His troops, discontented as they were, and weary of perpetual warfare, were yet proud of themselves, and incensed against those who had forced upon them fresh marches and fresh exertions. They fell upon the rebels with a trained orderly rage, against which no undisciplined levies, whatever their numbers, could hope to stand. The Kajars and Turkomans were scattered like chaff. Thousands of them were slain or blinded, and great pyramids of heads were set up as a warning for the future. The Lesghians, venturing away from their native mountains, were broken and dispersed with heavy loss, and there also the ghastly pyramids rose from the blood-stained ground. Taki Khan was beaten and captured. Persians still talk of his fate. One of his eyes was put out, his wives were given over to the soldiery, and he suffered the last indignity that could be inflicted upon a man. The miserable Ispahánis were crushed to the earth with a double burden of taxes, so that all seditious spirit should be broken among them.

The flame of revolt had been stamped out. The ashes were smouldering still, but for the present they were not dangerous; and Nadir, free from apprehension for the country behind him, turned again to face the Turks.

A PYRAMID OF HEADS, 1744

From Hanway's 'Travels'

CHAPTER XXXVI

NEARLY three years had passed over Sitara's head since the day when Nadir struck her down. With the infinite patience and fidelity of her race she waited still, hoping always that some day the man whose love was her life might once more summon her to his side; and when she heard that he was again within a few days' journey from Verawa, the longing to risk all and return to him came upon her with redoubled force. With all her gratitude and liking for the Agha Bashi, she rebelled more hotly than ever against the inaction to which she was condemned. He seemed to have forgotten her; his messages came more and more rarely, and for months she had not had a word from him. Was her whole life to be sacrificed to the fear of doing him harm?

She had always believed that the concealment of her escape from death at Nadir's hands had been a grievous mistake, and as the long years went by, the conviction had become stronger and stronger.

Her instinct had not failed her. She knew Nadir better than any one knew him, and her woman's heart had told her the truth.

But her woman's heart told her also that three years were a long time for a man to remain faithful to her memory. Must she be silent still and let him forget her?

One beautiful evening in spring she was sitting with Miriam at her favourite spot, looking down upon the plains, and westward to where Nadir's camp was said to be. The air was exquisitely clear, with the crystalline clearness of Central Asia. She could see, miles away in the plain below, a long line of camels marching along the Hamadán road, and she pointed them out to Miriam.

'It is little more than a week's march to the camp,' she said. 'Oh! if I could go with the káfila. You have been very good to me, and God knows I am grateful. What should I have done without you? But it maddens me to think he is so near and that I cannot go to him.'

The Armenian took the hand that rested on the earth beside her.

'Patience,' she said; 'you have borne it bravely so long. Be patient a little longer. All will come right in time.'

'I do try to be patient, but sometimes I cannot. They say the snowy range over there is beyond the camp. It is so near, between Hamadán and Kasvin. And I know the Agha Bashi was wrong. The Shah never meant to hurt me. If he saw me he would forgive everything and be glad. The Agha Bashi would not be punished. Oh! I cannot wait any longer. I cannot. I must go.'

Miriam was silent for a few moments. She half believed that Sitara was right, but the messages from the camp, though few of late, had been as decided as ever.

'Khánum, wait a little longer. You know what they say about the Shah, how angry he is over all these rebellions. Wait till things are going better.

You are a Christian now, and you say the Book has helped you. Have faith. In God's time your prayers will be answered.'

'I know I am faithless. The Book has helped me. I think I should have gone mad without it. But I cannot wait and do nothing. He is forgetting me, perhaps learning to love others as he loved me. Alas, alas, that I never bore him a son! It is more than I can endure. For God's sake, help me.'

Miriam had taken to her home an Armenian girl, little more than a baby, whose mother had died in giving her birth. Her father had afterwards been killed by one of the Kizlbash for resisting some extortion. The child had attached herself to Sitara, and had become her special charge.

'I thought,' Miriam said, 'that the child had brought you comfort, and that you were happier. What will she do without you?'

'Poor baby. She has been a great happiness, almost as if she had been my own. But she would not miss me long. And my duty is to the Shah. If he is angry and sore at the ingratitude of the Persians, what wonder is it?'

'Khánum, they have had much to bear of late.'

'I know, but think of all the Shah has done for them. You say they abuse him and curse him now, and it maddens me to hear it. I used to be able to help him when there was trouble. Perhaps I could help him now. I believe the Book would say I ought to go. Let us open it and take a verse and see what it says. If it says I should go, you will help me?'

'Khánum, we must not do those things. The Book is not Háfiz or the Korán, and we are not Mussulmans. Listen. I will write and send a special messenger.

Promise me you will wait for an answer. It will come in two or three weeks.'

Two or three weeks! To her that day, in her impatience, with the spring working through all her young blood, it seemed like asking her to wait two or three years.

'You will write strongly?' she said. 'You will tell them I cannot bear it any longer—that it is killing me?'

'You shall see what I write. I will say anything you please. But without leave and an escort you must not go. I promised my husband and the Catolicos. And you would not be safe. You would fall into the hands of the Kizlbash, and God knows what would happen to you. Think how they have treated others.'

Sitara shuddered. 'I will wait,' she said. 'But come and write the letter.'

The letter was sent off, and as the time for a possible answer came, Sitara grew so restless that she could not remain indoors. Every day she sat for hours on the lookout, watching the road from the city below. Two weeks passed, and three, and four. The sweet white iris faded and dropped, and the lilac and the may. The roses came and the nightingales. The rounded head of the Tuchal showed more green than white, and in the daytime the heat haze gathered over the plain. But still there was no answer.

One evening Sitara had been sitting at her post idly counting the snow patches on the mountain. There were just a score of small streaks. One had gone since the day before. The child was sitting on the ground by her side close by. An ant lion had sunk its little cone in the sandy soil under a blade of grass. An ant climbed upon the blade and the child shook it off. The poor little creature made a desperate effort to get up the side of the hole, but its enemy flicked a shower of sand over it, and brought it struggling down to the bottom, where it was seized and dragged under. The child shrieked with glee, and Sitara turned to see what the matter was. With her Hindu feeling for animals she was vexed, and protested vigorously, and the child pouted.

Suddenly she called out, 'Khánum, look, a horseman coming up the road.'

Sitara watched the man as he rode slowly up along the stony track. At last! It was Miriam's messenger, dusty and worn with days of riding.

'You have come from the camp?'

'Yes, Khánum. I have ridden straight here.'

'You have brought a letter?'

'Yes, Khánum.'

He saluted and rode on. Sitara waited impatiently for a few minutes, until she thought Miriam had read her letter, and then followed. Her first look at Miriam's face was enough. There were tears in the older woman's eyes.

'It is bad news?'

'Khánum, I am grieved for you. My husband says you cannot go. The Shah has marched by this time across the Turkish border, and he is more angry than ever. No one dares to speak to him. You must wait.'

Sitara dropped on her knees by the window-sill and covered her face with her hands. The child stood watching her for a minute, and then came and tried to pull them away. Sitara kissed her and got up.

'Do not grieve for me,' she said to Miriam, with a brave attempt at a smile. 'Sooner or later God will hear me, and the summons will come.'

CHAPTER XXXVII

THE Armenian's news was true. Relieved for the time by the suppression of some of the revolts in Persia, Nadir had determined to try his fortune once more against the Turks.

For months he had toiled unceasingly to bring his army into a state of numbers and efficiency which would enable him to move and strike a heavy blow. From early morning till noon he sat in his Diwan Khaneh, the front of it open in all weathers, inquiring into every detail, and issuing orders. Often he was there again till late at night. His apathy seemed to have gone, and his application to business amazed all about him.

Nadir had need of all his powers. The country in his rear had become a waste. Depopulated villages and untilled fields attested the crushing nature of his exactions. The incessant fatigue of long marches, and the rigour of the seasons, had ruined the Persian cavalry. Nadir's own horses had suffered in common with the rest. His officers and many of the men had their arms and accoutrements ornamented with gold and silver, and their pay was extraordinarily liberal, but they were weary of war; and the recruits who were being brought in were of an inferior stamp. Nadir held out to all the prospect of immense rewards when his standards should be planted on the walls of

Constantinople. Gradually, by dint of untiring exertions, the army was brought into order; and though the quality of the troops was no longer what it had been, yet the force made a fine show, and in the hands of a great master of the art of war it was a formidable weapon. Harassed as he was, and surrounded with difficulties, Nadir was still a foe to be dreaded. The Turks knew it and made all possible preparations to meet him.

In the summer the great standards of red and yellow were struck, and the Persian army crossed the border. It had some success. The Turks were forced backwards, and shut up in Kars, and the famous fortress was soon invested by Nadir in person. But it did not fall. The Turks, always an obstinate enemy, defended their crumbling walls with desperate valour, and the besieging force began to suffer from want of supplies. The winter was approaching, and Nadir, though he was, as some one said of him, 'guerrier de toutes les saisons,' could not afford to let his last army face its rigours in the open field. Sullenly he raised the siege, and marched back to the warmer and more fertile country near the Persian border. There he once more rested his troops and prepared for another campaign.

The Turks redoubled their efforts. Their Asiatic forces were supported by contingents from Servia and Bosnia and Roumania; and when in the spring Nadir again set his troops in motion, a vast army was gathered in his front.

His heart was heavy as he gave the order for the standards to be struck, and once more crossed the border. He felt that the day for easy and decisive victories was over. The Turks were stronger than ever before, and his army was not what it had been. But for the terror of his name his enemies would have driven it before them. He could no longer hope to annihilate them, and sweep across an unresisting country to the shores of the Bosphorus. Worse than all, he was growing old. In his winter-quarters he had suffered from illness, and at times a dreadful lethargy settled upon him. His day was over, and he knew it. Never again would he march triumphantly into an enemy's capital, and make all the world ring with his name. But, hopeless as he was, the old spirit blazed up once more as he rode away to the last of his great fields. He would yet strike one resounding blow, and show that he was still the Nadir men had known.

Alas! a few days' march sufficed to bring on another attack of his malady, and as he entered the Georgian uplands he was borne in a litter, faint and in pain.

The Turks came forward to meet him, and the news of their approach stirred his blood like a trumpet-call. Once more the Kizlbash saw him in the saddle, fierce and impetuous as ever, and once more they pressed forward, sure of victory.

The Turks met them boldly, and the issue was long in doubt. Nadir was forced to throw into the fight even his last reserve, the priceless veterans of the Six Thousand, and to lead them himself, battle-axe in hand. Two horses were killed under him. But his skill and the terror of his name prevailed in the end. A last gleam of glory shone upon his banners, and the relics of the Ottoman host, broken and panic-stricken, sought shelter again within the walls of Kars.

He had conquered, and Turk and Russian alike were

awed by his greatness, as he stood, defiant and terrible still, on the threshold of their dominions.

But Nadir was not deceived. He knew that behind him lay a country wasted with years of warfare and seething with revolt. If he were to suffer one defeat he would be irretrievably ruined. The army under his banners was the last he could hope to raise, and even that he could hardly maintain. But for his Indian treasure he could not have held it together. There was nothing for him but to make peace while he could, while his enemies still feared him, and then to quench once for all the spirit of revolt in his own dominions.

Fierce with illness and remorse and disappointed ambition, he vowed an awful revenge upon his own people, upon the hated Persians who had ruined his schemes of conquest, and set bounds to his great career.

He offered peace to the beaten Turks, and marched his army back to Persian soil. Soon afterwards he was once more in the ancient capital of Ispahán.

Then there came to Verawa fearful tales of the torments he was inflicting upon all around him.

'From an incessant fatigue and labour of mind,' to use the words of a contemporary writer, 'attended with some infirmities of body, he had contracted . . . a diabolical fierceness, with a total insensibility of human sufferings.'

Upon the wretched Ispahánis especially he poured the vials of his wrath. To replenish his exhausted treasury, and to punish those who were disloyal or suspected, he had recourse to dreadful tortures. His ministers and generals were flogged or blinded or slain, until even those who would have been true to him were driven by terror into the ranks of his enemies. The frenzy of rage and cruelty which had seized upon Nadir's mind increased day by day, and at last he seemed to be, in truth, a madman. The hero who had once been loved and worshipped as a god was hated and feared like an incarnate devil.

CHAPTER XXXVIII

It was a beautiful afternoon in November. For some days there had been heavy clouds and snow upon the mountains; but the west wind had swept the clouds away, and then dropped, leaving the air clear and still. The great cone of Demavend was white all over, and along the range the snows lay in dazzling purity under a deep blue sky.

Sitara took the child with her and walked out to her favourite seat. How well she knew every detail of the landscape before her. Year after year she had sat there gazing out over the plains. It was a wonderful picture. Some of the trees still showed traces of green, but most had taken their autumn colouring. Here and there on the grey of the stony plain was a walled garden, in which the yellow of the mulberries and poplars mingled with the deep red of the chinárs. Beyond them were the blue hill ranges, and above them the cloudless sky, the whole a blaze of intensely vivid colour in the clear dry air.

The sun went down, and the warm light on the snowy range died slowly away, until Demavend alone stood out, rose crowned. Then the glory faded on Demavend, and the long line of peaks lay cold and white against a steel blue sky.

Then came the afterglow, and from a point to the eastward, just clear of the great white cone, there shot into the sky long bars of rose and blue, which broadened overhead and lost themselves in the west, above the sunken sun.

Sitara was watching in silence when the child, who was sitting on her lap, pointed to the slope below.

'Look, Khánum,' she said. 'What are they doing?'

Sitara's eyes followed the child's finger. A troop of horsemen was advancing at a gallop across the open ground. They were a mile or two away, but she could see them clearly. One seemed to be riding alone some distance ahead, with the rest in pursuit. Here and there she caught a faint glimmer of steel. Some puffs of smoke broke from the galloping line, and the sound of distant shots came up the long slope.

At first Sitara thought nothing of it. More than once she had watched the Persian horsemen galloping and wheeling on the stony plain, firing from the saddle after the Persian fashion at some mark on the ground. But they rarely came so far up towards the barren hillsides, and this time it did not look like play. There was no wheeling or pause. The whole troop was coming on together, evidently at full speed. They were heading straight for the village.

Sitara rose to her feet. The gateway was a couple of hundred yards away, and she had not much more than time to reach it. Something might be wrong, and though there was always a watchman on the corner turret of the village wall, it would be well to give warning and get into shelter. She took the child's hand in hers, and ran towards the village.

As they got to the gateway, she saw that the alarm had been given. Several men were running up to

PERSIAN SPORTS

From a Sketch by James Morier

the parapet with weapons in their hands. Others were closing the heavy iron-bound leaves of the gate. They called out to Sitara to be quick, and as she passed in with the child the gateway closed behind her, and the massive wooden bars dropped into their sockets.

She went into her own house, and ran up the steep brick stairs to the roof. From the roof a wooden bridge led to the top of the village wall. In another moment she was standing by the parapet looking over. As she reached it, she saw, two or three hundred yards off, a single horseman riding straight for the gateway. He was waving his arm to the villagers and calling for help. Behind him came the troop she had seen below. Their long gallop had tried the quality of their horses. A few were within musket-shot of the man they were pursuing, the rest were strung out along the stony track. But all were pressing furiously forward.

Sitara bent over the parapet. She heard shouts of warning and encouragement from the Armenians, and saw the first horseman look over his shoulder with a face of terror. The next instant he had sprung from his horse and dived through a small postern door in the side of the gateway.

There was a yell of rage from the riders behind him, but he was safe, and as they came up to the village they reined in their horses.

Sitara had been too long with the camp not to recognise them. From their long spears and loose half-Arab head-dress she knew they were Kurds, perhaps the wildest savages among all Nadir's soldiery. Between them and the Armenians of the western border there was a long-standing feud. When they saw that their prey had escaped them and that the gateway was securely held, they brandished their lances and shouted out curses and threats.

Then Sitara saw one of them, who seemed to be the leader, ride backwards and forwards among them, giving orders. She could not hear what he said, but he pointed to the rear with a drawn sword which he held in his hand, and gradually the troop turned and retired out of musket-shot, leaving him alone. He was a fine-looking man, tall and powerful, with a fierce, dare-devil look which became him well.

When his troop had retired, he turned to the men on the wall above the gateway.

'What village is this?' he said, 'and who are you that shut your gates in the face of the Shah's servants?'

The head-man of the village answered, respectfully enough, but firmly:

'The name of the village is Verawa, and we are peaceful cultivators. In these times we keep our gates shut against all armed men whom we do not know.'

'You know well enough that we belong to the Shah's army. Now in the name of the Shah I call upon you to open your gates, and let my men come in. They have made a long march to-day and want food and a night's rest.'

There was a laugh among the younger men at the Kurd leader's effrontery, but the head-man checked them.

'Have you a firmán from the Shah?' he said. 'Without that we cannot open.'

The Kurd's eyes flashed.

'Dog of an Isavi,' he said fiercely. 'Once for all, will you obey my order, or shall I report you to the Shah? You know what mercy he has for rebels.'

His words were received with an angry murmur. 'Robber. Murderer. Worshipper of the Devil.' More than one musket-barrel was laid on the parapet. The Kurd faced them with a glance of haughty contempt, and Sitara could not help admiring his courage. The head-man answered quietly:

'We are not rebels, but we cannot open our gates without a written order from the Shah. As to food and rest, the town is not far away, and we are poor.'

The Kurd raised his sword in the air.

'Then listen, you accursed infidels. I will go now and report how we were received when we asked for shelter in the Shah's name. When I return I will show you how the Shah treats rebels. Before a month has passed every man among you will have become food for the village dogs, and your maidens will be in the tents of my horsemen.'

A shout of anger answered him, but he sat motionless on his horse till it died away, then spat on the ground and turned his back on the gleaming musket-barrels. He rode slowly to his men, and the whole troop filed away towards the plain.

The villagers watched them from the wall until the swift eastern darkness came down and hid them from sight among the stony sand-hills.

That night, after the evening meal was over and the child had been put to sleep, Sitara sat for some time alone. Miriam had gone away to Tehrán for a day or two, and there was no one in the house but the servants. Sitara's thoughts naturally went back to the scene at the gateway, and a vague uneasiness came over her. The threats of the Kurd had been so fierce and so confident that she could not altogether dismiss them from her mind. He was only boasting, she said to herself, angry at his defeat and trying to frighten them; but there was something about him which made her anxious. The Armenian who had had that desperate ride for his life reported that the Kurds were evidently bent on mischief of some kind. He had ridden up from the town by a short cut through the sand-hills, and had come in to the regular track ahead of them. They were marching towards the mountains, and the track practically led nowhere except to the village. He had seen them first, and had broken into a canter, meaning to keep at a safe distance, but they had at once shouted to him, and as he rode on, had fired a shot. He had heard the bullet whistle over his head. Then they had broken into a gallop and hunted him like a hare to the gateway. It looked suspicious. But after all, a score or so of horsemen could hardly have meant to attack a walled village. And it was unlikely that if they were now to complain to the Shah's governor in Tehrán they would get help. Nadir had always treated Armenians well, and the village, though heavily taxed, had never been seriously molested. It was unlikely that any great harm would befall it now.

The girl went to her room at last, and in spite of the excitement of the day, she was soon asleep.

Not long after midnight she was woken by a sound of wind and hail. A storm had come up along the mountains. She rose to fasten a wooden shutter which had been blown open. The night was very dark and cold. Some hail and snow were falling. She got back to bed and went to sleep again.

When she woke once more, she sprang from her bed in wild alarm. She had been dreaming of her Indian home. In her ears was a roar of musket-shots, mingled with shouts and screams of terror, and the clash of steel. Too well she knew what it meant. The village was being attacked, and the enemy had got in. For a moment she stood by her bedside in doubt and fear, then taking from under her pillow her dagger and seal, and throwing on her cloak, she caught up the child, and ran for the staircase which led to the roof.

One look down into the village was enough. The sky was overcast; but a sprinkling of new-fallen snow made the darkness less intense. Some lights were flickering in the houses, and in one of them something had caught fire and was beginning to blaze. By the confused, uncertain light she could see men fighting or running here and there. She turned towards the gateway, and as she did so some figures sprang up upon the wall above it. At the same instant there was a crash below her, and some armed men broke into the courtyard of the house. She sprang across the bridge to the outer wall, and ran along the line of parapet away from the gate, towards the corner tower. There was a shout, and glancing back, she saw a Kurd racing after her, musket in hand.

Only one chance of escape remained. Calling to the child to hold tight, she clambered over the low parapet, hung by her hands for a second, and dropped into the darkness outside. As she did so her pursuer reached the wall above her. Some snow had drifted against the corner of the tower and broke the fall, but the shock tore away the grasp of the frightened child. As Sitara picked her up from the snow there was a shot above their heads.

Sitara ran on through the darkness until she had got behind a line of mulberry-trees, and then stopped, breathless and exhausted, to think what she should do. The child clung to her, sobbing and moaning. Sitara kissed her, and tried to comfort her, but she would not be quiet. 'It hurts—it hurts,' she said. Then Sitara felt that her hand was hot and wet with blood. The child had been shot through the body near the shoulder.

There was no other village within miles, and at any moment she might be pursued. She thought of her underground room in the kenát. If she could reach the shaft unseen, they would be safe for the moment. She went on again, moving as smoothly as she could, so as not to hurt the child, but she had lost a shoe in the fall, and the snow was not deep enough to cover the stones. More than once she trod barefooted on a sharp point, and stumbled.

At last she reached the line of kenát holes, and groped her way to the shaft. To make sure, she laid down the moaning child in her cloak, outside the bank, and climbing over, felt for the wooden step. The inside of the bank was slippery with frost and snow, but she found the step and the rope. Some pigeons fluttered up past her head.

She came out, and took up the child again, fastening the cloak tightly round them both so as to leave her limbs free.

The descent was not so difficult as she had feared. The first few steps were slippery, and her numbed hands and feet almost failed her, but before she had gone down far she found the wood was dry. In a minute or two she was at the bottom.

The underground room was much warmer than the upper air. She unfastened her cloak, and laid the child on the ground. Then tearing off some strips from her own clothing she steeped them in the running water of the kenát, and washed and bound the wounds as well as she could in the darkness. They were not bleeding much.

She had left her flint and steel behind, and could not light the chirágh, and it might not have been safe. She sat with the child in her arms until the first glimmer of light came down the shaft. It broadened quickly, and soon Sitara was able to see, but this helped her little. There was nothing to be done. And the light brought with it a new fear, for she knew that if any of the Kurds chose to follow her, they would be able to track her steps easily enough in the snow. She might crawl away down the water channel, but not with the child. Still, if any one tried to come down the shaft, he would be at her mercy for a second, and she resolved to defend herself.

She waited, as it seemed to her, for many hours. Looking up the shaft, she saw that it was broad daylight, and the sun was shining. The child's hands were hot with fever, and she still moaned a little, but feebly, and seemed unconscious. Sitara moistened her lips with water, but she took no notice. Then she shivered, and sighed gently, and was dead.

Sitara sat for some time with the little body in her arms. Then she got up and took from a niche in the wall the knife she had used to bury her gold. She dug out a shallow grave, and laid the child in it.

When she had done so, and waited a little longer,

her restlessness became unendurable. By this time she thought the Kurds must have left the village. She could not bear the suspense any longer.

She took her cloak again and secured it about her, placing her dagger where she could lay her hand on it. Then she climbed slowly up the shaft, listening at every step. There was not a sound but the murmur of the water below her, and the beating of her own heart. When her head was a few feet from the top of the shaft, so close that she feared any one looking down might see her, she stood for a full minute hardly daring to breathe. Suddenly she was startled by a shadow crossing the sunlight. She shrank against the side of the shaft, but as she did so there was a faint whistle of wings, and a pigeon alighted on the earthen bank above her. She knew there could be no one near, and climbed up the last steps. The pigeon flew away, and she came into the sunlight, and crouched on the inside of the bank, slowly raising her head until she could see over the edge. Her first look was towards the village. It was hidden by the ground, but a heavy smoke was going up from it straight into the blue sky. From the position of the sun she guessed that it was an hour before noon. She looked carefully all round her. There was not a living thing in sight.

She came cautiously out of her shelter in the shaft, and stooping low, crept up to the top of the nearest hillock. There she lay down among some rocks. Then she ventured to raise her head and look over.

The hillock commanded a view of the slope towards the plain, and of the plain itself. As her eyes came over the crest, they fell upon a sight which made her crouch down again in terror.

On the track leading to the town, and only a few

hundred feet away, the Kurd horsemen were riding slowly down, their spear-heads moving and glittering in the sun. For a moment Sitara lay with her face hidden on the ground. Then her courage came back to her. If she had been seen she had only just time to run for her last refuge, the open shaft. She raised her head again. The Kurds were riding steadily on.

This time she watched them carefully, and saw that their backs were turned to her. The band was much larger than it had been the day before. There were about a hundred spears. Among them she saw, with a thrill at her heart, that there were some women.

Sitara lay for an hour watching the Kurds march away, and examining the country all round her. There was no sign of life within sight except the long line of horsemen. She saw them leave the track leading to the town, and file away to the westward. At last they disappeared in the distance behind some sand-hills. She was feeling chilled and cramped, for though the sun was warm, the snow still lay among the stones. One of her feet was bruised, and she began to feel the want of food. At last she decided to go to the village and see whether she could find any one alive. If not, she would try to reach the town and find Miriam.

She got up and made her way, limping over the stony ground, to the line of mulberry-trees, and watched the village again for a few minutes. It was burning fiercely. None of the Kurds would have remained there so long.

Finally, she summoned all her courage, and with a beating heart came out from the trees, and walked towards the gateway. The gate was wide open, and she passed in.

A horrible sight met her eyes. On every side the

houses were blazing up, and the crash of falling roofs was all round her. Among the burning ruins and in every open spot the bodies were lying, men and women and children. Not one showed a sign of life. Some village dogs were tearing the carcase of a mule, and Sitara shuddered at the remembrance of the Kurd leader's words.

For some minutes she wandered about the village, wherever the gathering flames allowed, calling and listening, but no answer came. The Kurds had done their work too well. Then one of the dogs yelped and ran for the gateway, where some beams were catching fire. The rest followed, and Sitara saw that unless she went too, she would be cut off. A moment more and she was standing in the sunlight outside, sick with horror. When she had recovered herself, she walked round the walls towards the mountain-side, calling aloud. On the way she found the shoe she had dropped. In a field close by she came upon two dead women. They had tried to escape as she did, but had been shot down. It made her wonder the more at her own escape.

Against the wall were standing three rough ladders made of newly cut branches. The Kurds had succeeded in bringing them up in the darkness, and had scaled the wall unseen, or seen too late.

At last she gave up all hope of finding any one alive, and turned to the thought of getting down to Miriam in the town. It was a long way to go, and the gates would be closed by sunset. It might be safer to wait till dark. But she felt that she ought to go at once. It was the only hope of rescuing the girls who had been carried off, and of punishing the Kurds. If any one offered to harm her she had always her dagger.

She remembered that in an orchard near the village she had seen some apples lying under the trees. She went and picked up a few, and tied them in her cloak, eating them as she walked back to the shaft.

She dug up her hoard, and secured it about her. Then she cut a rude cross in the wall above the child's grave, and kneeling down, said a few words of prayer.

After that, she washed her wounded foot in the running water, bound it up with some rags torn from her clothing, and climbed up her stairway again.

The village was burning fiercely as she set out on her journey, and when she looked back from the last turn of the road where it was visible, she saw that the gateway had fallen outwards.

Sitara limped up to the city gates a few minutes before sunset, having met no one on the stony track till she was close to the walls, and in comparative safety. She passed in unchallenged, holding her cloak over her face, and before the winter night had fairly closed in she was once more in Miriam's house, heavy hearted with the tale she had to tell, but free from danger.

CHAPTER XXXIX

THERE was still some wealth among the Armenians of Tehrán, and it was known that Nadir had always shown them favour.

After some delay the governor of the town was induced by large presents to make an effort for the capture of the Kurds, and in the course of the next morning horsemen were out trying to follow their tracks, while a special messenger galloped westward along the road to Kasvin to warn the governor there. But the country was disorganised, and the two governors were not friends. Nothing more was ever heard of the raiders, who made their way safely to their own country, hiding and bribing and fighting by turns, until all pursuit was over.

The attack on the village had been an organised plot. The main body of the Kurds had remained hidden in the sand-hills, while the smaller party tried to obtain admittance. The arrangement had been upset by the accidental meeting with the Armenian on the road; but the result unhappily had been the same.

Little was found in the smouldering ruins of Verawa but the charred bones of the dead; and whatever of value was found, the governor seized and kept, 'pending the orders of the Shah.'

A month after the night of the attack the Armenian Ovanes started from Ispahán to look after his affairs in Verawa, and Sitara awaited his arrival with deep anxiety. The accounts which had been coming up from the Shah's camp were worse than ever. Nadir's exactions and the awful punishments inflicted by him were in every one's mouth. It was openly said that he was mad, and that all the Persians in his service were in daily terror of their lives. There were rumours of conspiracies against him among his most trusted servants, and in his own family. All seemed to agree that matters could not go on as they were, and that some catastrophe was impending.

These stories came to Sitara's ears, and once more there arose in her heart an overpowering desire to go back to him. More than ever she believed that her long concealment had been useless, and worse than useless. She began again to reproach herself, as she had often done before, and to feel that if she had gone back at the beginning she might have prevented much of what had happened. Her longing to go now had become unbearable.

She resolved that when Ovanes arrived she would make another effort.

But it was not needed. The Armenian rode in one afternoon, and late that evening Miriam came to her room and summoned her to meet him. There was something in the beautiful old face that made Sitara's heart beat.

'What is it?' Sitara asked. 'Has he any news for me?'

Miriam took her hand. 'Come,' she said, 'and my God guide you. Come.'

Sitara went with her to the room where Ovanes was awaiting them; and it seemed to her that in his face too she saw the same look of mingled joy and regret.

He met her inquiries and her condolences with a quiet inclination of the head, and a few words of thanks. Then he said, 'Khánum, I have news for you. God grant that it may be for your good.'

Sitara looked at him with an eager question in her eyes.

'Khánum, you have heard what is happening at Ispahán. There is much discontent and murmuring on all sides, and among those who are faithful servants of the Shah there is great trouble.'

Sitara's face flushed.

'Whatever the Shah has done must have been necessary. The Persians are always discontented and disloyal.'

'Khánum, the Persians have suffered much. They are becoming desperate. You know that when the Hakîm went away he never returned. He was a great loss. Since then the Catolicos and the Agha Bashi have done all they could, but they can do no more. They are now afraid to speak. Unless there is a change, some great evil may happen. They think there is danger to the Shah.'

'I ought to be with him. They ought never to have kept me away from him. For God's sake, let me go now. I cannot stay here any longer.'

'You still wish to go? You will be risking your life.'

'My life! What is my life? What has it been all these miserable years? Oh! forgive me. God knows I am not ungrateful for all your goodness. But I ought never to have left him. Help me to go now.'

'Khánum, if you are ready to go, it is no longer impossible. The Catolicos and the Agha Bashi have thought much about it, and about all you have said.

For the Shah's sake they are willing now to run any risk to themselves. They think that you may be able to do something. If you cannot, no one can, and God knows what will happen.'

Sitara's hands were clenched together, and her face was alight with joy.

'At last!' she said. 'Oh! thank God, thank God!' She sprang to her feet. 'Let me go now—to-night. I can be ready in an hour.'

A smile came into the Armenian's eyes. 'Khánum, there is plenty of time. The Shah is starting for Meshed by way of Kirmán, and you could not overtake him. If you go straight to Meshed from here you will arrive before the camp. But sit down and listen. You will forgive what I say?'

'I will forgive anything, but do not try to stop me.'

'Khánum, the Agha Bashi begs you to think carefully before you decide. He says, forgive me for speaking, that the Shah has never mentioned your name since—since that day. The Agha Bashi has tried several times to lead up to it, but in vain.'

'If the Shah had been really angry with me he would not have remained silent. I know he never meant to do me harm.'

'I hope it is so. But Khánum, think. It is a long time. And forgive me—the memories of men are short.'

'Would you have forgotten Miriam in a few years?'

Miriam took the girl's hand and held it hard. Her husband smiled.

'Well, Khánum, I will say no more now. Go and think it all over quietly. To-morrow, if you are determined to go, we will make up our plans, and you shall start as soon as it is any use.'

Sitara turned to Miriam. 'You always said it would come. You kept hope alive in my heart all these years, and gave me strength to live. You taught me to pray to your God, and now He has heard me. Henceforth, to the day of my death, I will bless Him and trust Him.'

CHAPTER XL

NOT many days later, on a bright winter morning, Sitara rode away from Tehrán with a káfila bound for Meshed.

There had been a fall of snow, but the sky was cloudless again. All round her the white plain was glittering in the sunlight. The air was clear and keen as it seems only to be on the great plateau of Central Asia.

In spite of her parting from Miriam, her heart was singing within her, and her young blood tingled with the joy of living.

She had chosen to ride in preference to being carried in a kejaveh. She longed to be on a horse once more.

'I shall have to ride again when I am with the camp,' she said. 'I must get used to it beforehand.'

Ovanes rode beside her. He was going to rejoin the camp too, in pursuit of his business.

As they came to the top of the low stony pass a few miles to the eastward, Sitara reined up and looked back at the city. Its mosques and towers stood out against the snow, and she could see the roofs of the palace where her sorrow had come upon her. She thought of the blinded Prince living there year after year in his helplessness and misery. At last, for her, that time of sorrow was over, but for him?

She turned away her eyes to the northward, to the long gentle slope which touched the foot of the great Tuchal. Mountain and slope alike were dazzling white against the blue of the sky, and so clear that every building could be seen. The ruins of Verawa were hidden in a fold of the sand-hills, but she could see the dark clump of trees above it. She sighed at the thought of the fate which had come upon the peaceful village, and the people who had been so good to her.

The old Armenian sat on his horse beside her.

'Come away, Khánum,' he said. 'It was a sad time for you. Please God, you will be happy now.'

Her eyes lingered on the scene for a moment more. 'I shall never forget all you and yours did for me,' she said. 'I have been very ungrateful. It was a time of peace, and I can never forget.'

Then she turned and rode on in silence, and in spite of the hope in her heart her eyes were full of tears.

It was a long and dreary march to Meshed, six hundred miles of stony road and winter weather. Often as she rode slowly along with the caravan she was chilled to the bone, for there were days when the sun was overcast, and snow fell. At night it froze hard, and the 'serais,' where they found shelter at night, were bare and comfortless, with no privacy or warmth. As a rule, Sitara had no sleeping-place but a shallow alcove in the wall of the courtyard, which was crowded with mules and camels. Even that sleeping-place was shared with other women. The cold and dirt and noise were at times almost unbearable.

All along the road she was made unhappy by the

INTERIOR OF A PERSIAN CARAVANSERAI

From Porter's 'Travels'

signs of suffering and discontent which she could not avoid seeing. A great change had come over the country, and the feelings of men, during the years she had spent at Verawa. The road passed by deserted villages and untilled fields. Her fellow-travellers of the caravan, and even the soldiers who escorted them, spoke openly against the Shah, cursing him for a bloodthirsty tyrant. Sometimes the talk of the women about her was almost more than she could bear. Nothing but the earnest warnings of Ovanes against betraying herself prevented her from many an outburst of fiery indignation.

But youth and the great hope in her heart bore her up; and at last, weary and travel-worn, but strong and well, she saw before her the walls of Meshed the Holy.

During those long weeks, riding side by side, the old man and Sitara had discussed over and over again their plans for the future. Travellers from Meshed meeting them on the road reported that the Shah had not arrived. If the camp was there when the caravan marched in she was to see the Agha Bashi, and to arrange with him for making herself known to Nadir. She had made up her mind, as far as she could do so in advance. She would choose a time when Nadir was alone and ask for an interview. He would not refuse to see a woman. Then she would trust to his old love for her and raise her veil. There should be no attempt at concealment or preparation. He had loved her, and she believed his heart would turn to her again at the sight of her face.

Day after day and night after night she went over all the details of the meeting that was to be. Sometimes a dreadful fear gripped her heart, fear not for her life but for what was far more to her.

Perhaps another had taken her place, and he would turn from her in coldness and indifference. Perhaps he would find her aged and altered; and her old power over him would be gone. That would be worse than death. But her dark moods were not many.

'He did love me—he did love me,' she said to herself again and again. That was her sheet-anchor. And she knew that she was still beautiful. It was with hope and confidence that she faced the meeting. She would see his eyes light up with pleasure, as she had seen them of old, and in a moment all her doubts would be over. As to those who had deceived him to save her life he would forgive them gladly. All would be well.

When she rode into Meshed her first news was a disappointment. The camp was still far distant, and no one knew when Nadir might arrive. She might have to wait for weeks or months before her fate was decided.

And when Sitara had settled down among the Armenians of Meshed her first disappointment was succeeded by other and worse tidings.

Though much was kept from her, much came to her ears, and all that came was dreadful to her. She soon learned that even in Nadir's own province, where the exploits of his earlier days had made him idolised, his name was now execrated by all. The very children babbled curses, and spat on the ground at the mention of him. Worse than all, men spoke openly of the conspiracies forming against his life, and prayed for their success. It was even said that his nephew, Ali Kuli, whom he had always treated as a favourite son, was among the disaffected. The Persians talked of him as the man who would sooner or later overthrow the

A ROADSIDE SCENE IN PERSIA

From a Photograph by Captain Crookshank, R.E.

tyrant, and deliver them from the insolence of his cursed Afghans and Tartars.

Much of all this Sitara tried to disbelieve. 'The Persians were always the same,' she said to Ovanes, 'always ungrateful, and always liars and boasters, brave at a distance, but cowards at heart. When the Shah comes we shall hear a very different story. They will cringe before him then, and swear there was never a king so great and good.'

But the old man shook his head. 'Khánum,' he said, 'do not deceive yourself. The times are bad and there is danger. God grant that all may yet go well, but things are not well now.'

And day by day the truth of his words came home to her till her heart was dark with the shadow of fear.

Then she set to work to find out everything she could, so as to be of use to Nadir when he came. Ali Kuli's Christian wife, her old friend, was in Meshed, but Sitara was afraid to go to her now. It was more than ever necessary to keep herself in concealment. But in so far as she dared she worked hard to get information, and Ovanes helped her gladly. It was only too easy. Before long she knew that the man she loved was ringed round with hatred and treason, and that his enemies were growing daily more fearless and dangerous. The conviction came upon her that unless Nadir could be turned from the course he was pursuing he was doomed.

She did not love him the less because her eyes were opened. He was maddened by remorse and misery, she thought, but his real nature was the same as of old. She knew him as no one else did, and she would save him from himself. The God who had spared her life would help her, and she would save him.

CHAPTER XLI

THROUGH those long winter months Sitara remained in Meshed, waiting impatiently for the coming of the camp, and always the news grew worse and worse.

From time to time fearful tales came from the South, tales of devastation and woe. It was said that the Shah was at Kermán, ravaging and torturing and slaying like a madman. Men spoke of harmless peasants and traders mutilated or blinded or put to death with horrible torments, of great pyramids of heads marking the halting-places of the army. And as they spoke they poured out threats and curses.

Ali Kuli had left Meshed for Herát to put down a revolt. It was openly said that he would never return, that he had gone to join the rebels, and would soon declare himself.

The whole air seemed full of horror and doubt, men's hearts failing them for fear, or hardening into a desperate resolve to endure no more.

Turn where she would Sitara heard nothing to cheer her. Not a voice was raised in defence of the man who had delivered his country, and raised her to the heights of glory and empire. All was forgotten except that he had hated and tormented his people.

The winter gave way to spring, and hope came back to Sitara's heart. But it was an anxious hope, full of fear and doubt.

Then at last definite news came that the army was

marching for Meshed, and parties sent on in advance began to arrive; and one morning, when the trees were green again, Nadir made his entry into the town.

Sitara's longing to see him was more than she could endure, and the old Armenian, yielding reluctantly to her entreaties, let her come with him, hidden in her long cloak and veil, to mingle in the crowd.

It was a dangerous crowd, full of mullas and theological students, always turbulent and seditious. But Sitara would not be denied.

Her impatience took them into the street long before the hour fixed for the Shah's arrival, and the time of waiting was a weary one. Though it was spring, the day was dark and gloomy, and at times rain fell. All about her the crowd murmured and jeered; and when a body of Afghans forming part of the advanced guard marched into the town they were received with scowls and curses. They evidently knew the feeling against them, for as they rode by, big bearded men in yellow sheep-skins, they cast to right and left glances of hatred and contempt. After them came troop after troop of Turkomans, with their flat Tartar faces and huge sheep-skin caps. At them too the Persians jeered and murmured.

'See, see, the Adam farúsh, the man-sellers. May dogs defile their graves!'

Mulla Abdul Kerim, standing among a knot of students, cursed them in a loud voice and spat on the ground. One of the Turkomans brought down the point of his spear, and the mulla dived into the crowd with a cry of terror. The Turkoman rode on laughing, and there was a laugh all round. The Persians had no love for the mullas, even in Meshed the Holy.

More troops went by, thousand after thousand, steady and cool and careless, bearing upon them the unmistakable stamp of men to whom war was a trade. Then there was a distant muffled roar which rolled nearer and nearer, and the crowd began to heave and push to the front; and Sitara, her heart beating wildly, knew that the moment she had longed for was coming at last. There was a sound of martial music half drowned by the roar of the crowd; and between the heads and shoulders of men in front she caught sight of the red-tipped turbans and steel cuirasses of the Guard, as they swung by grandly, rank after rank, the proudest infantry in the world. Through a rift in the cloud there came a sudden gleam of sunshine, which fell like a glory on their waving banners of crimson and gold.

And then, towering high above the serried lines of his veterans, and the heads of the surging crowd, she saw him again, the man she had worshipped, her conqueror and King. What then to her were the murmurs and the forebodings of evil that had darkened her spirit? He rode by, tall and straight and powerful as ever, his war-horse moving proudly under him. She saw again the golden helmet, and the strong, black-bearded face, and the stern eyes that had grown soft for her.

His hand rested as of old on the battle-axe that all men knew. Once it had struck her to the earth, stunned and bleeding, but she never thought of that. She stood gazing at him with parted lips and eager eyes, all her woman's heart going out to him in a passion of pride and love. At last! At last!

It was over. His bodyguard had ridden in behind him, and he had passed away from her sight. She had caught in the distance the last gleam of light from the golden helmet. The crowd began to press and jostle about her, talking and gesticulating. The old Armenian touched her arm and brought her back to herself. She sighed a long sigh of contentment, and turned to go. As she did so, Mulla Abdul Kerim brushed past them, and twitching away the skirt of his cloak, cursed them for a couple of Christian dogs. But she cared nothing for jostling or curses. Her heart was full of triumph and happiness. Why had she ever doubted and feared? What danger could touch him in all his strength and glory, with his splendid veterans about him, and his lofty spirit dominating all? Coward and faithless that she had been!

CHAPTER XLII

THAT night was one of the happiest in Sitara's life. The burden of sorrow seemed to have fallen from her heart. He was close to her. Next day she could see him again, and perhaps before another night passed she would be in his arms.

Even the old Armenian seemed to have been encouraged by the bearing of Nadir and his army of veterans. It was true that the crowd had shown none of their old enthusiasm at the sight of him. Before he came there had been murmurs and curses instead of joy. But when he rode by the curses had ceased, and Nadir had extorted from them, in spite of themselves, some signs of wonder and admiration.

Ovanes was in better spirits, and as Sitara talked on with flushed face and glowing eyes, full of confidence and joy, he seemed to catch something of her courage.

Next day the Kurk was to march in, and then, he said, he would see the Agha Bashi and bring news. Meantime Sitara could go, safe in the concealment of her long cloak and veil, and join the crowd at the Diwan Khaneh, where Nadir was sure to be sitting at his work as usual.

In her excitement the girl slept little, and soon after daybreak she was ready to start. They went together to the open space in front of the hall of audience, and saw Nadir ride up and take his seat. They could not get close to him, but Sitara was near enough to see that he was as of old very simply dressed in white. In his turban shone the great diamond of the Moghuls, the Koh-i-nûr. As of old he had his axe in his hand, and laid it beside him on the takht.

Then began the long day's work she remembered so well. It seemed but yesterday since she had seen him sitting there, with the groups of tribesmen and soldiers going up before him one after another, and Ali Akbar standing beside him reading out papers. It was all exactly as it had been. She watched for hours, and could have watched for many more, impatient, and longing to get nearer, but intensely happy. She was back in the old life which she feared she had lost for ever. Even the crowd seemed the same. There was no cursing now, nothing apparently but the old curiosity and love of a 'tamashá,' a show.

When they had stood till the old man was tired, and longing to get away, Ali Akbar came down the steps from the Diwan Khaneh and walked through the crowd. Nadir had sent him to get some papers. He passed close by them, and Sitara noticed that he was changed. He looked older, and walked heavily, and his face had no longer the same merry expression. But his eye was as quick as ever. He recognised Ovanes, with whom he had had dealings, and nodded with his old pleasant smile. Sitara fancied that his glance rested on her, and she shrank back with a sudden thrill of fear. Ali Akbar went on, and she knew that he could not possibly have recognised her under her veil; but the meeting had made her uneasy. When Ovanes proposed that they should go back, as the Kurk might soon be marching in, she agreed at once.

For the rest of the day she remained at home, anxiously looking for news. About sunset the Armenian, who had gone out again, returned to the house. He reported that the Kurk had come in, and that he had spoken for a moment to the Agha Bashi, who would, if possible, get leave that night and come to see her. She awaited his arrival in a fever of impatience.

Late at night, when they had almost given up hopes of seeing him, he arrived, and Sitara received him with a joy that she made no attempt to conceal. He seemed almost equally pleased to see her.

But directly the first greetings were over Sitara saw that he too was greatly changed. He looked aged and shrunken, and his dark face had lost the old look of peace and good-humour. He had become nervous and unquiet in his manner. And when he began to answer her eager questions about his master his depression and anxiety were only too evident. He said Nadir was not ill, that for the moment the march seemed to have done him good.

'But, oh! Khánum, he is so different from what he used to be. Ever since the blinding of Reza Khan he has been growing more and more fierce and pitiless. And now, Khánum, not one of us dares to look him in the face. If he had only listened to you and the Hakîm, all would have been well. But he was deceived, and grief has darkened his mind. To me he has always been good, and I am ready to give my life for him, but to others he is always suspicious and angry. All are in terror for their lives. Khánum, it cannot go on like this. I can see that fear is making all about him desperate. No man, however faithful, can hope to escape for long. They are becoming mad and reckless, for they have no hope, and God knows what will be the end. Khánum, I am afraid for his life.'

The negro's hands were trembling, and his eyes full of tears.

Sitara listened with a sinking heart. 'But the troops are staunch,' she said. 'So long as they remain true to their salt no one can do anything.'

'Khánum, but for that it would have ended long ago. The Shah still shows favour to his Afghans and Uzbegs, and they are faithful. So are some of the Kizlbash. But you know the Shah hates the Persians and shows them no mercy. Many even of the troops are disloyal.'

This and much more he told her, until her newborn confidence was sorely shaken again. And when she pressed him to let her go at once to Nadir and make herself known, he seemed afraid. He urged her to be cautious. She must do nothing rash. He would watch for an opportunity and let her know. He spoke irresolutely, without any confidence. It almost seemed as if he repented having sent for her, and dared not put it to the touch.

But Sitara was in no mood to be stopped now. She had never believed in the wisdom of concealing from Nadir the fact of her being alive, and now, seeing that the negro had lost all faith in himself, she felt that she would no longer let herself be led by him. She must act on her own judgment. In proportion as his courage sank her own rose to supply its place.

Boldly and firmly she put aside his pleas for delay.

'No,' she said, 'I know the Shah. I know that he never meant to harm me. I know that he will not be angry with me now. You were very good to me, and for your sake I acted against my own judgment. Now if all you say is true, it is a question of saving him. Agha Sahib, I cannot be silent any longer. I do not want you to help me if you think there is danger. I will go to him myself. He will not refuse to see a woman. For his sake I must go.'

In the end her courage and confidence prevailed over his fears. Hesitating and anxious, but carried away by the strength of her will, he gave a reluctant assent. Before they parted it was settled that next day, when Nadir had returned from the Diwan Khaneh, and was alone, Sitara should present herself and ask for an interview. The Agha Bashi would do what he could to help her without putting himself forward. If any question arose she would tell the Shah that the Hakîm had saved her life and concealed her.

To do him justice the Agha Bashi was not thinking only of himself; and when she had screwed his courage to the sticking-point, he behaved bravely enough. He made no pretence that he was not afraid, but he resolved to face all risks, and meet his death, if need be, in the attempt to save his master.

'Khánum,' he said, 'you have put me to shame. You have the heart of a lion. I will stand by you whatever happens. It is for his sake. God grant that all may go well.'

'All will go well,' she said. 'I know it. My heart tells me so. Do not fear. To-morrow all our troubles will be over.'

The Agha Bashi rose to take his leave, his whole being dominated for the time by her fearless spirit. Before he went she asked him one question which had been trembling on her lips.

'The Shirázi,' Sitara said; 'is she here? Can she still do harm?'

'She is here, Khánum, but she is not in favour. For the sake of Ali Akbar the Shah keeps her with him, but he distrusts Ali Akbar now, and he rarely sees her.'

Sitara hesitated and flushed hotly. Then she laid her hand on the African's arm, and raised her eyes to his face.

'Is there any other who is—who is more to the Shah?'

'No, Khánum. Since you have been away the Shah has never listened to any one in the Anderûn. No one has ever been to him what you were.'

Her eyes shone with triumphant joy. 'I knew it,' she said, 'I knew he would not forget.'

CHAPTER XLIII

At sunset the next day Nadir left his Diwan Khaneh, and rode back to his private quarters. Sitara and Ovanes, who had been waiting in the crowd, followed him quietly, and stopped near a gateway where the Agha Bashi had told them to wait.

Soon after dark a negro servant sauntered up to them and saluted.

'Who are you?' he said to the Armenian, 'and what is your business? Is it the business of the Armenian Khánum who lives at Verawa?' The words were a sign agreed upon the night before.

'We are here by order of your master the Agha Bashi,' Ovanes said. 'My name is Ovanes.'

The negro saluted again. 'Good, you can remain here. The Khánum will please to follow me.'

Sitara stepped forward. 'God protect you and bless you, my daughter,' the old man said in Armenian. His voice broke, and she laid her hand on his for an instant.

'Do not fear for me. I know all will go well,' and she passed through the gateway with head erect, and firm step.

The negro led her across a courtyard to a door in the palace wall, and then along a passage ending in a small waiting-room, where he left her. They had met no one.

A minute or two later the Agha Bashi came in. He looked ill and excited, his dark face almost grey with fear. Sitara could see that his hands were trembling.

'Khánum, are you quite sure you can do it?' he said. 'If you have any doubt, for God's sake wait a day or two. It is not too late.'

Sitara raised her veil. Her face was pale and her eyes very bright, but there was not a sign of unsteadiness about her. She smiled up at him.

'I have no doubt. I am quite ready.'

The Agha Bashi looked at her in astonishment.

'It is wonderful,' he said.

He told her that a servant would inform the Shah, who was alone, that an Armenian woman begged to be allowed to see him on important business. If he refused, the servant was to say that she was a friend of the old Hakîm Alavi Khan. If he still refused, there was no other way but to send him her seal.

'You have brought it as I asked you?'

'Of course, but I do not wish to send it. I must go to him myself. If he sees me, all will be well.'

'But if he will not see you otherwise?'

'Then I will send it.'

The Agha Bashi went out and gave an order. When he returned he sat in silence, nervously clenching and unclenching his hands.

They waited a few minutes only, and then the negro servant came into the room.

'The Shah is alone, and will see the Khánum at once.'

Sitara rose and followed him. All had gone so easily that she could hardly believe she had succeeded, and as often happens in the crisis of a life, she was wondering at her own calmness and freedom from concern. But when she stood before the curtain which hung across the door of Nadir's room, there came to her a sense of all that the next moment would mean to her; and the sound of the deep, well-known voice telling the servant to bring her in, almost overcame her courage. For a moment her heart stopped beating. But the brave Rajput blood saved her from giving way. She steadied herself with a desperate effort and walked in, her figure erect and her head up. As she came before the takht on which Nadir was sitting, he raised his eyes, and she saw him start and look at her closely.

But the deep voice showed no sign of emotion.

'Who are you and what is your business?' he said. 'Raise your veil that I may see you.'

Sitara's hand went up. It was trembling now.

'My Lord, forgive me,' she said, and she stood before him with uncovered face and pleading eyes.

A hoarse cry broke from him, and he sprang to his feet with a look of amazement that was almost fear. She threw herself on her knees before him, but he seized her arms and drew her up, gazing into her face.

'Great God! They told me that I had killed you, and all these years I have been in hell. Why did you leave me? God knows I never meant to harm you.'

'My Lord, I always knew it, and tried to go back, but I could not. I was ill, and you had marched to Daghestán, and they would not let me go.'

'Who dared to stop you? Who dared to deceive me? By God! they shall die this hour.'

Sitara looked in his face with smiling eyes.

'I know that you have forgiven me now, and all that misery is past. You will not darken the first hour of my happiness? You will forgive them too. I know you will forgive them.'

Ovanes waited long, forgotten, by the palace gateway. It was late in the evening, and he was worn out with anxiety and fatigue, when Sitara came to him. She insisted on going herself to make amends for her forgetfulness, and to bring him the good news he was longing to hear. On her way she spoke a word of comfort to the Agha Bashi, who had also forgotten him.

And then for the first few hours Sitara felt that the whole world was hers. That night all thought of the troubles which threatened them was put aside.

When at last Nadir slept, the darkness had cleared away from his spirit. He lay with open brow and restful face. One night at least of peace and perfect happiness heaven had vouchsafed to them.

And kneeling by his side Sitara poured out her soul in words of passionate gratitude to the God who had heard her prayers.

CHAPTER XLIV

But in the meantime the news of her return had spread through the Anderûn, and while she was drinking the first draught of her new-found happiness, the old snares were being woven about her.

To the Shirázi the tidings had come with a cruel shock, and her hatred blazed up again as fiercely as ever. The night was still young when she came to her brother's quarters. He was deep in his cups as usual, and in no humour to be worried with serious business, but her first words startled him into attention. She broke into the subject with characteristic abruptness.

'Listen,' she said, disregarding his polite inquiries, for Ali Akbar was always polite.

'Listen. The Indian girl has come back, and is with the Shah again. God knows by what sorceries she has been raised from the grave to torment us.'

'Allah! It is impossible. She has been dead for years.'

'Dead or not dead, she is in the palace. The Agha Bashi, upon whose head be cúrses, told me so himself, grinning like a black devil with joy. I could have stabbed him.'

'Wonderful! But after all, what harm can she do?'

'You will drive me mad. What a fool you can be. Has she not always been against us? She and that filthy negro? Whenever we have had to do with her we have eaten dirt. She hates us, and will use all her Indian devilments against us again. And the blood-drinker has no love for you now.'

'He wants money more than ever, and no one else can get it for him. I am not afraid of a girl.'

But he was afraid. He felt that Sitara had always distrusted him and his sister. Probably now she knew they had tried to lure her to her death. He had a superstitious feeling that things had not gone right with him since he had joined the plot against her.

And now he was standing on dangerous ground. He was very deep in treason. Partly from vanity and love of intrigue, partly from fear, he had become involved in a widespread conspiracy against his master. He was, in fact, the leader of the Persian malcontents, the brains of the party which aimed at Nadir's downfall. For a long time past he had seen that he was no longer in favour, that Nadir would never forgive his enmity to Reza Khan, and only endured him for his usefulness. He had resented it, and revenged himself by making all the mischief he could. Everything Nadir did had been used by him to stir up bad feeling. And Nadir, in his madness, had given ample opportunities to a watchful enemy. Every act and word against the priesthood, every favour shown to Afghans and Tartars, every sign of hatred and contempt for Persians, every one of Nadir's pitiless punishments, from which Persians were the chief sufferers, had strengthened Ali Akbar's hands. He was not brave, or capable of lofty patriotism, or even of fierce hatred. A little regard for his feelings, and love of ease, a little consideration for his 'izzat,' his honour in the sight of men, would have disarmed him. But Nadir treated him with ever-increasing harshness and contempt, wounding his vanity, and arousing his fears. So gradually he had let himself be drawn deeper and deeper into treason.

Of late he had come to the conclusion that the conspiracy he had fomented was drawing to a head. The mullas and the Persian military chiefs who attended the informal meetings at his house, were becoming more and more outspoken and definite in their threats. He had heard of a half-formed plot to murder Nadir on the first opportunity. He knew that Nadir's system of secret intelligence had become less active and accurate. From overwork, or over-confidence, Nadir had begun to show less care in managing the spies who had served him so well, and his information was not as good as it had been. Altogether it seemed to Ali Akbar that his master's sands had nearly run out.

He was in this frame of mind when he received an answer to a letter which he had written to Nadir's nephew and favourite, Ali Kuli, at Herát. With infinite care and circumlocution, but in words which were plain enough to a past master in Persian intrigue, and were supplemented by verbal messages, he was informed that Ali Kuli had turned against his benefactor, and would soon declare himself. The prince expressed the strongest goodwill towards Ali Akbar, and full reliance upon Ali Akbar's support, which would be well rewarded.

This message finally turned the scale, and Ali Akbar had resolved to throw his whole weight upon Ali Kuli's side. The more the conspiracy could be hurried on now the better. His very fears emboldened him to the verge of rashness. A frightened man is capable of anything.

So, although he was trying for the moment, with characteristic indolence and love of ease, to drown his cares in wine, his sister found him in a mood upon which her keener energy and will could work with effect.

He had not told her everything, for he distrusted her petulant vanity and her over-ready tongue. But she knew much, and now she made good use of her knowledge. With fierce volubility she pressed upon him the danger of the situation if Sitara should regain her old influence over Nadir's mind. Nadir was still strong, and it would not take much to turn the scale in his favour again. The girl had always been on the opposite side to them. She had done her best to save Nadir from the great error of his life, the blinding of Reza Khan. She would do all she could now to check him in his career of frenzied cruelty. His Afghans and Tartars were still with him. If he were persuaded to be more merciful and conciliatory towards others, it was impossible to say what the consequences might be. The Persian soldiery were always fickle and easily led. Many of them still regarded him with awe and admiration. He might win them over to his side again. God only knew what might happen. And certainly Ali Akbar and she would suffer. The black girl had always been against them. She would be doubly against them now, and all her Indian devilments would be set to work again.

Somehow or other she must be removed. Their very lives were no longer safe.

Ali Akbar listened in silence. He felt that his sister's hatred misled her into exaggeration. He laughed inwardly at her credulity and superstition. Sitara, after all, was only a girl, and a girl whom they had easily duped before. Her return could not really be so dangerous. Nevertheless he felt uneasy about it. Great events often depended on small causes. There was no saying what mischief a woman's influence might do. It was very unlucky that she should have reappeared just now. Certainly it would not make Nadir better disposed towards him.

He sympathised with his sister, and promised that he would help her again in getting rid somehow of her successful rival. That was always the thought uppermost in her mind. They had done it once, he said, and they would do it again. He did not tell her about Ali Kuli's letter, or the conspiracies of which he knew. She was not to be trusted. He could not be sure that she would welcome the success of a plot against Nadir's life. Much as she seemed to hate him, she might for the sake of her own position shrink from the prospect of his death. And if her own interests were involved, she was capable of any treachery. So he stuck to her side of the question. Inshallah, they would get rid of the girl somehow. He would work out another plan.

The Shirázi went away happier than she had come.

But when she had gone, Ali Akbar sat thinking it all over from a different point of view. What she had said about Sitara's influence was true enough in a sense. And he was now so deeply committed on the other side that he would find it hard to extricate himself. Better go through with it now. The sooner matters came to a head the better. He would set to work next day and push things on. Ali Kuli's letter was a grand card to play.

He poured out another goblet of Shiráz.

'Aho! What a fool I was ever to mix myself up with these tyrants and murderers. Ali Kuli will be just as bad as the other—worse, very likely. Curse them all! Why was I not a dervîsh?'

CHAPTER XLV

THE next morning Nadir went to his Diwan Khaneh as usual. With astonishment and intense relief those who were in attendance saw again the Nadir they had almost forgotten. He rode up with an unclouded face, and as he took his seat on his takht he acknowledged their obeisances with his old cheery salute instead of the gloomy scowl to which they had become accustomed. He went through his work in his usual quick, decided way, but without any of the outbursts of rage which had made him a terror to all about him. He detected a frightened wretch in a lie, and let him go with a contemptuous smile. And when they brought before him some men accused of concealing their property to evade the exactions of his tax-gatherers, he contented himself with imposing a fine instead of some horrible mutilation.

Holding Sitara in his arms that morning, he had pressed her to tell him what gift in the world he could bring her, and she had dared to answer: 'Promise me that no one shall suffer death or sorrow to-day.' And he had promised.

The people looked at one another and murmured their astonishment.

'It is wonderful,' they said. 'What has happened? What good news has come to him? It is like old times.'

He dismissed his Durbar soon after noon, and rode back with a look on his face that men had hardly seen for years; and on a thousand faces around him his happiness was reflected.

But Ali Akbar, borne away to his house in his takht i raván, said to himself: 'It is too late. If he had always been like this I would never have gone against him. Afsôs, afsôs. What a pity it is. He is worth a hundred of Ali Kuli. But it will not last. To-morrow he will be a mad Shaitán again, torturing and killing. It is too late.'

That evening, after dark, there was a gathering at Ali Akbar's house. All who came were trusted adherents of the Persian party, mullas and seyyids, descendants of the Prophet, in voluminous turbans of white or dark blue, and some Persian officers of the Kizlbash.

As the kaliáns went round they began to talk of the Shah.

'What does it mean?' one of the soldiers said. 'I was at the Diwan Khaneh to-day, and he was as he used to be in the old times before he went mad, and took us to be shot down by those cursed Lesghis. The Kizlbash are all talking about it. They say his brain has got cool, and that there are good times coming again.'

The Mulla Bashi took the kalián from his mouth, and blew out a cloud of smoke, contemptuously.

'Truly you men of the sword are wise,' he said with an evil sneer. 'Cannot you see that it is all a trick? Only yesterday he was cursing you all for cowards and traitors. He means to get the Kizlbash off their guard, and then he will fall upon you with his Afghans and Uzbegs and slaughter every Persian in the army.'

He turned to Ali Akbar. 'Have I not spoken the truth? You know what he means to do.'

Ali Akbar looked sad. 'I fear it is true. I have often heard him say when he was angry that he wished he could cut the throat of every Persian in Irán. And lately I have seen signs that he is thinking over some deep plan. I am trying to find out all about it. Meanwhile the Kizlbash should be on their guard, and not let themselves be deceived.'

There was an outburst of curses. When it was over Ali Akbar spoke again.

'I have something to tell you,' he said. 'You all know that Ali Kuli was a friend of Reza Khan, and that he has long been disgusted by the Shah's tyranny. He is a friend to all Persians.'

'Yes,' the Mulla Bashi said. 'Every one knows that. He is just and merciful, and has always been our friend. Our hope is in him.'

'Listen. I know what is in his heart. He cannot bear the Shah's tyranny any longer, and is ready to declare himself. He has received an order to come in, but has sent excuses; and he only wants to be sure that the Persians are with him, to defy the Shah openly. I have told you that there is a plot forming to slaughter us all. I expect to get proof of it in a day or two. If I do, will the Kizlbash show they are men and strike before the plot is ready, or will they let the Afghans cut their throats like sheep?'

There was a fierce murmur among his hearers, and one of them, Mûsa Beg, who had lost his ears at Charjui, took up the challenge. He had now risen to be a sort of Quartermaster-General of the Persian troops, but he hated Nadir with a deadly hatred.

'The Kizlbash will show whether they are cowards,'

he said. 'Their hearts are burning, and if we can give them proof of the plot, they will not leave an Afghan alive. Did they not scatter the Afghans before, like lions driving deer? I swear by the mother that bore me that they are Rustems. Every one of them is worth ten Afghan dogs. Give them the proof and you will see. Meanwhile I will prepare them.'

'I can answer for my men,' another said.

'And I.'

'And I. Only give us proof. There are some who are still unwilling to go against the Shah, though they hate the Afghans. If we get proof of the plot no one will hold back.'

'And what will they do?' the Mulla Bashi said.

'What will they not do? They will spare none—not one, whoever he may be.'

'Afrîn! Will they dare to do what is necessary? It is not the Afghans who are planning this devil's work.'

The soldiers looked at one another. Then Mûsa Beg answered for them.

'The Kizlbash are not fools. They will strike at the head, and the arms will fall.'

There was a moment's silence. Ali Akbar's face had grown pale.

'I am not a man of the sword,' he said. 'It is not for me to mix myself up with these things. I can only tell you what I know, and you must do what you think best. But for God's sake be careful.'

The Mulla Bashi sneered again. 'Give us the proof,' he said. 'We shall know what to do.'

The meeting broke up soon afterwards, with many oaths and vows of secrecy. The Mulla Bashi and Mûsa Beg met again before the night was over. It was settled between them that the story of the plot should be carefully circulated among the leaders of the Kizlbash, and that as soon as proof could be found to convince the wavering, a picked body of men should rush Nadir's quarters at night, and put him to death.

But proof must be found as soon as possible. If Nadir showed signs of changing his ways, the Kizlbash might be difficult to manage. Among the men and the subordinate officers he was less hated than among the leaders.

CHAPTER XLVI

MEANWHILE Nadir had gone back to the palace, and contrary to his custom, had spent the afternoon in the women's quarters.

He would have found it hard in any case to keep away from Sitara, but the night before she had resolutely put off 'till to-morrow' any mention of his many troubles; and in the pathetic solitude of absolute power, he was longing to talk over with the one being whom he knew to be perfectly faithful to him, the difficulties by which he was surrounded. He still trusted the Agha Bashi, but the Agha Bashi was too much afraid of him to speak plainly, and he felt that he was alone.

Nadir did not deceive himself about the state of affairs. Although his information was not as good as it had been, he was too clear-headed not to know that he was in danger. The widespread revolts of the past few years would have been warning enough if he had needed warning, but in truth he needed none. He knew that his exactions and cruelties had made the Persians hate him as much as he hated them, and that among his own people he had hardly one trustworthy friend. He saw that his troops were weary of war, and that all except the foreign mercenaries were discontented, if not disloyal. In the gloom and misery of the last few years he had thrown prudence to the winds, and had indulged, with a desperate recklessness of consequences, every passion of the moment. But in the worst paroxysms of his frenzy, which at times seemed very like actual madness, he saw clearly enough the results of his acts. It was remorse and despair rather than over-confidence that drove him to his worst excesses. Doubtless he had been over-confident. He had trusted too much to the terror of his name, and to the power of brain and will of which he could not help being conscious; but if he had been less unhappy he would have been less fierce.

Now he felt that the toils were closing round him, and that the future was very dark. Sitara's return had been like a gleam of sunlight breaking through the clouds. It had given him fresh hope and strength. But as he rode back to the palace the gloom was gathering again. In spite of the joy and hope she had brought him, he knew that he would have to exert all his powers if he was to prevail against the thickening ranks of his enemies.

And when he was with her again, the news she brought him was not good. She had determined that at all costs she would open his eyes to his danger, and try to make him see that he could escape it only by going back to his old ways, and conciliating all whom he could still hope to conciliate. At all costs she would save him from himself. Boldly and unsparingly, with love in her eyes, and love in her caressing hands, but with words that could not be misunderstood, she told him all she had seen and heard. She spoke of the wasted country and deserted villages; of the swarms of wretched men, blinded or mutilated by his orders, who begged on the streets and highways; of the horrible pyramids of rotting heads that had risen all over Persia; of the disorder that was spreading everywhere; of the thousands of desolate women who called upon Heaven night and day to avenge their wrongs; of the children lisping curses on his name. She told him of the murmuring among his soldiery; of the rumoured conspiracies among his highest officials; of the belief among the people that those of his own blood were no longer to be trusted. Even Ali Kuli, she said, whom he had treated like a favourite son, was believed to be disloyal.

And to it all Nadir listened in silence, gazing before him with a face of stone, making no defence. He knew that all she said was true, and he knew she loved him so well that, in spite of all, she had come back to share his danger, to die with him if need be.

His strange silence and gentleness cut her to the heart, and she held fast in hers the hand that had once struck her down, pressing her face and her lips upon it.

'Oh! my Lord,' she said, 'forgive me for speaking as I have. I know how they treated you long ago, and I hate them for it. I know how ungrateful they have been. They have deserved their punishment. But as you are great, be merciful. They have suffered enough. Be merciful now henceforward, and all will be well again; and you will be beloved by all and happy as you used to be. That is all I care for. That is why I speak.'

Nadir was silent still, gazing before him with a stony face.

'My Lord,' she said in sudden fear. 'Will you not speak to me? Have I said too much?'

He turned towards her, and she saw in his eyes a look of misery and despair. He lifted the hair from her temple, and gazed at the scar that she would never lose. Then with a groan he threw up his hands and covered his face.

'Oh my God! my God! I am rightly punished. First Reza Khan, my son, and then you—the only one who was true to me, the only one who tried to save him.'

And then Sitara saw what no woman who has seen it ever forgets, the dreadful agony of a strong man's tears. She threw her arms round him in remorse and terror, soothing and imploring. A moment, and the storm had swept over him, leaving him calm again, but the look of despair was still on his face.

He spoke quietly now. 'I know that all you have said is true. If I had listened to you before, all would have been well. But now it is too late. I have gone too far to go back. I know the Persians. If I show them kindness now they will think it comes from fear. It is too late.'

She argued with him eagerly, passionately, telling him there were many who were true to him still; that they would rally round him gladly; that the Kizlbash had never forgotten his victories; all she could think of to change his conviction; but he shook his head.

'Little one, do not deceive yourself. There is no one true but Ahmed Khan and his Afghans. I must rely on them. Even Ali Kuli, my brother's son, who has always been like a son in my eyes, even he has turned against me, and if he has gone, who else will be faithful? I ordered him to come in, and he has sent excuses, saying he has not yet subdued the rebels. I received his answer to-day. What you have heard of him is true, no doubt. I half believed in his excuses.

He has never failed me before, and he is the son of my brother Ibrahim. Now I know. It is too late.'

As a last hope of persuading him, Sitara asked him to call in the Agha Bashi.

'As you will,' Nadir said, 'but it is useless. He does not understand.'

The Agha Bashi came, and supported her as far as he dared, and Nadir received his advice without resentment. But he was evidently not persuaded.

Still, in spite of all, Sitara fell asleep that night with hope in her heart. She had been terrified to see Nadir shaken and unmanned. But his weakness had been momentary, and he had shown that he understood his mistakes. He would yet go back to his old ways, and all would be well.

CHAPTER XLVII

For the next few days it seemed as if she were right.

Some of the old gloom had come back to Nadir's face, but it was no longer what it had been. Though he believed it was too late, he tried to follow her advice as far as possible. His temper was more under control. His punishments were less fierce and cruel. Those about him saw that his mood was changed. A few of them rejoiced to see it; most of them distrusted him.

'It will not last,' they said with Ali Akbar. 'He will soon begin again.'

And Ali Akbar himself, committed now to Ali Kuli, and spurred on by his fears, was casting about him for some means of bringing the conspiracy to a head.

At this time, after a few days' stay in Meshed, Nadir broke up his standing camp, and moved out again, with the bulk of his force, towards the north-west. A colony of Kurds who had been settled in the neighbourhood had been giving trouble, and he suspected them of being in league with his nephew against him. He had always acted on the principle that in war secrecy and surprise are the foundation of success. He now resolved to attack and destroy the Kurds before they could do serious mischief, and he resolved to do it himself. The Kizlbash should see that he was still the Nadir of old days, that his right hand had not forgotten its cunning. He would strike one of those swift and sudden blows which had done so much in the past to build up the terror of his name.

The resolve once taken Nadir worked out his arrangements with characteristic promptitude and thoroughness.

A strong body of Afghan and Kizlbash cavalry was to move out at sunset to a point he had selected; and at daybreak next morning, when they had rested, he would gallop out and join them. A forced march during the next day and night would enable him to surround the Kurds, and at daybreak on the second morning he would surprise and exterminate them.

The main force was to halt for a day, and to march on the second day to a place called Futtehabad, where it was to await his return. Riding in fast, he would be in Futtehabad the same night. The Kurk was to remain with the main force at headquarters.

To make all clear Nadir wrote out his orders. It was only during the latter part of his life that he had learned to read and write. To the end his writing was bad, with none of the rounded elegance which the Persians admire. His rough, angular characters were a subject of derision to those about him. But they served his purpose, and at times, when he wanted to explain his meaning, he would take a sheet of paper and dash off in his swift, imperious way a rough sketch-map, which, however rough, was clear and to the point.

That afternoon, as he was in his native province, and thoroughly knew the ground at Futtehabad, he drew out a plan of the new camp, showing the position to be taken up by each division of the force which would remain after deducting the troops he was taking himself. Having done so he sent for Mûsa Beg, who also knew the ground thoroughly, and made him take down in writing the position of the several Persian contingents. He did not show Mûsa Beg the plan, but dictated the list of the Persian contingents in their proper order.

Then he sent for Ahmed Khan and an Uzbeg chief who commanded the non-Persian parts of the force. He explained to them the numbers and composition of the troops which were to be detached, and the position to be taken up by each of the foreign contingents that remained. He warned them to hold those contingents in readiness for immediate action, and to keep a close watch upon the Persian part of the force. To make sure that they understood, Nadir made them each take a copy of his plan. When they had done so he dismissed them, and having no use himself for the rough original, which was not a secret paper, crumpled it in his hand and tossed it aside.

Neither Mûsa Beg nor Ahmed Khan was told what Nadir was going to do with the force he was taking away himself. In such cases he always kept his own counsel. He merely told them that he would start at dawn, and rejoin the camp at Futtehabad on the evening of the following day.

At night, when all arrangements had been made, Nadir came as usual to Sitara's tent. He told her what he had told the others, and she begged hard to be allowed to go with him. In her happiness and her anxiety she dreaded the thought of being separated from him. But he refused.

'No,' he said, 'I am going to show the Kizlbash that I have not forgotten my old ways. We shall make a forced march, and perhaps have some rough work. I want the Kurk to march with the camp to Futtehabad. I shall meet you there the day after to-morrow. You must trust me and do what I tell you. If I could take you I would, but I cannot.'

Much against her wishes, but obedient as ever, she answered that his will was her law. But the whole thing disturbed her.

'You know best, my Lord,' she said. 'If I shall be in your way I must stay with the Kurk, but my Lord, forgive me for speaking, is it safe just now? God knows what the Persians are thinking of.'

Nadir laughed. 'There is no cause for fear, little one. Ahmed Khan knows what I feel, and is accustomed to watching the Persians, who will not dare to give trouble. And I shall be with trusty Afghans. Do not fear for me.'

He seemed so eager, and so much more confident than he had seemed of late, that she felt reassured.

CHAPTER XLVIII

Yet Sitara's instinct was not at fault. It was for Nadir's enemies an opportunity which was not to be thrown away, and they saw it at once. The same night, while Nadir was talking to her, the Mulla Bashi came to Ali Akbar's tent. He broke into the matter at once.

'It is reported,' he said, 'that the Shah, curses upon him, will march early to-morrow morning, and will be away from camp two days. Is it true?'

'Yes. A force has left camp already for a night march. He is to ride out at daybreak and overtake it. He has just given me orders.'

'Are you to go with him?'

'No. This is one of his old expeditions. God knows what shaitáni he has in hand. I am to stay with the camp, and meet him at Futtehabad on the third day.'

'Alhemdulillah. Thanks be to God! Then our chance has come. Those soldier fools who were here last night are hard at work frightening each other and the Kizlbash. The Shah will be out of reach, and that Afghan hog, Ahmed Khan, will not understand. Now find proof of the plot you know of.'

Ali Akbar hesitated. He was not a brave man, and he had many times repented at intervals of having gone so deep into the conspiracy.

'I have found nothing yet,' he said with an anxious air. 'I cannot tell whether I shall find anything so soon.'

A look of contempt came over the Mulla Bashi's face.

'Proof is easy to find, and there is danger in too much caution. News of what is going on will reach him sooner or later, and then God help those who are suspected. If we wish to save our own heads it is better not to delay. Your head is not too safe in any case, for he does not love you, and some of the soldier fools are sure to talk.'

The Mulla Bashi remained an hour longer, and when he left the tent he had worked upon Ali Akbar's fears with decisive effect. Ali Akbar had promised to find the proof required.

Fortune played into his hands. The Mulla Bashi had hardly left him when he was told that a Georgian 'ghulám' or slave of Nadir's wished to see him. The Georgian had the reckless courage of his race, and Nadir had taken him into service as a reward for an act of bravery in the field. For a time he had been faithful, but when Nadir's nephew, Ali Kuli, became disaffected, the man had been corrupted through the agency of a Georgian girl, and now he was a paid spy of Ali Akbar's. He came that night to report upon the conference which had taken place between Nadir and the foreign commanders. He said he had been on duty at Nadir's tent, and had managed to overhear something of what passed. Nadir had spoken in a low voice, and he could not catch much that was said, but it was something about the Persians. Nadir had warned the foreigners against them. Finally, Nadir had given the foreigners a paper to copy. After they left, Nadir had come out of the tent with the paper in his hand, and then had crumpled it up and thrown it on the floor. Thinking it might be of some use the Georgian had picked it up, and found it was in the Shah's writing. He had therefore brought it to Áli Akbar.

A glance at the paper was enough to show Ali Akbar that it was of no value. But as he sat holding it in his hand a sudden thought flashed into his quick brain. He gave the Georgian a gold 'tumán.'

'You have done good service,' he said. 'If you are faithful and do what I tell you, and all goes well, I will make the tumán ten. But you must be faithful, and do all the service you can.'

The Georgian's eyes glistened.

'I will do faithful service,' he said.

'Khaile khûb: very well. Now listen and I will tell you how you can earn the money.'

The Georgian listened, and before he went away he had learnt what he had to do. The lesson took a long time, but it was thoroughly mastered in the end.

After he had gone Ali Akbar sat for hours alone with pen and paper, writing and rewriting a list of names. When the list was finished he compared it letter by letter with the writing on the Shah's sketch-plan. The two were exactly alike. Any one who knew Nadir's handwriting would have sworn that both were his.

Ali Akbar burnt his rough drafts, and sat for a minute or two with a look of satisfaction on his face. Then he took the sketch-plan itself, and drew some arrows between the names of the foreign contingents and the names of the Persian contingents. The arrowheads pointed towards the Persian names.

On the following day, after Nadir's departure, Ali Akbar went to see the Mulla Bashi and remained with him some time.

The same evening the leaders of the Persian party assembled in the Mulla Bashi's tent. There was a feeling of unrest and expectation among them, for each had been summoned verbally by a confidential servant, and warned not to fail, as there was important business to discuss. Priests and soldiers alike felt that a crisis was imminent. They sat looking at one another with questioning eyes, speaking little and in low tones. When they had been together a few minutes there was a slight stir at the doorway, and Ali Akbar entered the room. He saluted them with his usual pleasant smile and manner, but his face was very pale, and he looked furtively about him as he took his seat on some cushions which were disposed on the floor at the Mulla Bashi's right hand.

There was a moment's silence, a silence of extreme tension, and then the Mulla Bashi spoke a few words. He said that Ali Akbar had something to tell them, and he earnestly begged all present to hear it in silence. If any one had any questions to ask they would be fully answered when Ali Akbar had finished, but there must be no interruption. His hearers stroked their beards and turned to Ali Akbar.

It was with a very low voice, and hesitating manner, that he began to speak. His hand played nervously with the corner of a cushion beside him, and his first words were hardly audible. He told them that a Georgian slave in Nadir's household had come to him that morning, and had told him what had passed at the interview between the Shah and the foreign leaders the day before. The man, he said, was well known to him and thoroughly trustworthy. He had been on duty in Nadir's tent, and had managed to conceal himself within hearing.

There was a low stir among Ali Akbar's hearers. He paused, and looking round him he saw that they were following his words with eager interest. His voice became firmer.

Nadir, he said, in slow, deliberate tones, had announced to Ahmed Khan and the Uzbeg that he had discovered the existence of a conspiracy against his life among the Persians, and had decided, if the Afghans and Tartars would stand by him, to put to the sword every Persian in his camp.

Here a low murmur arose. The Mulla Bashi held up his hand, and Ali Akbar went on.

'After that,' he said, 'the Shah promised that if the foreigners carried out his wishes all the property of the Persians and all the women should be distributed among them.'

Again a murmur broke out, this time a fierce murmur of curses and threats. Again the Mulla Bashi raised his hand.

'Then,' Ali Akbar went on, 'the Shah called upon them to swear that they would carry out the massacre. They swore by Allah and the Prophet. Their faces were full of joy. The Shah then said that to disarm suspicion, he was going away, but would return on the evening of the second day, when the camp would be in Futtehabad. During the night the foreigners would all get under arms. A little before dawn a rocket would give the signal, and the foreign troops would fall upon the Persians according to a plan he had worked out.

'The Shah then produced a paper in his own hand, showing the plan of the camp, the places of the several contingents, and the portion of the Persian force which each contingent was to attack.'

Ali Akbar's hearers were leaning forward with angry eyes. There was not a sign of doubt on their faces. Ali Akbar drew a small packet from the breast of his coat and slowly unrolled the muslin in which it was wrappped.

'Here,' he said, 'is the plan. You all know the Shah's writing. In a moment I will show it to each of you. But listen. There is something more.

'When the foreigners had seen the paper the Shah told them to make copies of it, and they did so. Then he took out another paper, also in his own writing.'

Ali Akbar paused again, and saw that all were watching him with intense excitement.

'Afsôs! Alas that a Shah of Persia should be so faithless and ruthless! This second paper contained a list of names. The Shah went over every name with the foreigners and told them each man on the list was his special enemy, and that not one must escape. You will see that the name of every one present to-night is on the list. There are two names with a mark against them. These are the names of men who have lately been executed by the Shah's orders. One is the Bakhtiari chief who was strangled two days ago.'

The muttered curses broke out again. There were scowling faces and clenched hands. 'Khûn Khor. Blood-drinker. Tyrant. Murderer. Faithless Turkoman dog!'

'I have nearly done,' Ali Akbar said. 'When the foreigners had gone the Shah sent for a box which is always kept by the Agha Bashi in the Anderûn. The Georgian saw him put the papers into it. I have long wanted to see into that box, and at last only a few days ago, by the help of a woman in the Anderûn who is in love with the Georgian, he got a key made to open it. Last night he gave the key to the woman. He dared not take the paper then lest the Shah should want it before starting this morning, but when the Shah was leaving camp and the Agha Bashi was outside with him, the woman took the chance. By the mercy of God she was successful.'

Ali Akbar looked on the faces of his hearers. This was the least likely part of his story. But the Persians in their anger and suspicion were ready to accept anything he told them. There was no sign of disbelief.

'Now,' Ali Akbar said, 'here are the papers. Let every one examine them and see for himself. Mûsa Beg can say whether the order of the Persian troops is correct. I know the Georgian and believe he has spoken truth, alas that I should have to say it! But if any one doubts, he is here to answer any questions.'

The papers were handed round. The Mulla Bashi, who received them first, examined them carefully.

'There is no doubt,' he said. 'It is the Shah's writing. No one can mistake it.'

Mûsa Beg said the same, with a curse.

One man after another looked and agreed. There were some exclamations of astonishment, but none of doubt. Among those present were two or three who had till then been regarded as waverers. They had no doubts now. There was only one feeling—rage and hatred towards their treacherous master.

'Shall I call the Georgian?' Ali Akbar asked. There was a murmur of dissent.

'What is the use? It is all clear enough. He can say no more.'

Then the Mulla Bashi spoke. 'There is one thing that astonishes me. If there was a man among us who still trusted the blood-drinker, and would not listen to a word of reason, it was Sáleh Beg of the bodyguard. Why is his name on the list, and the name of his father?'

The Mulla Bashi knew well enough, but the question seemed natural. Sáleh Beg was young and full of soldierly enthusiasm. He was of Nadir's own tribe, the Afshar, and devoted to his great master, who had given him command of the bodyguard and made him Intendant of the Household. What possible reason could Nadir have for putting his name on the list?

Hasan Khan, of the Six Thousand, also an Afshar, answered the question.

'It is wonderful,' he said, 'but the Shah is mad and a devil. For some weeks Sáleh Beg has not been in favour. He was always a fool, and when the Bakhtiari was going to be killed, Sáleh Beg spoke for him.'

'That is quite enough,' another said. 'The Shah has killed many a man for less.'

The rest agreed. No one was safe now. The Shah took dislikes for nothing, and a moment's dislike meant death.

'Then,' the Mulla Bashi said, 'let us send for Sáleh Beg. If he once sees the truth, there will not be a waverer left. We cannot send for all on the list. It would take too long. But Sáleh Beg is at the Shah's tents close by.'

'And if he does not understand?' some one said. 'He is a hot-headed fool, and might betray us all.'

There was a pause and then Mûsa Beg laughed. 'Leave that to me,' he said. 'What is Sáleh Beg? If he chooses to be a fool, well. But I swear by the mother who bore me that he will not have the chance of betraying us.'

The others understood. 'Khaile khûb,' they said: 'very good. Whose dog is Sáleh Beg?'

In a few minutes Sáleh Beg appeared. He was a soldierly-looking man of about thirty, in the white uniform of the Six Thousand, with a golden axe, the badge of the bodyguard, chased upon his cuirass. He walked into the tent with his head up, and a look of displeasure on his face. Then he saluted the gathering respectfully, and remained standing.

'What is it your Honours want of me?' he asked.

The Mulla Bashi answered him.

'Sáleh Beg, do you know the Shah's handwriting?'

'Chirá. Why not? Am I not the Shah's servant?'

'Are these papers in the Shah's hand?'

Sáleh Beg glanced at the papers.

'Of that there is no doubt,' he said, handing them back.

'Khaile khûb. Now listen. Those papers were given to the Afghan Ahmed Khan and the other foreigners yesterday. They are to massacre all the Persians in camp to-morrow night. Those whose names are on the list are to be killed first. The foreigners have special orders that not one is to escape. Your name is there, and your father's.'

Sáleh Beg started, and his face flushed. 'It is not true. It is a trick. We have eaten the Shah's salt, and he knows that we are faithful.' He spoke bravely, but there was trouble and doubt in his face.

'Was not the Bakhtiari faithful? And how many more of the Shah's faithful servants have you seen handed over to the Nasakchis? And was the Shah pleased with you when you defended the Bakhtiari? Afsôs, afsôs, but it is true. Will you see all your people butchered by the Afghans, and your women in the hands of Turkoman dogs?'

Sáleh Beg laid his hand on his sword with a fierce gesture. But he was not convinced. 'I do not believe it,' he said. 'It is a trick.'

'Listen. The Shah promised them that all the women of the Persians should be distributed among them if they carried out his orders, and they swore to do it. Look round you and see who are here. All present know that it is true. Are we all fools to be deceived by a trick?'

'It cannot be true. I was on duty when the foreigners came to the Shah's tent. There was nobody who could have heard what was said, and the foreigners would never have told the story.'

'Was there no one on service at the door?'

'No one but the Shah's ghulám, the Georgian. He would give his life for the Shah. No one could have got near without his seeing.'

The Mulla Bashi looked at Ali Akbar, who left the tent. A minute later he returned with the Georgian. Sáleh Beg gazed at them with a face of astonishment.

'Great God!' he said.

The Mulla Bashi turned to the ghulám.

'Tell us what you have to say.'

The Georgian seemed ill at ease, and began his story

in a hesitating voice, but like Ali Akbar he gathered confidence from the faces of his hearers. Sáleh Beg listened in silence, but his eyes grew more and more excited. When the man had finished no one spoke, but all turned towards Sáleh Beg. He stood a moment with white set face, gazing before him and seeing nothing. Suddenly he threw up his hands with a gesture of despair and a wild cry:

'Allah! Allah! Traitor and murderer! I have eaten his salt and I have been faithful. But in my heart I knew it all. I was mad and faithless to my own people. Now it is over. He shall die. I swear he shall die. Traitor and murderer! Traitor and murderer!'

He turned and was striding out, with rage and misery in his face. Mûsa Beg sprang up and stopped him. He mastered himself and came back.

'Forgive me. I am mad. From this hour I am on the side of my own people. Tell me what you want. I am ready.'

Then it was all settled. Nadir's plan of the camp showed that his tents would be pitched as usual in the centre of the force, with the Persians on one side and the foreign troops on the other. In the evening, when the troops had marched in, all the Kizlbash would be held ready to repel an attack. At midnight, if Nadir had arrived, seventy chosen men, led by Muhammad Khan, Commandant of the Six Thousand, would be in hiding near the network surrounding the Anderûn. When all was quiet word would be brought out to them by Sáleh Beg, who would show them how to avoid or rush the eunuch guard on duty, and Nadir would be killed. His fall would paralyse the foreigners, from whom there would be little to fear.

If Nadir did not return to his tents the Persians would stand to their arms all night, and repel his attack whenever it came. But probably he would return as he had arranged, to disarm suspicion.

When the gathering broke up all the details had been worked out.

CHAPTER XLIX

THE next morning at daybreak, the great camp was astir, and with the quickness which came from long use, the troops formed up for the line of march.

Sitara had slept little, for left alone again, she had begun thinking back over the occurrences of the last few days; and as the night wore on her thoughts became more and more anxious. She sought, and found, comfort in the remembrance of her meeting with Nadir, and of all he had been to her since. As long as she lived she could never lose him again. Yet she was anxious and troubled. She could not forget that there was discontent and disloyalty all round him. He seemed hopeless of regaining the ground he had lost. He was no longer confident in his star as he used to be. Fits of gloom and depression alternated with his stronger moods. Once she had seen him break down completely. She hoped and believed that if he could now refrain from the mad deeds which had made him hated he would in time be again the idol of his soldiery. But could he do so? Had he gone too far? Was it as he said, too late to go back?

When she mounted in the bright June morning to ride with the Kurk, some of the shadows of night passed away from her heart, but she was anxious still.

Most of the way she rode by the side of the Agha Bashi; and it was like old days, the days in which, as it seemed to her now, she had been so perfectly happy. But the negro was less cheerful than he used to be. His face, always sad, had now got a settled look of worry and apprehension. He tried to speak hopefully of Nadir's change of mood.

'We have had some dark years, Khánum, but Inshallah, now that you have come back, all will go well. Inshallah.'

He sighed as he said it, but he had always had a trick of sighing.

Before they reached camp, the Agha Bashi asked her whether she would object to changing tents with the Shirázi.

'No,' she said. 'But why do you wish it? She will be angry.'

'I think it is better, Khánum, and her anger will do no harm.'

'Very well.'

But Sitara rode on in silence, thinking what it meant.

Early in the afternoon, the troops filed into their appointed places at Futtehabad. It was hot, and she lay in her tent waiting for sunset.

'A few hours more and he will be here,' she said, and the thought made her happier.

After sunset the Agha Bashi, who had gone out, came back to the Anderûn, and asked to see her. He was looking depressed and nervous.

'What is it, Agha Sahib?' she said. 'Nothing wrong?'

'There is nothing wrong, Khánum, and I may be foolish to speak at all. My heart has turned to water of late. I do not think it is anything. But, Khánum, I feel uneasy to-night.'

'Why? What is it?'

'I don't know, Khánum, and you must not be alarmed. But I have been to see Mûsa Beg and the Afghan. Things do not look as usual. Mûsa Beg's manner was not pleasant, and there is no "árám," no quiet, in the Persian camp. The troops seem restless. There is much moving about and talking. Ahmed Khan says some of the Kizlbash have seemed unfriendly all day. Nothing has happened. Maybe it is only that the Shah is absent. Would to God that he were here.'

'Is Ahmed Khan on the watch?'

'Yes, Khánum. You know how he hates the Persians. He is watching them carefully. He says they dare not move a finger, that his troops are all ready, and that at the least sign of trouble from the Persians he would sweep the camp, and make flour of them.'

'Then what can they do?'

'God knows. I cannot say. You know the stories about Ali Kuli. They might march away in the night and join him.'

'They would have gone last night if they had meant to go, and it would do little harm if they did. But they would not dare. And there must be many still faithful to their salt.'

The negro sighed. 'Not many, Khánum. A few perhaps.'

Fear for Nadir himself was always uppermost in her mind. 'The Guard is trustworthy at least?'

'Khánum, I think the men are faithful enough. But many of the officers of the Six Thousand are discontented and dangerous. Muhammad Khan, the Commandant, was always a friend of Ali Kuli. A few weeks ago the Shah was suspicious of the Six Thousand, and I suggested pitching his tents among the Afghans, but he said I was a fool—that it would seem as if he were afraid, and would make bad blood. The bodyguard are picked men, and mostly Afshars, as you know, but they are few.'

'There is Sáleh Beg? The Shah trusts him, I know.'

'Yes, Khánum. Sáleh Beg is faithful, but he is only one man. I have spoken to him, and he will keep a strong party of the bodyguard on duty all night just outside the Anderûn, towards the Persian camp.'

'I wish the Shah were back. No one will dare to give trouble then.'

The negro sighed again. 'Inshallah,' he said. 'Inshallah.'

The evening passed quietly, but to Sitara, waiting alone in her tent, the hours seemed very long. At every sound from the Persian lines, every swell in the dull murmur which rose from the great host camped around her, she listened with straining ears. The Agha Bashi's nervousness seemed to have infected her.

'He was always timid,' she said to herself. 'There is no real cause for fear. The Afghans are all ready, and the Persians can do nothing.'

But she could not shake off the feeling of doubt and anxiety.

'If he would only come,' she kept saying to herself.

Two hours before midnight there was a sudden noise outside; a shouting and trampling of horses, and sharp words of command. She sprang up with a beating heart. One of her women came into the tent.

'The Shah has come back, Khánum.'

'Thank God,' she said. 'At last!'

The woman looked at her in surprise, and smiled. What a love-sick fool the Indian was!

CHAPTER L

MEANWHILE Ali Akbar and his sister had been acting after their kind.

The night before, when the conspiracy of which he was the moving spirit had come to a head, Ali Akbar had been seized with a sudden access of terror.

What would happen if some one among the conspirators had been a spy of Nadir's? Or if one man's nerve failed before the fatal hour came round, and made him betray the rest? Or if the attempt on Nadir's life were to miscarry? Any one of these things was likely enough, and if all did not go right, what would be his chance of escape?

Lying in his tent during the night, these thoughts came to him with ever-increasing force, and before morning he was cursing his folly for having been led away. He had committed himself hopelessly. His life was in the hands of any one among a score of mullas and soldiers. Lured on by vanity, and pride in his cleverness, he had been bold and confident. Now he was cold and faint with fear. God, what a fool he had been!

He slept a little at last, after emptying two flasks of Shiráz, and dreamt that he was being strangled in front of the Diwan Khaneh, while Nadir looked on and laughed.

When he woke, he lay waiting for daylight, while

the sounds of the camp began to stir around him. The servant lying outside the tent door sat up and yawned, and stretched himself. 'Ah-h-h,' the man muttered in a voice of sleepy discontent, 'there is but one God.'

Ali Akbar called to him, and asked for a cup of wine. When he had drunk it he felt a little better, but his mind was made up. He would get away from the camp in the evening, before Nadir returned, and await the event in safety. If all went well he could come back. If not, he would make his way to Ali Kuli's camp or elsewhere. The soldier fools would bungle the whole thing in all probability, and anyhow he was better out of the way. There might be fighting with those mad devils of Afghans. God knows what might happen.

And his sister, should he take her with him? He pondered over that question in his takht i raván, on the march to Futtehabad, with the result that he decided to say nothing to her. She could not be trusted to keep the secret, and she would hamper his movements. Besides, Nadir might find out that she was gone, and suspect them. No, he would go alone. After all, she could take very good care of herself. She was not likely to come to any harm.

The Shirázi made the march on horseback, with the Kurk, cursing Sitara and the Agha Bashi at intervals, and Nadir. When she arrived at Futtehabad she was tired and out of temper. Her irritation was not lessened by finding that the Indian woman had been given her tent.

The Pîsh Khanch had begun to arrive that morning early, before daybreak. The camels had straggled during the night march, and a smart young 'ferrásh,' or tent pitcher, who had charge of a portion of the Anderûn, had come in before the rest. He pitched his tents, and then feeling tired, he selected a quiet corner, curled himself up in his baráni, rain coat, and went to sleep. He slept long and heavily. When he woke the sun was high, and he found to his horror that the rest of the tents had been pitched, that some of the eunuchs and slave girls had arrived, and that he was a prisoner. If he tried to get out now he must be seen, and that meant death. His only chance was to lie still and hope he might remain concealed until the Anderûn broke up again next morning.

But his hope was soon at an end. In the afternoon, after the Kurk had marched in, the Shirázi came wandering through the dark passage where he lay, and her quick eyes caught sight of the long bundle in the corner.

Thinking it was a slave girl asleep, and feeling irritable, she walked up and touched the figure with her foot, telling the girl sharply to get up. As there was no answer she bent down, and twitched away the baráni.

Another woman might have screamed at the unexpected sight of a man's face in the Anderûn, but the Shirázi's nerves were proof against most things, and his look of terror put her at her ease. The next instant he was kissing her feet, and imploring her in a whisper to hear him before she betrayed him. 'For God's sake hear me, Khánum. I am innocent. For God's sake, Khánum. Az baráe Khudá.'

It was an adventure, and the Shirázi liked adventures. Moreover, the man was young and good-looking. Even as he grovelled at her feet she could not help noticing his handsome face and slight, athletic figure. She heard his story and laughed. 'Stay quiet,' she said. 'I will get you off. Wait till I come back.'

In another minute she had brought him a woman's cloak, and without meeting any one on the way she smuggled him safely into her own tent. Against one side of it were two camel trunks containing her travelling wardrobe. Their curved backs, shaped to fit a camel's body, stood out from the tent wall, and left a tunnel along the foot of it. With the help of one or two rugs and cloaks thrown over them, they made an excellent hiding-place.

The ferrásh crept in behind the trunks, thanking heaven for his deliverance, and the Shirázi threw herself down on some cushions near his head, and laughed till she cried.

In the course of the afternoon, the two had a long and interesting conversation, the ferrásh proving to be, when reassured in mind, a young man of considerable tact and humour. Like many Persians of his class he could quote poetry with freedom and point, which appealed to the Shirázi's cultivated taste, and his manners were admirable.

Before long they were on the best of terms, and in the evening, with the help of the Shirázi's confidential maid-servant, who enjoyed the whole thing nearly as much as her mistress, they had a very pleasant supper together. It was dangerous, no doubt, but it was an adventure after the Shirázi's own heart.

She was eating sweetmeats and enjoying the conversation of her ferrásh, who had drunk several cups of Shiráz, and was making himself most agreeable, when the noise of the Shah's return startled them both. In a moment the ferrásh was back in his hiding-place, and the maid had removed from the carpet all signs of the feast.

It was fortunate for them that they lost no time. Things had hardly resumed their usual appearance when the curtain was suddenly raised, and Nadir himself walked into the tent.

With all her readiness and courage the Shirázi could not restrain a low cry of terror. For an instant she thought all was discovered, and her heart stood still with the fear of a horrible death. But Nadir's first word showed her that she was safe.

'You!' he said with a frown, as she struggled to her feet. 'What are you doing here? Where is Sitara Khánum?'

When she had shown him Sitara's tent, which had been her own, she cursed them both furiously, in spite of her relief.

An hour or two later, as she was again sitting in conversation with her ferrásh, the canvas above her head quivered to a sudden jerk, as some one tripped over a tent rope, and the next instant two men with drawn swords were within the curtain. For the second time that night she started up in deadly fear. Even in the dim lamp-light she knew them both, and one was Nadir's trusted follower, Sáleh Beg.

She began to plead for her life. Sáleh Beg smiled contemptuously. 'Be quiet,' he whispered. 'Where is the Shah?'

'In the tent of the Indian woman.'

'Where is it? Come and show me.'

'Mercy, mercy, for God's sake! I swear I am innocent. I swear by the head of the Shah.'

'Be silent, shameless one. You deserve death, but if

you show me I will do nothing to you. My business is with him.'

A suspicion of the truth flashed upon the Shirázi's mind, and with it came a thrill of joy. Her revenge would be sweet.

'You will not tell him? You swear by the Prophet that you will do me no harm? You will let me go?'

'I swear it. Show me, or, by God, I will kill you now.'

'I am ready. I will show you.'

'The back of the tent, and be quiet. If you make a sound you are dead.'

Sáleh Beg signed to Mûsa to stay and watch the ferrásh. Then he followed her. Near Sitara's tent they crouched in the darkness and listened. All was still. Nadir was sleeping.

When they returned it was arranged that Mûsa should remain with the Shirázi, to see that neither she nor the ferrásh gave the alarm, while Sáleh Beg went back to bring up the rest of the band.

He made his way to the spot where he had left them. There had been seventy. There were now twelve. The rest had disappeared. The waiting had been too much for their nerves.

'What has happened?' Sáleh Beg asked of their leader, Muhammad Khan.

'What could I do? One or two went off first, and then the rest all together. They were afraid of the Shah.'

'Cowards! come on quickly, before they betray us.'

Silently and swiftly the thirteen made their way to the Shirázi's tent. Hardly were they safe inside it when they heard a quiet footfall coming from the opposite direction. Sáleh Beg looked cautiously out through the curtain at the doorway. It was the Agha Bashi keeping watch over his master. He stopped close by, listening, so close that Sáleh Beg's hand tightened on his sword hilt. Then the negro turned and went slowly back.

CHAPTER LI

After her long waiting, Sitara had been surprised and distressed at hearing from her women that Nadir had gone to the Shirázi's tent. She was the more rejoiced when a minute later he raised her curtain and walked in. She welcomed him with shining eyes.

'Did you think I was not coming?' he said. 'I went into the tent of the Shirázi. Your places have been changed. Why have they done it?'

'My Lord, I know nothing. The Agha Bashi wished it. She was not pleased.'

'What a Shaitán she is. The sight of her face has become hateful to me.'

'What is the Shirázi, my Lord? Do not let the thought of her trouble you. You are weary and want rest.'

'Yes. We were on the march all yesterday and all last night, and I did not sleep; and to-day I have ridden in fast.'

'My Lord was successful as always?'

Nadir looked tired and depressed.

'We were too late. I do not understand it. I had told no one, not even you, where I was going. Yet some one must have sent warning. The Kurds have been giving trouble. I wanted to surprise them and punish them. We surrounded the settlement in the night, but when we advanced at daybreak we found the forts deserted. The Kurds had left lights burning to deceive us, but they were gone. My face has been deserted.'

'They knew they had deserved punishment, and were frightened when they heard the Shah was within reach.'

'It is possible, but I fear there was some treachery. These Persian dogs have been playing me false as usual. Nothing goes right now.'

His voice and eyes were weary, and Sitara hated to say anything that could depress him further. Yet she felt that she must warn him.

'All will go well again. What are the Kurds? Cowardly thieves who ran away at the very thought of the Shah.'

'The Kurds are nothing. But there is treachery on all sides. There is no rest for a King of Irán.' He sighed deeply. 'Ali Akbar is the worst of all, because he is the cleverest. He was not here to-night to receive me. I have noticed of late that he seems to keep out of my sight. He knew I was displeased with the Kurds, and he knows my ways. He may have guessed and given warning. By God! if I find him out, his life will be short.'

Nadir spoke fiercely now, and his eyes grew hard.

'My Lord, have you seen the Agha Bashi since you came in?'

'Yes. I did not speak to him. He always looks frightened and irritates me. Why do you ask?'

'My Lord, he seems anxious to-night.'

'He is always anxious. What is the matter?'

'He is faithful, and thinks of the Shah day and night. I have told him it was nothing—that when the Shah came back all would be well, but he is troubled. He says the Persians seem restless, and more unfriendly to the Afghans. He thinks perhaps they are in doubt about Ali Kuli.'

Nadir was silent for a minute.

'Ali Kuli,' he said at last, 'Ali Kuli! the son of my brother Ibrahim!'

He put the thought aside. 'The Persians hate the Afghans because the Afghans are faithful to me. And when I am not there they dare to show what they feel. Ahmed Khan was awaiting me when I rode in. He told me some of the dogs had shown insolence to-day, not openly, but after their manner. I wish he had killed a few of them.'

'My Lord, I am sure the Kizlbash are faithful still. They remember your victories, and all will be well now.'

'Inshallah! But they are Shaitáns, ungrateful and treacherous.'

'The Afghans are watching them carefully?'

'Yes—as always. God! that it should be needed. There is no peace for a King of Irán—but in his grave. I have not a friend, not one.'

'Oh! my Lord, you have thousands—hundreds of thousands. There is not a King in the world who is so great.'

Nadir shook his head. 'They fear me, yes. But how many can I trust?' He smiled bitterly.

'Ahmed Khan, and the Agha Bashi, and you—an Afghan and a negro, and an Indian girl. And her I nearly killed.'

His head dropped on his breast. She thought there were tears in his downcast eyes. His whole attitude was one of the deepest dejection.

'You never meant to harm me, and you have made

me perfectly happy now. My Lord, you are weary, and you have not eaten to-night.'

'I ate something in the day. I cannot eat now.'

'You are weary, and want sleep.'

She got up and filled him a cup of Shiráz.

'Now sleep. In the morning you will be rested, and all will be well.'

She knelt by him, her hands wandering over his great limbs and shoulders with gentle pressure, till gradually he grew quiet and the lines faded from his face. His eyes closed. He opened them with a faint smile and kissed one of her caressing hands.

'Ján i ma,' he said, 'my life.'

Long after he was asleep she knelt by him, watching him anxiously. His sleep was uneasy. At times he started, and his limbs twitched. Even in the dim light of the oil 'chirágh' she could see how grey he had become, and how his temples and cheeks had fallen. The huge frame was powerful as ever, but he looked old, worn and sad and old.

Sitara had left him at last, and gone to sleep herself, when a hoarse cry from him woke her into sudden consciousness. He had started up with a face of horror, and seized his axe.

'Great God!' he said, his eyes still wild. 'Great God! What a dream!'

She was kneeling by his side again.

'What is it? Is anything wrong?'

'No, thank God. It is nothing, only a dream.'

He tried to laugh. 'I am like a child to-night. Go to sleep, little one. It is nothing.'

But she saw that he was shaken and excited.

'Tell me what it was. I cannot sleep unless you tell me.'

'It is nothing. You remember I told you once long ago how the messenger came and took me away to Ali? And Ali gave me a sword and told me to watch over Persia?'

'I remember.'

'I dreamt that the messenger came again and made me get up and follow him. As before he brought me to the tree, where Ali was sitting. Ali's face was dark, and his eyes were burning with anger, like fire. And he said to the men about him, "You see this dog Nadir Kuli? I chose him to guard my people who were scattered like sheep without a shepherd, and he has become a wolf. Take him and slay him." Then they seized me and were killing me—and I woke.'

He tried to laugh again.

'It was only a dream,' he said. But he looked in her face with eyes of doubt.

'You are a Christian. You do not believe in dreams, or in Ali?'

Sitara's heart was beating fast. His words and manner had frightened her in spite of herself. She smiled bravely.

'My Lord, you are tired and have been thinking too much about these faithless Persians. What is Ali? He was only a man. He cannot harm you. I have prayed day and night to Hazrat i Isa, the Son of God. He will protect you.'

'Inshallah! For your sake he will protect me. God knows what has come to me to-night. I am like a child.'

She made him lie down, comforting him like a child—the mighty King and conqueror of whom men said that he feared nothing, neither man nor God. Soon his weariness overcame him and his eyes closed.

An hour later she sprang to her knees again, to find him once more gazing at her with horror in his face. His forehead was damp with sweat.

'Stay with me,' he said. 'Do not let me sleep. I have dreamt it all again. Oh my God! I am afraid.'

He passed a trembling hand over his forehead, and there was madness in his eyes, the madness of fear.

Sitara knelt at his side, and in his weakness he held her fast, clinging to her as if for protection. At times his eyes would close in spite of himself, and the next instant his head would go up with a start. Brain and heart were disordered by over-fatigue and over-anxiety.

It was long past midnight, and all was still in the camp. Nadir lay silent with drooping head. Sitara still knelt by him, his hand holding hers. Suddenly she felt his grasp tighten. He raised his head. A faint sound came from outside. One second more and Sitara heard it distinctly—the sound of approaching footsteps, soft and stealthy, but unmistakable, the footsteps of several men moving swiftly. Then there was a cry of alarm, quickly cut short, a scuffle and fall, and a rush.

Nadir was on his feet, his axe in his hand, rage and despair in his eyes, but no fear now. His deep voice thundered out a roar of warning and defiance. The curtain dropped to the ground, cut loose with sword strokes; and through the doorway the lamp-light fell on thronging faces and the glitter of steel.

As the foremost men sprang in, Nadir was upon them. Mûsa Beg went down under a blow which crashed into his brain. A tall officer of the Six Thousand reeled back, his life-blood spouting from a deep gash between neck and shoulder. The rest gave ground to right and left. But as Nadir wrenched away the axe blade, and turned upon the nearest, his foot caught in the fallen curtain, and he staggered headlong through the doorway. Before he could recover himself, Sáleh Beg's sword came down, striking him to his knees. As the Persian's arm rose for another blow, Sitara's dagger was buried in his heart, and with a passionate cry for help she was stabbing fiercely at the ring of murderers who pressed in upon their fallen King.

. . . . .

Ahmed Khan stood in the torch-light, his sword red with Persian blood, and looked down at the headless trunk of the great leader he had tried to save. Near it lay the Rajput girl, the dagger still clenched in her stiffening fingers, faithful to the end.